The Roots of Capitalism
John Chamberlain

Capitalism is a system that can stand on its own attainments, believes the author of this book, and he offers here a fast-paced, provocative look at the intellectual forces and practical accomplishments that have created American capitalism.

In clear, unequivocal language, John Chamberlain discusses the ideas responsible for our economic institutions, the originators of these ideas, and the times in which they first became important. The political theories of the men who hammered out the Magna Charta and the Declaration of Independence, the thinking of John Locke, James Madison and Adam Smith, the deeds and discoveries of the James Watts, Eli Whitneys and Henry Fords—all these diverse elements are shown to be part of the tradition of a free society in which American capitalism has grown and flourished.

Chamberlain admits to "a mature preference for the uncoerced man" and reveals the weaknesses of those thinkers, from Robert Owen and Marx to Keynes, who theorized about planned or dictatorial economic systems. He also gives considerable attention to two important disruptive factors which are often neglected by economic historians—invention and technological improvement—and observes their relation to rising standards of living and the many ways they can be encouraged or suppressed.

"With eloquence, fluency and wit, Mr. Chamberlain makes a vastly persuasive case for capitalist theory and practice. . . . A notable contribution to the cause of economic freedom."—*Barron's*

JOHN CHAMBERLAIN has enjoyed a varied and illustrious career as critic, editor and journalist. His newspaper column is syndicated by the King Features Syndicate, and his most recent book is *The Enterprising Americans: A Business History of the United States.*

The Roots
of Capitalism

John Chamberlain

LibertyPress

Indianapolis

Liberty*Press* is a publishing imprint of Liberty Fund, Inc., a foundation established to encourage study of the ideal of a society of free and responsible individuals.

The cuneiform inscription that serves as the design motif for our endpapers is the earliest known written appearance of the word "freedom" (*ama-gi*), or liberty. It is taken from a clay document written about 2300 B.C. in the Sumerian city-state of Lagash.

Library of Congress Cataloging in Publication Data
Chamberlain, John, 1903–
   The roots of capitalism.

   Includes index.
   1. Capitalism.   2. United States—Industries.
I. Title.
HB501.C517   1976   330.12′2   76–52492
ISBN 0–913966–24–X

For the late Garet Garrett, who provided the lead;
and for Claude Robinson, who provided the impetus.

Contents

Preface

For many years the system we call capitalism was on the defensive. It existed in the here-and-now, and its imperfections, whether inherent or not, were plainly apparent to everybody. Socialism, on the other hand, was something to be attained in the future, a thing of shining colors wrapped in the gossamer tissue of a dream. Its imperfections, if there were to be such, were still concealed in the womb of time.

When contrasted with a dream of perfection, capitalism was manifestly at a disadvantage. But with the advent of socialist economies (Communist Russia, China) and the semisocialist, or "mixed," systems of Scandinavia, Britain and New Deal America (to say nothing of the "national" socialisms of Nazi Germany and Fascist Italy), capitalism no longer requires apologists. Under any comparative audit of systems it comes out very well indeed. It may have its islands of poverty, its "contradictions," but it does not murder people as a matter of policy or shut them up in concentration camps. It does not force men and women to accept uncongenial occupations or goods that are subjected to the approval of a small "planning" bureaucracy.

It does not reduce life to a continual round of abject permissiveness.

The title of this book, then, parades itself unashamedly: capitalism is a word for a system that can stand on its own attainments. As for the plan of the book, the effort has been to explain the categories and institutions of economics in terms of their origins, the men (whether originators or not) who first made them famous, and the times which brought them to fruition. The exposition of categories and institutions has been accompanied by a running critique. Most histories of economic thought are, to me, unbearably eclectic. They have their virtues—but economics is, after all, a subject with its pluses and minuses, if not its rights and wrongs. Ever since the beginnings of social life men have swung between extremes of freedom and coercion, of voluntary association and community compulsion, of family "mutualism" and state-imposed "order." Men can live under any combination of the two extremes. But it seems to me obvious that they can only live creatively when cooperation is a matter of free election, of the voluntary approach. The running critique in this book is based on what is, to the writer, a mature preference for the uncoerced man.

Professional economists may consider the book an indefensible mixture of theory and technology. No apologies will be offered for the mixture. The writer has spent ten years of his working life doing corporation and industry studies for *Fortune* magazine, for *Barron's National Financial Weekly,* and for the *Wall Street Journal.* The experience left him with the ineradicable impression that economists in general have overlooked the importance of the "x" of invention and the "y" of technological improvement in their equations. In my years as a writer of economic topics I have never once caught the capitalist system at a moment of "equilibrium." This is not to say that equilibrium models are not useful for purposes of illustration and analysis. But an economic model, to be a true reflection, should allow for disruption. And the pace, the incidence, of disruption must remain a largely unknown quantity unless the economist can isolate the causes of invention, of creativity, itself.

This book was written before I had a chance to read *The Sources of Invention* by John Jewkes, David Sawers, and Richard Stillerman. But I find justification for my combination of theory and technology in the Jewkes-Sawers-Stillerman statement that "future historians of economic thought will doubtless find it remarkable that so little systematic attention was given in the first half of this century to the causes and consequences of industrial innovation. Material progress, it had long been taken for granted, was bound up with technical advance and technical advance in turn, with change, variety and novelty; but whence this novelty, how closely it was related to rising standards of living, whether and how it might be stimulated or stifled: all this ground remained largely untrodden by the economic historian or the economic theorist."

We have, as Professor John Kenneth Galbraith has said, an "affluent society." But it is affluent because it has been free. Its freedom has been hammered out by theoreticians, by pragmatic experiment in shop and marketplace, and on political barricades and hustings from Magna Charta on. Because of the many sources of the economic freedom which makes for affluence, this book inevitably presents a mixture of political theory, economic theory and the practical accomplishments of business and shop innovators such as Robert Owen, Eli Whitney, Frederick W. Taylor and Henry Ford. I hope the logic of the mixture is apparent— but that is for the reader to decide.

Thanks are due to the editors of *Fortune,* the *Wall Street Journal, National Review* and *The Freeman* for permission to use pieces of this discussion which have appeared in their publications.

JOHN CHAMBERLAIN

Cheshire, Connecticut
January 1959

The Roots of Capitalism

Time, Place, Principles, Beginners

In 1776 Adam Smith's *The Wealth of Nations,* an economic treatise which had grown out of its Scots author's preoccupation with the wider problems of free choice as a foundation of moral philosophy, was first published. That same year Thomas Jefferson, a man whose predilection for free choices had endowed him with many accomplishments (he could "calculate an eclipse, survey an estate, tie an artery, plan an edifice, try a cause, break a horse, dance a minuet and play the violin"), retired for seventeen days to an upstairs room in a bricklayer's house in Philadelphia and produced the Declaration of Independence.

Between the two events there was more than the casual relationship of coincidence. Each document was the summary of an epoch, the distillation of what hundreds of people had been thinking and saying, usually with considerably less felicity. Each had come out of the same "forcing house"; the period of the fifteen years that stretched between the end of the Seven Years War—or the French and Indian War, as the conflict was known in America—and open defiance of the efforts of a "planning" king, George III, to remake the world in a mercantile planner's image. Each, in different ways, carried to completion the thinking of John Locke, the libertarian philosopher of the English Revolution of 1688. But the truly important connection between the two documents lay in the future, not in the past. The one was a prophetic economic blueprint, not without its flaws, for the vast outpouring of human energy which was to create the modern world; the other was a simple guarantee that the blueprint could be made palpable within the physical growing space of a new continent.

When Adam Smith, a mild, professorial, inquisitive and absentminded man, was expanding his classroom lectures into a book between 1759 and 1776, he was sanguine for the future, both of his own fledgling science of political economy and of what were still the British colonies of North America. Writing in the spring of 1776, he spoke of the "late" disturbances across the water as if they were shortly to be settled. Despite the "planning" predilections of George III, the British Constitution, as amended in various grants of liberties through the centuries, seemed to stand eternal guardian of the immemorial rights of Englishmen. Speculating on the moral and mental causes of "opulence" or decay in different societies, Smith had said: "The difference between the genius of the British Constitution which protects and governs North America, and that of the mercantile company which oppresses and domineers in the East Indies, cannot perhaps be better illustrated than by the different state of those countries."

Yet even as Smith was writing, the attempted counterrevolution from the top against English liberties was gathering increased momentum. The counterrevolution was embodied in that worst of menaces to the human spirit, a political executive with a "let me do it" complex. (It is of such people that the Chinese say: "A great man is a public calamity.") King George III, the first of the Hanoverian line of monarchs to be born on British soil, came to the throne at the close of the midcentury French wars with his mother's famous "George be a king" resounding in his ears. Young (he was only twenty-two), handsome, moral and proper, with a taste for upright country life (he raised turnips), he had resolved from the outset to do his people nothing but good, even if it were to kill them.

Such purism was an attempt to revive the spirit of the Stuart kings, and England had long since had enough of that. For a generation the realm had been governed by the great Whig landowners, who believed in a wise laxness. The Whigs were close to the soil of the shires, but they were also interested in their alliances with all the new forces that were compact of the liberating energies of scientists, tinkerers, shopkeepers, commercial chance-takers and overseas adventurers. The Whigs were not above corrupting Parliament to get their way, but it was creation, not coercion, for which they wished to clear the road. Meanwhile the first two Hanoverian Georges let the English world wag, preferring to take their ease in their ancestral lands in Germany to reigning on the spot in London. Under the Whigs, England prospered, the standard of life rose, and the nation won its battles. But George III, a perfectionist, had read his Bolingbroke and absorbed the idea that a king should be above faction and party—which, in an England that depended on Parliament, meant corrupting or browbeating a majority to royal whim. During George III's reign the attempt was made, by way of a shift in the Poor Law, to legislate a basic free income for every man or woman, whether able-bodied or not, with no tests required. The result was to divide England, not into Disraeli's "two nations" of rich and poor, but into workers and drones.

Prior to George III's assumption of authority, England had paid lip service to the mercantilist theory that a state prospers by gathering gold, not goods, and by licensing a few favorites to do overseas business with an eye to the personal aggrandizement of a court circle. But, as a popular gag has phrased it, England was not so much a mercantilist state as "a piece of land entirely surrounded by smugglers." Even the ministers of the Crown, though they were sworn to uphold the laws, were not above smuggling: when he was chancellor of the Exchequer, Sir Robert Walpole, the leader of the Whigs, had bought contraband lace from Holland; and, as a younger place-holder, he had boldly used an Admiralty launch to slip wines past the customs. Indeed, Sir Robert had his pet smuggler, a rough sea captain who waited periodically at the doors of Houghton, the Walpole country estate, for settlement of his bills.

The North American colonies, too, had raised smuggling to a fine art. The colonists ignored the Molasses Acts, lured British coast-guard ships into shoal waters where they grounded, and traded in and out of the Caribbean for rum and sugar quite as they pleased. The standard of life rose in North America every time a king's agent was bilked, a tax avoided. Wages were high in New York, money earned good interest, yet the necessaries of life were cheap. Said Adam Smith in 1776: "The price of provisions is everywhere in North America much lower than in England. A dearth has never been known there." America was doing very well, thank you, without any Benevolent or Enlightened Despot's Five-Year Plan, and once the menace of the French had been removed by British and colonial successes in Canada during the French and Indian War, there seemed less reason than ever to put up with any nonsense that violated the immemorial rights of Englishmen on North American shores.

It was at this point, as we are sometimes reminded on July 4, that George III grew particularly stuffy about his relations to overseas Englishmen. There was, first, the Stamp Tax, a slight impost on colonial legal documents designed to raise money for keeping British troops in America. Though the Stamp Tax was a mere nothing, the colonists rioted over it, for it was the same "taxation without representation" which had set their forefathers against the Stuarts and helped cause the settlement of New England in the first place. The tax was repealed, but there were even more obnoxious laws—the tea tax, for instance—to come. When the colonists finally rose in resistance, then in rebellion, Horace Walpole expressed his fear that if King George III were to win a victory in his American war the sequel would be chains on Englishmen at home. Sir Edmund Burke, the elder Pitt, and the other great Whigs more or less openly took the part of the Americans; not without reason they felt that the colonists, in rebelling, were defending the liberties of Englishmen in London, Leeds, Sheffield—and everywhere else.

George III failed in his mania to revive benevolent despotism in England. He failed largely because he was defeated by the colonists in America. The common energies of his age, as expressed by the rising tide of individual self-sufficiency, were against him. It was not without struggle, however, that Adam Smith's "natural liberty"—or Edmund Burke's "natural society"—prevailed and the bonds of mercantilist caution were broken in England. And it was only after considerable travail that Thomas Jefferson's Declaration of Independence—that "all men are created equal, that they are endowed with certain unalienable Rights"—was transmuted into the American constitution, which says that Life, Liberty and Property shall not be touched without due process of law.

Smith had to wait upon the slow processes of technology, the diversionary effects of the Napoleonic wars, and the collapse of markets after the wars, before the energies for which he had designed his blueprint could roll up and force the issue of freedom in the economic realm. And his revolution could hardly take place in a day in a North American colonial world devoted mainly to agriculture. But the physical space was there in America; there were no inhibiting feudal laws and institutions preventing the free transfer of property; and, thanks to the Founders, the requisite freedom-in-federation was soon to come.

The categories, the institutions, of capitalism, which is the economic expression of the morality which says a man must be free to choose between alternatives of good and evil if his life is to have Christian meaning, were all present in *The Wealth of Nations*. In the America of Thomas Jefferson's Declaration these categories and institutions were to have the opportunity which they were never fully to achieve in their constricted English home.

Chapter One

The Freely
Choosing Man

Adam Smith, so it is said, once fell into a tannery pit while he was absorbed in explaining the division of labor to his friend and patron, the Right Honorable Charles Townshend, who is famous in history for having given King George III the bad tax advice which resulted in the American Revolution. An absentminded man who could roll bread and butter around in his fingers and stick the mess into a pot under the delusion that he was making tea, Smith plunged into the subject of economics almost as inadvertently as he fell into the tannery pool. He was led into political economy, a new subject in his time, when, as part of his lecturing kit on the science of jurisprudence, he found himself dealing with the policeman's duty to provide cleanliness, safety and *cheapness or plenty* to the population of a city or a state.

On the subject of cleanliness and safety, there wasn't much to be said beyond stipulating their necessity to economics if the energies of man are to be protected against disruption by marauders, fires, accidents and diseases. But cheapness—or "opulence," as Smith preferred to put it— was quite another matter. How could cheapness best be brought about? In the world of the eighteenth century the authorities had set ideas on the subject. For instance, they believed that plenty was a prerogative of the few, to be conferred upon the many only within the bounds of a certain discretion.

In the early Middle Ages, when a distinctive European society was being forged in the face of Moslem beleaguerment from the East and the breakdown of Roman law within, discretion dictated a subordination of the very notion of plenty to the safety of the manor. It is an old story, not to be repeated here, that the free yeoman gladly turned in his titles to freedom in order to gain the protection of costly armor and the well-trained horseman-knight. When Adam Smith began his lectures on the "moral sentiments" in the mid-eighteenth century, the need for the chivalric order within the boundaries of any West European nation-state had long since passed. But the institutional hangover had not: despite the revolution of the seventeenth century in the arts of government, despite the rise of towns, the thought of plenty as a product of the uninhibited flow of energy had not really penetrated.

True, it had begun to bubble and seethe in unlikely places. In France, where the Bourbons assumed a God-given right to absorb, seize, dictate or stop anything, the Physiocrats, led by a physician named Quesnay, were preparing their famous *Tableau Economique,* a chart which endeavored to explain the circulation of wealth as something analogous to the circulation of blood. Wealth could not get around in a system which exalted the tourniquet of government control over the free pumping of the heart. The Physiocrats had the queer notion that agriculture was the one truly productive branch of economic activity, the source of all value-blood in the circulatory system. Nevertheless, despite their patent animus against industrial production—or "value added by manufacture"—as "sterile," the Physiocrats had achieved an important insight: the "policeman" could best confer plenty on the many by leaving the producer alone.

Adam Smith knew the Physiocrats. He talked with them during his sojourn on the continent as a tutor to the young Duke of Buccleugh from 1764 to 1766. In particular he had many meetings with Turgot, the French minister who persuaded Louis XIV to abolish forced labor and various restraints on the grain trade. But it was not Turgot or his Physiocratic brethren, with their ideas which resulted in the slogan of *"laisser passer, laisser faire,"* who had originally set Smith's mind to racing—it was a simple predilection for freedom which he had picked up at a far earlier age from his old instructor at the University of Glasgow, Dr. Francis Hutcheson.

Hutcheson, an Ulster Scot, had a passion for "natural liberty and justice," those hallmarks of an ideal society, which he communicated to his students by lecturing to them in English instead of the Latin which had hitherto been the prescribed language of the schools. As part of "moral philosophy," the concept of "natural liberty" clicks easily into place. Man, as an ethical integer, is either free to choose between good and bad courses within the limits of his circumstances, or he is not. If he is not free, if he can only accept what is handed to him from above (by fate, or by decree of the human agents of fate), then there is not much use in talking about morality or ethics. To make any sense of the idea of morality, it must be presumed that the human being is responsible for his actions—and responsibility cannot be understood apart from the presumption of freedom of choice.

As with the Physiocrats, economics with Adam Smith began as part of a wider science of choice; only secondarily was it a science of wealth. Smith saw clearly that man, as a choosing animal, was a self-starter, one who could best add to the sum total of human wealth if he were permitted to act without waiting for a command from above. Natural liberty, he was to say in *The Wealth of Nations,* was good because it discharged the sovereign, the "police," from the "duty of superintending the industry of private people and of directing it towards the employments most suitable to the interests of the society."

After a century or more of describing economics as the study of wealth, the economists have finally returned to the idea that their subject is merely a subdivision of a greater and more encompassing science, the science of human choices. "Choosing," says the fertile Ludwig von Mises in his *Human Action,* "determines all human decisions. In making his choice man chooses not only between various material things and services. All human values are offered for option." In other words, the saint who elects to abstain from consumption affects a sales curve or an energy-disposition curve as much as the gourmand who overdoes things; every choice, whether narrowly economic or not, affects every other choice. But there can be no inhibition on choices within the orbit of any individual's rights without demeaning man as a moral integer, one who has the moral duty to make up his own mind between good and evil alternatives.

Thus the economic wheel, with the von Mises school, has come full circle: what began as an almost inadvertent offshoot of moral philosophy has returned to it. Choice is fundamental to economics because it is fundamental to the moral nature of man.

Today, with the evidence all about us, the virtue of free choice in the economic realm ought to be apparent to everybody. (This is not to say that it *is* apparent to more than a small and sometimes helpless minority.) And, as Isabel Paterson has pointed out, the longer the circuit of human energy, the more important that no tourniquets of government dictation be interposed to burden the free pumping of the heart. The idea that a proper long circuit of energy could be set up from above, by state decree without reference to the thousands of free choices of individuals, becomes immediately absurd if we reflect, for example, on how the self-starter got into the automobile, or on how the continuous strip mill became standard to the economical production of steel plate.

The automobile self-starter came about as the result of human self-starters from away back. It came as the result of two streams of individual choosing, one dating to Eli Whitney's discovery of how to manufacture interchangeable parts for guns, the other to inventor Charles F. Kettering's early apprenticeship as a telephone linesman in a rural Ohio district which required that linesmen be ingenious. If Eli Whitney had not shown President Thomas Jefferson in particular and the arms industry of Connecticut in general how to make standard parts from standard dies, Henry Leland, a Colt Arms employee, would not have learned an important secret of mass production to apply in his later years to the making of Cadillac and Lincoln cars. Nor would Leland have been in a position to decide, all on his own, that the rest of the automobile industry was crazy in thinking that a self-starter was impractical. Furthermore, if Charles F. Kettering had not been free to apply his telephone experience to tinkering with electric circuits in a Dayton, Ohio, barn loft, in his spare time, Leland would have had to look long and far for someone capable of inventing the self-starter on order. The "long circuit" that led from Whitney to Leland to Kettering could not possibly have been "planned" from above.

Similarly, if an American Rolling Mill man, John Butler Tytus, had not been free to apply to steelmaking his father's experience in rolling out paper from water-soaked woodpulp by continuous methods, we would not have had the continuous strip mill. Such things as the automobile self-starter and the continuous strip mill could not have been planned by government, for they were dependent on the sort of voluntary cross-fertilization that is almost vagrant in its nature. (They were also dependent on the willingness of private individuals to "waste" their savings on pure hunches, which is something that cannot be done by bureaucrat budgeters in the nature of things.) Nobody can plan from a central conning tower the happy chance conjunction of separate streams of energy, for the man in the conning tower must be preoccupied with control of a going circuit, not with its distortions and disruptions by the sudden intuitions, the divine spontaneity, of the freely choosing individual man.

In the eighteenth-century world of Adam Smith, a world of simple husbandmen, simple craftsmen, and simple merchants, the values of free choice as the systole-diastole of an energy stream were not immediately apparent. Even so, evidence had just begun to accumulate that free individual hunches were, on balance, better for everybody than the system of constraints dictated from above.

Smith is a continual surprise to commentators because he supplied a complete rationale for the manufacturing and trading system arising out of the industrial revolution even before that revolution had been well begun. When Hutcheson was expounding his principles of freedom to Smith at Glasgow, and when David Hume* was throwing out his speculative leads that surely affected the thinking that went into Smith's own teaching, the great linkages of coal and iron were still in the fairly distant future. The word "manufacturing" still connoted "making by hand"; villagers still supplied their own food, "cloathing" and furniture; and the internal trade of the British Isles was carried on over a road system that in many places was still virtually impassable from autumn till late spring. It would still be a two-generation span before Matthew Boulton, James Watt's partner in the manufacture of the first crude, noisome steam engines, would remark about his Birmingham factory: "I sell here, sir, what all the world desires to have—power." But already, in laggard Scotland as well as in burgeoning England, a great change was in the air.

The change in Scotland could be dated some time after 1707, the year of political union with England. By the terms of union, Scots merchants—including Smith's friends, the great tobacco importers of Glasgow—found themselves on more or less equal footing with those of England; and as English foodstuffs came north to forestall or alleviate

* Hume, a pioneer in many things, set forth the economic doctrine of comparative advantage years before Smith. But it was *The Wealth of Nations* which successfully "brokered" the thought to the world.

Scots famines, the awakening curiosity about "farming for plenty" led also to the importation of improved English farming methods. The "simple system of natural liberty" was already discernibly at work, proving to Smith, the student, that man, "by pursuing his own interest . . . frequently promotes that of society more effectually than when he really intends to promote it." As he was later to write in *The Wealth of Nations,* industry needs only one encouragement—"the establishment of a government which . . . [affords] some tolerable security" that business "shall enjoy the fruits of its own labor."

The Wealth of Nations is full of references to the sudden expansion of the eighteenth-century horizon. These references mock Robert Heilbroner's recent contention that much of England in Smith's day was "a dog's hole." On one page Smith speaks of "that stunted breed [of cattle] which was common all over Scotland thirty or forty years ago, and which is now so much mended through the greater part of the low country, not so much by a change of the breed . . . as by a more plentiful method of feeding them." On another page he remarks on "all sorts of garden stuff" which had become cheaper—"turnips, carrots, cabbages; things which were formerly never raised by the spade, but which are now commonly raised by the plow." "Luxury," he says at another point, quoting a "common complaint," "extends itself even to the lowest ranks of the people . . . the laboring poor will not now be contented with the same food, cloathing and lodging which satisfied them in former times . . . "

These observations and many others like them, though not published until 1776, actually predated such milestone events as Watt's invention of the steam engine and Arkwright's patenting of the spinning throstle or water frame, both of which came in 1769. Curiously, it was Smith's own University of Glasgow which helped extend to James Watt the "natural liberty" that resulted in the steam engine. In 1756, when Watt applied to the city of Glasgow for the right to open a workshop, the trade corporations, invoking their medieval privileges, objected. But where the city and the restrictive guilds of the time refused Watt the common courtesy of a toehold, the university had no fears. Watt was given a workshop within college confines and named mathematical instrument maker to the university. It was in his college workshop that Watt, in the course of repairing an old-fashioned Newcomen engine, first started on the line of conjecture that led to the idea of the separate condenser, which was to provide the power that would unleash the industrial revolution.

The steam engine and *The Wealth of Nations,* then, came independently out of the same university matrix, a fact which clearly disproves that ideas are merely the "superstructure" of materialist forces. It is the mind, rather, which forces matter to do its will. But to give mind and matter their play, the principle of free will must be assumed even in the face of such things as guild restrictions.

The rising energies of England depended on one thing: the weakening of the old idea that government could be something other than a brake on human activities. In June of 1740, when Adam Smith rode his horse southward from Glasgow to take up residence at Oxford for six years, he was struck from the moment he crossed the border with the comparative richness of an England which had won a good measure of economic freedom in 1688. There were the fat oxen, the plenteous garden stuffs, the native "apples and onions" which, a century before, had been imported from Flanders. Though the great cotton textile spinning and weaving inventions were still to come, there was the considerable improvement in the "coarser manufactures of both linen and woollen cloth." As Professor G. M. Trevelyan has pointed out, capital in the mid-eighteenth century was flowing in two directions: landlords and agriculturalists, taking their profits from the enriched dimensions of the soil, were employing it in factories, mills and County Banks, from which a stream of wealth was frequently plowed back again into the exploitation of new methods of tilling, draining, sowing, manuring, breeding and feeding of cattle, and the rebuilding of farmsteads.

The enclosure of the open land, the conversion of heath and fen and moorland pasture into controllable fields, was just getting under way in 1740. In East Anglia, hitherto a depressed agricultural area, new systems of drainage, crop rotation and the fertilizing of light soils were shortly to create the immense riches of men like "Turnip" Townshend and "Coke of Norfolk," who raised their rentals some tenfold in a generation without working hardships on their exceedingly prosperous tenants. The scientific breeding of stock began in those years, the average weight of sheep and cattle doubled, and rye, oats and barley were progressively abandoned for wheat and white bread.

We have heard, almost *ad nauseam,* about the wrongs visited upon the English peasantry by the Enclosure Acts: the deprivation of rights to feed a cow or two or a flock of geese on the common, the forced sales of tiny plots, and so on. There is a little verse that goes:

They put in jail the man or woman
Who steals the goose from off the common
Yet let the larger felon loose
Who steals the common from the goose.

But the enclosures, which enabled farmers to raise root crops and artificial grasses behind protective hawthorne hedges to feed to cattle and sheep in winter, took England off a scurvy-producing salt-meat diet. It also enabled many more people—including those who had been saved by the improving medicine of the times—to live and live comparatively well. (So where does the pendulum come to rest in this matter of "guilty" enclosures?) Fresh beef and mutton were coming regularly to the English table when Adam Smith ate his first meals at Balliol—and a servant, seeking to rouse Smith from one of his absentminded reveries, did so by telling him that he had never seen such a piece of beef in Scotland as the one which was sitting before his eyes on the table.

During the quarter-century when *The Wealth of Nations* was growing from the egg of the few stray lectures of 1749–51 to the finished product of 1776, improving road and canal communications were giving internal mobility to an England which had hitherto depended on rivers and the sea. Significantly enough, it was private enterprise which built the new English roads. In the seventeenth century, the parishes were charged with road upkeep, which meant that nobody did anything about mud, dust, ruts and quagmires of oozy clay. For six months of the year country folk were housebound or reduced to the limitations of struggling horses, the women riding pillion behind their husbands or brothers. But, in the years between 1700 and 1790, two thousand separate Road Acts were passed by Parliament allowing private turnpike companies to remake and maintain the highways. Private carriages became lighter and swifter, posting inns were established, redcoated guardsmen were seated on public coaches to deal with highwaymen, and heavy commercial wagons succeeded the packhorses which had hitherto transported coal in sacks. By 1786, fresh salmon, packed in ice, were traveling from Scottish rivers to London tables.

Meanwhile—as roadside England moved on towards the well-traveled times of Jane Austen and Charles Dickens—Francis Egerton, the Duke of Bridgewater who was the father of inland navigation in Britain, was sponsoring a rude engineering genius named James Brindley in linking the rivers together with canals. The Manchester-Liverpool canal was built in the 1760s, and the cottage industries of the interior suddenly found themselves on the great trade routes then opening to America and the Indies. However much the road and canal builders depended on state permission for their enabling acts, this vast multiplication of mobility was carried through by the free planning and free will of privately acting individuals.

When the laws stood athwart the choices of the free man, the Englishman of the eighteenth century, quite unlike his twentieth-century descendants, usually made short shrift of the laws. Only recently has England become the great law-abiding nation. All through *The Wealth of Nations* there are allusions to the ubiquitous smuggler. The tobacco merchants of Smith's own Glasgow used an "elastic" hogshead into which extra quantities of tobacco could conveniently be jammed. Even the clergy, as Trevelyan tells us, dealt with smugglers as tea drinking became fashionable: the year after *The Wealth of Nations* was first published Parson Woodforde, a good and respectable man, wrote: "Andrews the smuggler brought me this night about 11 o'clock a bagg of Hyson Tea six pound weight. He frightened us a little by whistling under the parlour window just as we were going to bed." (To the Parson, smuggling was not against the law of God.) Some years later, according to the historian Lecky, the younger William Pitt reckoned that out of thirteen million pounds of tea consumed in the Kingdom in a year, less than half of it had paid duty. In other words, stay-at-home Englishmen were even more insistent on a free trade in tea than their cousins in revolutionary America who had instigated the Boston Tea Party.

Even before steam power was applied to industry, mass production was coming into play in Adam Smith's eighteenth-century world. Smith's own famous example of the division of labor as carried out in the pin factory is a case in point: this "trifling manufacture" (Smith's words) had been so organized that ten persons could make forty-eight thousand pins in a day where a lone workman "not educated to the business" could scarcely make one. And even as Smith was writing about pins, Josiah Wedgwood, the peg-legged Staffordshire porcelain maker, was experimenting with methods and molds which brought good pottery within the reach of classes and masses alike. When Wedgwood couldn't get his cheap but often extremely tasteful porcelains to market, he too turned canal and turnpike promoter on his own.

What Smith had uncovered, then, was a set of principles accepting man as a self-starter which is good for any productive society, whether it utilizes steam, electric, or atomic power or merely depends on horses and human muscle. It was not until after the publication of *The Wealth of Nations* in 1776 that the manufacturers, working on Smith's principles of freedom, demonstrated the relevance of these principles to the world of modern power. Everything came with a rush in those first years after *The Wealth of Nations:* the application of coking coal to the making of good iron, the casting of the first iron bridges, the development of good boring and milling equipment for the making of machine parts.

The first commercially built steam engine was sold in 1777 to John Wilkinson, the ironmaster who had developed a precision cutting tool which enabled Watt and his partner Boulton to machine a steam cylinder which would actually work without leaking its energy all over the landscape. The steam engine, the prime mover of the industrial revolution, capped the revolution in production which had already begun to take place in the textile business during the years of Adam Smith's life. James Hargreaves, a weaver and carpenter, had perfected a spinning contraption of eight bobbins and eight spindles in 1764 and named it the spinning jenny after his wife or daughter. Then came Arkwright's patent of the throstle or water frame for spinning strong warps to go with the more delicate threads coming from Hargreaves' jenny. A "bag-cheeked, pot-bellied barber," to quote Carlyle, Arkwright may have stolen his invention from others; but the point for the future lay in the "barber's" ability to organize factory production around his own and Hargreaves' devices. In 1779, ten years after the water frame, came Samuel Crompton's mule—a cross between the jenny and the water frame which superseded both its predecessors.

Smith, Watt, Wilkinson, Hargreaves, Arkwright and Crompton were all illustrations of the same idea: let energy flow! Smith did not live to see the application of power to the mills using the great textile inventors' devices, but he would not have been surprised by the factory system that grew out of the inventions of his time. He was endlessly curious about industrial processes: he poked about the ironworks at Carron, near Edinburgh, with Edmund Burke during the latter's visit to Scotland in 1784, and his famous fall into the tannery pit occurred while he was busy observing the application of the pin-making division of labor methods to the processing of hides.

Much has been made of the ugliness which spread over the English landscape as the result of the tinkering which so entranced Smith. But the factory is not inherently unesthetic, and, as we shall see, there were many social causes connected with the long agony of the Napoleonic wars which explain the ugliness of the early nineteenth-century landscape even more than does the far more celebrated pioneering rush for riches. Certainly the emergence of the machine did not intensify the poverty of those at the bottom of eighteenth-century society, for it is a fact of record that factory competition for labor in the northern English counties kept rural wage rates above the line where the Poor Laws, as amended in 1795, would have required supplemental payments to farm laborers out of parish funds. In other words, there was less poverty in Lancashire, where the machines were huffing as Adam Smith's principles took hold, than there was in rural Berkshire, where agricultural labor had to be supplemented out of the rates.

Smith's theory of the utility of freedom clearly antedated his own mature observations of eighteenth-century economic life. But it was soundly based on a correct idea of the human personality. Man may not have an innate propensity to "truck and barter," as Smith assumed, but nobody can be spontaneously creative if he must first wait upon the decision of a board for permission to act. Smith had been led to freedom by Francis Hutcheson, of course; but beyond that he had a relish, somewhat perverse in a moral Scot, for Bernard Mandeville, author of the early eighteenth-century *Fable of the Bees.* Mandeville, who spoke in verse with a "coarse and rustic eloquence" (Smith's description of the ironist's style), was convinced that, economically speaking, "private vices are public virtues." Thus:

> . . . whilst luxury
> Employed a million of the poor,
> And odious pride a million more;
> Envy itself and vanity
> Were ministers of industry.

But where Mandeville saw the vices of the consumers as supplying the motive power which put people to gainful work, Smith thought more in terms of the "public vices" of the producer. It was with the capitalist-entrepreneur, not the glutton, in mind that Smith wrote: "It is not from the benevolence of the butcher, the brewer, or the baker that we expect our dinner, but from their regard to their self-interest. We address ourselves, not to their humanity, but to their self-love, and never talk to them of our necessities, but of their advantages."

That the publicly displayed "vice" of self-love could lead

to the "private" virtue of meat, ale and bread on the individual customer's table seemed obvious enough to Smith. But granted that Smith had hit upon a signal part of the truth, was it only "self-love" that kept the butcher or baker at work? Smith's own theory of the "moral sentiments"— which, in his estimation, derive from the element of sympathy for others—would seem to belie the overt cynicism of his frequently expressed relish for Mandeville. After all, butchers and bakers often have families to care for, and even an occasional charity to support. Is it self-love, or the far more Scottish virtue of self-reliance, which impels a man to seek an income and an estate sufficient to keep himself and his family from becoming a burden to others? Taking his two books, *The Theory of Moral Sentiments* and *The Wealth of Nations,* as complementary, the lesson of Adam Smith is that free choice, when disciplined by sympathy, becomes moral choice; and the man who stays "off the parish" (or relief, or whatever) is following the Golden Rule and doing as he would be done by.

In any event, Smith could see in his own lifetime that the "public virtues" of rulers were far more wicked in their effects on society than the "private vices" of either producers or consumers. His journey with the young Duke of Buccleugh to France, where he lived in Toulouse and in Paris, brought him into close contact with the economics of the Bourbon kings, who sought to concentrate all important decisions in the court at Versailles. Under French mercantilist policy, industry was regulated and the French people were taxed to a fare-you-well. In the country districts the Bourbon policy created a sullen—and eventually bloodthirsty—peasantry that was addicted to "playing poor" so that the tax collector would restrain his hand. And in the towns life tended to become static (only Paris and Versailles were alive).

In *The Old Regime in France* Alexis de Tocqueville, who is more famous in the United States for his *Democracy in America,* has unforgettably analyzed the condition of France during the very years of Smith's tour. Smith's Physiocratic friends were aware of what had happened to a great nation, and Turgot was trying to do something about it. But it was like pushing the rock of Sisiphus to heave against the regulations of the French economy. For example, it took more than two thousand pages to print the rules established for the textile industry between 1666 and 1730. Weavers had to negotiate with the government for four years in order to obtain permission to introduce "blackwarp" into their fabrics. The effect of the regulations was to freeze French textile production at a certain level, though smuggling and evasion of the manufacturing regulations did alleviate the situation somewhat. The violations of the rules often brought terrible penalties: for breaking the regulations governing printed calicoes some 16,000 people were either executed or killed in armed brushes with government agents. And in Valence, on a single occasion, seventy-seven people were sentenced to be hanged for breaking economic regulations, fifty-eight to be broken on the wheel, and six hundred thirty-one were sent to the galleys. Yet for the sake of "natural liberty," men continued to break the rigid mercantilist laws.

This was the "planned economy" at its worst, as evolved by the ministers of Louis XIV and his successors. In England, under the Whigs of the early eighteenth century, the movement was the other way. Even so, Adam Smith wrote out of a vivid acquaintance with mercantilist thinking in Britain. His pages about the mercantilist balance-of-trade fallacy—the idea that a country should devote its economic energies to building up reserves of gold and silver in the central treasury by giving bounties for exports and by levying strangulating duties on imports—are among the most memorable in economic literature. (A mercantilist economy was, by definition, a low-wage economy, for by keeping home labor costs down foreigners would be stimulated to buy—and pay gold—for its goods.) And when Smith comes to the working of the mercantilist system as applied to the American colonies his eager nose for detail gives a splendid picture of what King George III's "planning" did to alienate British citizens in North America.

It was not that George III was worse than his royal brethren in playing the game of the eighteenth-century "benevolent despot"; indeed, he was much softer than some of his Continental guides and mentors. As Smith says, it was only "with regard to certain commodities that the colonies of Great Britain are confined to the markets of the mother country." The "enumerated commodities" included such things as molasses, tobacco, "cotton-wool," beaver pelts, indigo and whale-fins, none of which could be produced in England itself, as well as pig and bar iron and naval stores, in which the home country was deficient. In addition to monopolizing the purchase of the "enumerated commodities," the government of George III prohibited the erection of "steel furnaces and slit-mills" in the American plantations. As for hats and woollen goods, the colonists were forbidden to export them from "one province to another," whether by water or by road. The colonists were, of course, expected to do their buying of manufactured goods, hats included, in England, whose merchants had exclusive rights of export and reexport to North America.

Adam Smith saw all this, and condemned it as "a manifest violation of the most sacred rights of mankind." In a less exalted passage he spoke of mercantilist regulations as "impertinent badges of slavery" imposed "by the groundless jealousy of the merchants and manufacturers of the mother country."

At home in England, though the new liberalism of the French *philosophes* and their English friends was percolating everywhere, Smith was annoyed at the persistence of certain feudal hangovers. He objected to the exclusive privileges of corporations and to the statutes of apprenticeship—the very same rules which had prevented his friend James Watt from establishing himself in Glasgow—as "real encroachments upon natural liberty." And he inveighed against the "law of settlement" which made it illegal for a workman who had been thrown out of employment in one parish to seek a job in another. He also attacked primogeniture and entail, the laws of inheritance which guaranteed that landed estates should go intact to the eldest sons and their progeny forever. It was primogeniture which effectively prevented the devolution of the estates of big proprietors into small, manageable parcels. Smith, a realist, conceded that "to expect . . . that freedom of trade should ever be entirely restored in Great Britain is as absurd as to expect that an Oceana or Utopia should ever be established in it." But the new freedom was working so well in mobilizing capital as a prime agent of production for such great enterprises as road building, the draining of fens, and the establishment of tobacco importing houses that Smith saw no good reason for continuing the medieval fetters on land and labor, the remaining productive factors.

In his feeling that all the agents of production—land, labor and capital—should be free to go to work at will, Smith was fortified by the experience of the American colonies. There, despite the mercantilist hobbles imposed by the Hanoverian kings, the fact that "waste lands of the greatest fertility" could be "had for a trifle" encouraged immigration and made for high wages and high profits. To keep a worker from taking up land of his own, an employer had really to bid high; and the need for capital to work new lands necessarily imposed a good rate of interest. There was no right of primogeniture in Pennsylvania and in parts of New England in Smith's day, and in the other colonies the presence of many unclaimed acres tended to render strict inheritance laws a harmless thing. Hence the engrossing of lands by a few large proprietors, which had helped destroy the free market in late Roman and early medieval times, had never become a colonial problem. Moreover, the North American colonies had never been forced to contribute more than a pittance to the support of Empire defense or to defray government expenses at Westminster. The mobility of life in the American colonies—and the freedom from onerous taxation—made for an economic progress which was a continual prod to Smith's enthusiasm, and his pages on the difference between England's American empire and that of Spain bubble with exuberance. By contrast, his treatment of the monopolies granted to single companies for trade with the Orient— the East India Company, for example—is a masterpiece of restrained rage.

The true reasons for colonial prosperity were entirely lost on the government of King George III, and as late as 1783—the year the Revolutionary War came to a formal end—Lord Sheffield's *Observations on the Commerce of the American States with Europe and the West Indies* predicted that American political freedom would be followed by the economic ruination of the new nation. To Lord Sheffield, the mercantilist system, the "guardian of the prosperity of Britain," had provided the colonies with a shelter. Lacking access to English ports, so Lord Sheffield said, the States would be unable to trade their raw materials for the manufactured goods they needed. And, lacking both labor and machinery, they would be unable to create a manufacturing system of their own.

Lord Sheffield and the surviving champions of mercantilism missed the great point of *The Wealth of Nations:* that freedom creates its own markets and machines. Yet they could not say that Smith's doctrines were too novel for comprehension in 1783. For as far back as 1755, or twenty years before the battles of Lexington and Concord, Smith had written in a paper which he read to a Glasgow economic society: "Little else is required to carry a state to the highest degree of affluence from the lowest barbarism but peace, easy taxes, and a tolerable administration of justice; all the rest being brought about by the natural course of things. All governments which thwart the natural course are unnatural, and, to support themselves, are obliged to be oppressive and tyrannical." This is what Burke and the Rockingham Whigs believed even as Smith was expanding his idea into *The Wealth of Nations.* It is what William Pitt, the Younger, was soon to accept as his guiding light of policy. If the shadows of the French Revolution and the long Napoleonic struggles had not intervened, the full Smith doctrine might have become English governmental policy long before 1835 or 1848.

Adam Smith died in 1790, on the eve of the Napoleonic cycle of wars and upheaval. Because of the wars, the attention of Britain was forcibly diverted for a full generation from the wider international aspects of the Smith doctrine. But as England turned to using the new machines of Adam Smith's contemporaries to manufacture for war purposes, the rising class of industrialists became impatient of the hobbles which were supported by Lord Sheffield and his friends. Meanwhile, in distant America, a young nation found ways in freedom of circumventing Lord Sheffield's gloomy predictions. The star of Smith was rising in a world to which freedom of choice suddenly seemed as natural as breathing. But first, there had to be created the political framework in which choice could move to its ends in the opulence which Adam Smith so prized.

Chapter Two

The Property Base

The market, which is the characteristic institution of capitalism, expresses a relationship of buyer and seller.
It is, in effect, what results when free choice is applied to
the disposition of property—or of what is made with the
use of property, by "mixing" labor with it. The compari-
sons which the market permits lead to the creation of value,
which is a compromise of individual judgments. The seller
seeks to cover the labor and energy he has expended, plus
a profit; the buyer seeks to save himself labor and energy
by making an exchange. Two subjectivities meet in an objective price. But behind the creation of value there must
be ownership—the right to dispose of a good or a service.

So we come back to property as the base for liberty. In
The Wealth of Nations, which is the first good book about
the market, Adam Smith had plenty to say about free
choice, about the simple system of natural liberty. But, like
other economists of an older day, he tended to assume the
property right. This right, in the pages of Smith, is something which is anterior to economics as such. Where property could not be freely traded he expressed his displeasure;
witness his attacks on primogeniture and entail, those laws

which kept much of the land of England and Scotland from coming freely on the market. But, in spite of the feudal hobbles which still existed in his day, Adam Smith took private ownership for granted. In doing this he was exercising his prerogatives as a freeborn British subject. But it was not until Smith's own time that Englishmen could take the property right for granted. That right had been bitterly contested in most previous generations, though usually in its political aspects rather than in its more purely economic.

Whether a discussion of "rights," either "natural" or legal, belongs to a book on economics is an arguable point. But "rights" have their important effect on the flow of human energy, and therefore on the creation of the wealth that reaches the marketplace for valuation in exchange. It is not too much to say that economics could not exist at all without the prior establishment of the rights to life, liberty and property—or, in the older word, "estate."

The "right" to life must be assumed if the race itself is not to perish: without it, human existence would indeed be "nasty, brutish and short" and only a few consummately clever murderers would soon be left to people the earth. The other rights of the famous triad can be deducted from the first: if one has a "right" to life, one must be at liberty to work and sustain one's self, and one must have access to the means of production, specifically land and tools. If one can be legally deprived of the right to acquire these, the right to life becomes a permission to be revoked at the politician's or the military man's will.

From the standpoint of economics, the three basic rights are necessary if there is to be any economic calculation. Under slave systems, or under the "planned" disposition of energy and goods that is part and parcel of any permissive system, the market simply ceases to function. Under planning one takes what one gets according to a superior's definition of good, and there's an end to it. Pricing is done by the whim or guess of the patriarch or the planner, without relation to the desires of buyer and seller, and the measurement of value thus becomes an impossibility. Without a method of measurement, of registering the comparative force of human desires, economics as a science must cease to exist.

In recent years, forgetting that the three rights are indissolubly linked (indeed, they are three faces of the same thing), fashionably smart people have fallen into the habit of opposing "human rights" to "property rights." Jefferson (or Franklin Roosevelt) stood for "humanity" where Hamilton (or Hoover) stood for property; therefore, down with Hamilton (or Hoover)! But, despite the fashionable notion, the property right is just as much a human right as any other. Where there is no property right, human beings are invariably kicked around—by the politicians, as in Soviet Russia; by the military, as in any warlord system; or by a priestcraft, as in Peru of the Incas.

Englishmen knew this both instinctively and from experience long before Adam Smith first listened to Francis Hutcheson on the subject of natural liberty. In the days of the barons, when property relations were regulated by a grand permissive system which envisioned the king (with his divine right) as the chief feudal holder and all others his vassals, there may have been no abstract "property right" in land. But if permissiveness governed all things in 1215, the year of Magna Charta, the barons who exacted the Great Charter from bad King John on the meadow at Runnymede were hardly disposed to admit it. With them, permissiveness had become prescription. They assumed that the land was theirs in exchange for the performance of duties (the chief taxes of the time). Much of Magna Charta is taken up with such things as the rights of heirs living under guardians, and the rights of debtors against bailiffs who would seize lands or rents without regard to the debtors' net worth in chattels. Prescriptive property rights, indeed, are the substance of Magna Charta, and the protection of these rights is pushed backward toward the protection of persons and forward again into the protection of the conditions or channels of trade. Thus, the indissolubility of life, liberty and property was recognized even as early as at the very start of the thirteenth century.

Under Magna Charta no freeman could be deprived of his freehold except by the "law of the land." All merchants were guaranteed safe and secure entry to or exit from England, with the right to tarry there and to buy and sell "quit from all evil tolls." Sheriffs and bailiffs were forbidden to take the carts or horses of freemen for transport duty, or wood which was not theirs, or "corn or other provisions . . . without immediately tendering money therefor." Fines and "amercements" imposed against the "law of the land" were to be remitted; Welshmen "disseised" of lands or liberties were to have their property or rights restored to them; and the "men in our kingdom" were to "have and hold all the aforesaid liberties, rights and concessions [of Magna Charta] well and peaceably, freely and quietly, fully and wholly, for themselves and their heirs, in all respects and in all places, forever, as is aforesaid."

If all this was merely "barons' justice," as has been frequently charged by those who try to make it seem that the common man had no rights in medieval England, then the barons of King John's time (or the churchmen who stood behind them) were extraordinarily sympathetic men. True, the villeins on their estates, the serfs who were bound to the soil, were not to achieve freedom for some time to come (either by deserting to the towns or by making individual deals with the landlord when labor became scarce after the Black Death). Nevertheless, the justice which the barons demanded for themselves was applicable to many others. The barons asked for reasonable fines, proportioned to the offense; for justice as a right, "not to be sold, denied or delayed"; for security of person as well as property; for uniform weights and measures; for freedom of travel; for a redress of church grievances; and, in general, for a recognition of common-law rights as the "law of the land." All this was applicable across the board—and twelfth-century "Anglo-Saxon writ" and thirteenth-century "Anglo-Norman writ-charter" thus became the basis of "the immemorial rights of Englishmen" which were the colonists' quite legitimate concern at the outset of the American Revolution.

The struggle for the property right was always a checkered one in the ages when the divine-right theory sanctioned the king as the feudal overlord of all landowners. Nevertheless, Magna Charta was confirmed under Edward I, with a kingly admission that no seizures of goods would be made for the Crown's use; and all through the later Middle Ages judges applied the rights of the Great Charter as the "law of the land." The king, ideally, was supposed to be "under God and the law."

In France, where anyone could be imprisoned if the king chose to sign a letter of arrest bearing the privy seal, there was no such safety of life, liberty and property as in England. Whether the English dispensation came "out of the German forest" (the old-time Angles and Saxons thought of law as a quest for the Creator's justice) or from the Roman Stoic philosophers who had elaborated the concept of "natural," or ideal, law is immaterial to the fact that Englishmen, from their twelfth- and thirteenth-century beginnings, held that rights came with birth and not from any permissive act of king or state. The common law was there before the king, for it originated in man's intuitive recognition of rules of conduct that were suited to the nature of man.

The Tudors broke with the theory of the thirteenth century by seizing the properties of the monasteries and distributing them among their handymen and court retainers. This lawless act not only put the property right in question, but it also saddled the state with the necessity of caring for the indigent and the aged who had hitherto been supported by the contributions of churchmen. True enough, Queen Elizabeth had the native good sense to refrain from pushing her assumed prerogatives too far, and adventurous Englishmen began acquiring wealth and property from all over the globe during her reign. Even so, the temperamental Elizabeth insisted on infringing the property right by granting trade monopolies to her favorites. Though she allowed the courts to speak their piece, it was more or less in vain that defendants cited Magna Charta in her later years to prove that any freeman of the town might buy and sell "all things merchantable in London."

So things stood at the onset of the seventeenth century, when the Stuarts came in to assert the divine-right theory even more forcibly than Elizabeth. This was the century when the courts (as championed by the doughty Chief Justice Coke) came to the "crunch of war" with the Crown.

Edward Coke, in his several activities as judge, member of Parliament, and commentator on Magna Charta, provided most of the groundwork for American constitutional law by his insistence that no one could be deprived of rights without full and fair hearing or in consonance with stated government powers. Coke's importance to economics resides in his clarification of the old English guarantees that no one can be ousted from a freehold or deprived of a livelihood without due process of law. The economic aspects of Coke's thinking were put on high ground by his assertion that monopolies and impositions on trade come under the heading of deprivations of liberty. Thus, once again liberty and property rights were accepted on high legal authority as being facets of the same thing.

The seventeenth century also saw Parliament (the focus of the forces making the Puritan Revolution) siding with the courts in the battle which finally established the "separation of the powers" as the physical guarantee that no executive authority could ride roughshod over the "immemorial rights of Englishmen." The Puritan Revolution was not fought over mundane things, for it was, in the bright dawn before the new "presbyters" became as intolerant as John Milton's "old priests," a struggle for the right of the individual to read the Bible for himself and to dissent in religious matters if he so pleased. However, the "property right" was deeply involved in the fight on all levels. First of all, the Puritans who objected to being forced to abide by the spiritual decisions of the Church of England also disliked paying the king "ship money" (a seizure of property) without parliamentary representation in tax matters. Hampden, whose personal assessment of ship money was a mere twenty shillings, brought the matter into court on the ground of libertarian principle, and the battle was joined. The Roundhead, or parliamentary, party saw clearly that all the immemorial rights of Englishmen were indissolubly linked in the struggle against the arbitrariness of the king.

Cromwell's army was an army of pamphleteers, and it had its individualist and primitive communist wings. The Levellers (not really Levellers, for they believed in the natural inequality that arises from the vast variety of human abilities) spoke for ancient rights which had been affirmed by Coke and championed by Hampden in the ship money case. The Diggers, who got their name because they insisted on squatting and "digging" to plant parsnips and beans where they pleased, were land communists. Their chief spokesman, Gerrard Winstanley, said equivocally: "Property there must be, but all must possess it." With the property right thus under attack from the two extremes of the political spectrum, the Stuart kings at one end and the Winstanley Digger Puritans at the other, it is scarcely cause for wonder that Englishmen began to think more clearly than ever before about the relation of private property to both the physical and spiritual needs of man. The result of the intellectual churning of the seventeenth-century struggle was some twenty thousand tracts—and two great works bearing on the property right and government, Thomas Hobbes' *Leviathan* and John Locke's *Second Treatise on Civil Government*.

In the conflicts and in the single basic agreement of Hobbes and Locke, the meaning of the seventeenth century comes clear. Hobbes was the older man: he was born in 1588, the year of the defeat of the Spanish Armada, and he died at the venerable age of ninety-one, long after the restoration of the Stuarts. Like the Calvinists, Hobbes believed in the sinful nature of man—in a state of nature, he said, it is "every man against every man," and life, in consequence, is "solitary, poor, nasty, brutish and short." In his shrewd guess that there had never been a "golden age" of primitive freedom, Hobbes, who had not had the benefit of modern anthropological research, rested his case on pure assumption. But it was a reasonable enough inference at a time when Oliver Cromwell's rule and that of his incompetent son, "Tumbledown Dick," was going to pieces. If men were "sociable one with another," said Hobbes, "like bees and ants," they would not need an "artificial covenant" to bind themselves to sociability. But, unlike the bees and the ants, men are "continually in competition for Honour and Dignity . . . and consequently amongst men there ariseth on that ground, Envy and Hatred, and finally Warre . . ."

Nor could the individual conscience, as disciplined by religion, prevent that "warre." After all, it was over religious differences as well as over tax matters and parliamentary supremacy that the rebellion of the seventeenth century had been fought. Hobbes distrusted Puritans, he distrusted Quakers, he distrusted Catholics—or any "boy or wench [who] thought he spoke with God Almighty." To keep the peace, said Hobbes, a strong "artificiall" creature, a "great Leviathan," was necessary. Hobbes considered that the Leviathan must have the power to overrule the individual judgment of men on all issues, whether of property or anything else. He was a totalitarian in all save one very English thing: he believed that government derived from a compact, or a contract, made between men to accept a ruler over them. Implied in the bond of this compact was the promise that the ruler would be just. Government was not accepted by men for the exaltation of the ruler, or for the mystical adoration of the state; it was accepted to obtain peace and protection in one's own estate.

As Hobbes put it, the "liberty of the subject . . . lyeth . . . in those things, which in regulating their actions, the Sovereign hath praetermitted: such as Liberty to buy, and sell, and otherwise contract with one another; to choose their own aboad, their own diet, their own trade of life, and institute their children as they themselves think fit . . ." And "the obligation of subjects to the sovereign is understood to last as long, and no longer, than the power lasteth, by which he is able to protect them. For the right men have by Nature to protect themselves, when none else can protect them, can by no covenant be relinquished . . . The end of Obedience is Protection. . . ."

In other words, a *quid* for a *quo*. Both in his trust in a ruler's "protective" benevolence and in his feeling that the ruler would naturally "praetermit" the liberty to buy and sell, to live where one chose, and to bring up one's children in one's own way, Hobbes took great chances. He had been a tutor in mathematics to Charles II before the Restoration, and he thus knew the Stuarts at a time when they were willing to promise much in order to regain the Crown. Though he did not believe in divine right, his doctrine, which he presented in vellum to Charles II in exile, was good enough for a restoration-minded king. For had not Hobbes said that it was a "disease" of a "common-wealth" to believe "that he hath the soveraigne power is subject to the civil lawes?" The Hobbesian compact gave total power to the king by free gift—and it was only another manifestation of "disease" to think the power could be "divided"

into parliamentary, executive and judicial comp&
each constituting a check on the other.

John Locke, whose phrases were to become the language of the American Revolution and the Declaration of
Independence, was fully as disgusted as Hobbes with the
excesses of the Puritan Commonwealth. Even as much as
John Milton he came to think that "new Presbyter is but
old priest writ large." But he did not react to the intoler-
ance of the Cromwellian "liberators" with the extreme
veneration for kingship that is implicit in Hobbes' *Leviathan*. Possessing a supple and sinuous mind, with a scientist's insistence on precision (he was a physician as well as
a philosopher), Locke was ultimately to show how a "compact" for a "soveraigne" could be made a two-way instrument, hedging the king about with agreed-upon limitations
of the ruler's own liberties, and giving Parliament a most
effective veto on the executive through control over the
power of the purse.

Locke was born in 1632, forty-four years after Hobbes,
and he was only nine years old when the great Civil War
of the seventeenth century broke out. His father, a fervent
adherent of the Puritan cause, captained a Roundhead
band in the West of England, where the seafarers of Bristol
were up in arms about the ship money exactions. Locke
himself had a strict Puritan upbringing, spending six years
at Westminster School in London where he was surrounded
by the tumult and the rumblings which led up to the be-
heading of Charles I. He went on to Christ Church at
Oxford when that royalist institution was officially being
"cleansed" by the Puritan party. But John Owen, the dean
of Christ Church, was a most tolerant Puritan at heart,
and the spirit of toleration survived throughout Oxford as

a whole during the entire Commonwealth period. The local Puritans permitted great scholars such as Dr. Edward Pococke, who taught Hebrew and Arabic to Locke, to remain at the university without taking the oath of allegiance to Cromwell. Locke's friends at Christ Church included unrepentant Royalists. It was from John Owen, the latitudinarian Puritan, that Locke in all probability picked up his key thought on toleration—that it is the duty of the state to let all religious sects alone except those whose aim is the subversion of the civil power.

By the time of the Stuart restoration Locke had pretty well lost his Puritanism. He welcomed the Restoration for its "quiet settlement," and hoped that men would be "kind to their religion, their country and themselves" by forgoing the "overzealous contention" of the Puritans. The "popular asserters of public liberty," he wrote, "are the greatest engrossers of it too." Continuing in this vein of subdued contrition, he said: "A general freedom is but a general bondage . . . all the freedom I can wish my country or myself is, to enjoy the protection of those laws which the prudence and providence of our ancestors established, and the happy return of his majesty has restored."

But if, like Hobbes, he trusted the Stuarts to be protectors of ancestral liberties, he was soon to suffer the second disillusioning experience of his young life: Charles II soon broke his word and permitted a revival of ecclesiastical tyranny. By 1667 Locke's departure from Hobbesian thinking was clear. In an early essay on toleration (not to be confused with the more famous *Letter on Toleration* which he wrote in exile in 1685), the whole theory of the proper limitation of the respective spheres of individual and governmental action is stated with admirable precision.

Like Hobbes, Locke begins in 1667 with the idea that governments are necessary to "preserve men in this world from the fraud and violence of one another." This is the seventeenth-century view of human nature, and nothing that has happened in the twentieth has done much to disprove it. But since men remain men even when they are governors, it does not do to take any ruler on trust. Some method must be found to guard the guardians; and to keep "magistrates" from going out of bounds it must be clearly understood that they have no role but the limited one of protecting men in their lives, their liberty and their "estate."

Since the rise of Marxian criticism in the nineteenth century, it has become the fashion to say that the Glorious Revolution of 1688, which unseated James II and brought William of Orange to the throne of England, was the work of property holders who were totally uninterested in the larger question of the rights of everybody in the community. But the view of Locke was that if the state would stick to the narrow issue of preserving "life, liberty and estate" against the violence of thieves, anarchs and outside marauders, freedom and tolerance in all spheres would follow as a matter of course.

A government, said Locke in 1667, if derived from the people, can only have the power necessary to "their own preservation." "This being premised," he continued, "...the magistrate ought to do or meddle with nothing *but barely* in order to secure the civil peace and property of his subjects." The business of government was to make as few laws as possible; there was no need for "laws to any other end but only for the security of the government and protection of people in their lives, estates and liberties . . ." And, so Locke asked in a bit of ringing rhetoric in defense of the religious tolerance which was his real overmastering concern, "can it be reasonable that he that cannot compel me to buy a house should force me his way to venture the purchase of heaven?"

In sum, Locke asserted that if a government began using force for any reason besides protecting individuals in their lives, liberties and estates against the presumption of force exerted by others, it thereby demeaned itself and no longer deserved to hold the allegiance of men. This amounted to a qualified right of revolution any time a government denied such things as freedom of speech, assembly and religion.* With Locke, toleration came first; the defense of property was the means to an end that could well be left to the individual without the intercession of government. Locke was property-minded because he was freedom-minded, not because he cared particularly for the material goods of this world as such.

All of Locke's basic distinctions were set down a full generation before the Glorious Revolution of 1688. They were set down in vivid recollection of the arbitrary compulsions in all spheres, whether religious, cultural or economic, of both the early Stuart regimes and the Cromwellian interlude. They were set down before Locke, as physician and tutor in the family of Anthony Ashley Cooper (or Lord Ashley), was drawn into a broad enterprise of his patron for colonizing the Carolinas. Locke

---

* Bertrand de Jouvenel and Willmoore Kendall observe that Locke provided for no defense against a possible "tyranny of the majority." His doctrine of parliamentary supremacy would allow a majority vote to "conclude the rest." But when Locke was writing, the House of Lords and the king's veto, to say nothing of the courts, constituted a check on pure majoritarianism. And in any event, Locke insisted the realm of "Caesar" did not include either religious teaching or economic decision.

served as secretary for Lord Ashley's colonizing group: he recorded the proposed constitution for the Carolinas in his own handwriting, and he is almost certainly the author of that part of the constitution which insisted on freedom for any religious sect which could muster as many as seven adherents.

The sole limitation to be placed on any "religion of seven" was that the liberties claimed by it should not include the liberty of attempting to coerce others to its beliefs. Applied to the modern day, Locke's "model" for a constitution would permit any party to exist that did not have for its aim the supersession or suppression of other parties. Clearly he would outlaw the Communist Party as long as it adhered to its belief in the necessity of a dictatorship. But for all groups which believed in freedom he would say to government: "Hands off!"

Twenty-odd years after his part in writing the Fundamental Constitution of the Carolinas, Locke published his systematic presentations of ideas on toleration and the limited role of government. Although he had set forth his matured views on government as early as 1681, when he wrote them down for his own guidance, he withheld them until final overthrow of the Stuarts made it safe to issue them. In the fashion that was increasingly to be followed by eighteenth-century thinkers, he ignored journalistic immediacy in favor of going back to first principles.

"In the beginning and first peopling of the great common of the world," he wrote in his famous *Second Treatise on Civil Government*, ". . . the law man was under was . . . for appropriating. God commanded, and his wants forced him, to labour. That was his property, which could not be taken from him wherever he had fixed it. And hence subduing or cultivating the earth, and having dominion, we see are joined together. The one gave title to the other. So that God, by commanding to subdue, gave authority so far to appropriate. And the condition of human life, which re-quires labour and materials to work on, necessarily intro-duces private possessions."

In the beginning, as anthropologists were later to surmise, "private possessions" were held in common by blood rela-tions, the gens—or the house—of Roman antiquity, or the ramified family clan which has persisted into modern times in the Scottish Highlands or the Indian village community. The conveyance of family-held lands to others could not be undertaken without the permission of all members of the clan. But if Locke—and Hobbes before him—knew nothing of anthropology, it still followed that labor, when "mixed" with raw materials, creates the original property right.

Following on from this, Locke argued that man must have a right to defend his own possessions and to bequeath or otherwise bestow them as he sees fit. But, since men are not angels, private judgment could not be relied upon to settle conflicting claims. "All private judgment of every particular member being excluded," said Locke, "the com-munity comes to be the umpire . . . those who are united unto one body, and have a common established law and judicature to appeal to, with authorities to decide contro-versies between them and punish offenders, are in civil so-ciety one with another . . ." The society, of course, derives from the consent of the governed, and civil government "relates only to men's civil interests, is confined to the care of the things of this world, and hath nothing to do with the world to come . . . the business of laws is not to provide for the truth of opinion, but for the safety and security of the commonwealth, and of every particular man's goods and person."

Again and again Locke hammered it home, both in the *Second Treatise on Civil Government* and in the *Letter on Toleration,* that the "political society is instituted for no other end, but only to secure every man's possessions of the things of this life." The soul, the things of the spirit and the transmission of possessions in the marketplace were "not to be compelled . . . either by law or force."

Before Locke, people had tended to confuse the concept of "society" with the concept of the state. Where Locke was a distinct advance on Hobbes—or on Aristotle, for that matter—was in his feeling that society and the state are two distinct things. The function of the state is to permit people to live in society by protecting them in their property relationships, and to keep them from killing, maiming or otherwise harming each other. But beyond that both individuals and society are to be left alone to order things by mutual contract or by the principle of voluntary association. The whole realm of governmental interference with economic matters—whether it concerns the fixing of prices, or the "planning" of industry, or the seizure of one man's substance to endow another, becomes, in the Lockean view of things, an invasion of the social individual's right to do his own planning and association or to undertake his own bequests or charities.

Locke's was the theory of the umpire as against the vampire state, and in distant America, where the colonists followed English doings with an avidity that was only intensified by the time it took to get news of the homeland, his ideas were read and pondered along with Coke's commentary on Magna Charta, and Blackstone's later eighteenth-century commentaries on the law of England. The Lockean distinctions and Coke's teachings about the "law of the land" lay around like so much dry tinder, awaiting the spark that would be struck when the Hanoverian kings, forgetting that their patents to the Crown derived from the Whig tradition of 1688, tried to revive the pretensions of the Stuarts to absolute rule.

Private property, as Russell Kirk has said, has been a powerful instrument for teaching men and women responsibility, and for giving them the leisure to think and freedom to act with prudence. In the America which read Locke and Coke, property was the rule rather than the exception: as Gouverneur Morris was to point out at the time of the Constitutional Convention of 1787, some ninety percent of the colonists were members of freeholders' families. They were used to thinking for themselves and exercising their own responsibilities.

They had, indeed, been Lockean men from the beginning: America had come into being by Lockean social compacts, such as the Mayflower compact, which instituted governments by popular consent. The colonists frequently departed from Lockean toleration, notably in the witch-burnings at Salem and in the persecutions that drove Roger Williams from Massachusetts Bay to Rhode Island and Hooker's charges to Hartford in the Connecticut valley. But the colonists, for all their moral frailties when it came to practicing what they preached, were accustomed to the distinction between society and the state, for their own Pilgrim or Quaker or Maryland Catholic (or even Cavalier) societies in the Old World had reacted to state persecution by emigration. As Trevelyan has put it, "twenty thousand Puritans had already carried their skill and in-

dustry, their silver and gold, their strivings and hopes" to
the New World before the successful outcome of the Civil
War revived hopes for their independent kind in England.

Naturally, the men who had dared to emigrate were at-
tuned to Locke's thinking and quite ready to make it the
"party line" of the American rebellion against George III.
The Hanoverian kings' "plan" for seaboard America—to
keep it a raw material country, to force it to buy tea from
the East India Company's monopoly and manufactures
from British merchants, and to seal it off from the Missis-
sippi Valley, which was envisioned as a preserve for the
fur trade with headquarters in Quebec—seemed to the
Lockean colonists to be a complete invasion of everything
that had been fought for in the English revolutions of the
seventeenth century.

As for the non-Puritan sections of seaboard America,
they had the Lockean tradition of tolerance as set forth in
the Carolina constitution. The lawyers in these sections
had also been reared on Coke's and Blackstone's commentaries, which insisted on the common-law rights of all Englishmen, regardless of where or in what status of life they
might be. Jefferson and Washington spoke Locke's language even as John Adams in Massachusetts; moreover,
though they had an obvious interest in the lands of the
Ohio valley, they spoke it from more truly disinterested
motives. After all, even though they groused at being in
debt to British merchants, it would not have mattered so
much to tobacco planters to be forced to remain in "raw
material" status as producers, for their big market for tobacco was in England.

When Thomas Jefferson, a truly disinterested Virginian,
repaired to his room in the bricklayer's house in Philadel-

phia to write the Declaration of Independence, his mind was full of the Lockean phrases. It was also full of rage against George III. The general principles of the Declaration—that men have inalienable rights to life, liberty and the pursuit of happiness (a Jefferson substitution which was by no means designed to subvert the property right)— were followed by a Lockean affirmation that governments are instituted by men to "secure these rights." Then came the full force of Jefferson's rage: George III was accused of a whole category of abuses, of "refusing" to assent to "wholesome and necessary" laws, of bribing judges, of rendering the military superior to the civil power, of quartering troops in colonists' homes, of cutting off the colonists' trade, of imposing taxes without consent, of depriving Americans of trial by jury, of plundering the seas and sending foreign mercenaries to "compleat the work of death, desolation and tyranny," and of suspending colonial legislatures and taking away colonial charters.

The rage behind Jefferson's short, stabbing phrases was real, but the form it took was an imitation that must have been artfully calculated to stress the relation of Anglo-Americans to English tradition. For Jefferson's bill of complaints follows the pattern of the complaints set forth in the English Bill of Rights of 1689, which was inspired by the thinking of Locke. Like the Declaration, the English Bill of Rights punched out a list of grievances in short, pithy sentences. King James II had "endeavored to subvert laws and liberties," he had levied money for Crown use without permission of Parliament, he had quartered troops "contrary to law," he had disarmed Protestants at a time when "Papists were . . . armed," he had violated the freedom of parliamentary elections, he had imposed excessive fines and illegal and cruel punishments, and so forth and so on. The whole list, with minor changes, had found its echo in the Declaration of Independence almost a century later.

When he was accused by his fellow Virginians and by morose New Englanders of copying Locke and stealing from George Mason's Virginia Declaration of Rights, Jefferson answered that he "did not consider it as any part of my charge to invent new ideas." All he knew was that he "turned to neither book nor pamphlet while writing it." It was "intended as an expression of the American mind." The ideas were in the air, they had been thoroughly debated everywhere throughout the colonies, and even after the hacking process of editing the Declaration was ended, the words stood for the bold consensus of an embattled people.

Whether the sole original substitution in the Declaration—that of "pursuit of happiness" for "property"—was a wise substitution has often been argued. However, the violation of the Lockean triad hardly matters if one looks into the furnishings of Jefferson's own mind for a clue to his intention. No one can deny that "pursuit of happiness" is an inalienable right of the individual. (No one can pursue happiness for another, and no one can benefit by trying to steal the "pursuit" from somebody else.) Moreover, no one can "pursue happiness" for himself without paying some attention to "property" as a means to the end of contentment and enjoyment of one's days. Jefferson had no animus against property in speaking for happiness; he merely wished to use an idea that would make the blood race a little faster.

Indeed, Jefferson's reading in the 1770s included, besides Locke, a number of works which inquired specifically into the origins of property. Jefferson was fond of quoting from Lord Kames's *History of Property,* a book which argued that if men did not devote at least some time to their own estate, then "independency" and "liberty" would both be destroyed. With Jefferson, both "independency" and "liberty" were absolutely necessary to the "pursuit of happiness." Again we come back to the indissoluble nature of all the "rights": life, liberty, property and the pursuit of happiness are all component parts of one great chain.

In any event, the colonists fought for "life, liberty and property" and eschewed happiness for the moment. When the long struggle was over at Yorktown, they returned to their property bases in the respective states. They soon found that neither life nor liberty could be sustained, or happiness pursued, without a special type of government which would guarantee respect for contractual relations among property holders who wished to trade in a single currency across state lines. So came the call for still another Lockean compact, the one that was to be hammered out at Philadelphia in 1787 by men who had read the *Second Treatise on Civil Government* and were bent on restating it in American terms.

As we shall see, this compact set the stage for Adam Smith's "simple system of natural liberty," providing a legal framework in which it could operate over vast spaces. Without the American political structure there would have been no dynamic capitalism. And when the structure collapses, dynamic capitalism will also cease to be.

Chapter Three

The Political Frame
for an Open Society

Capitalism presupposes an open society in which the
ends are determined by individuals, or by voluntary
associations of individuals. It is fundamentally incompatible with the idea of an all-encompassing state purpose, or
a single official Manifest Destiny—though it is thoroughly
compatible with a church whose own purposes are extra-
governmental, either "not of this world" or, if of this world,
devoted to leadership, mediation and charity in the realms
which do not belong to Caesar.

Theoretically, of course, it is quite conceivable that capitalism could flourish without a legal framework, either
under pure anarchism or under a beneficent landlordism,
or with the blessings of a "let alone" monarch. But, as we
shall see, it was James Madison, the scholar among the
Founding Fathers, who put his finger unerringly on the
need for a device which will put automatic checks on government if any freedoms are to flourish. Purely as a practical matter the institutions of an open society demand the
safeguards of a limited government.

This is not to say that limited government is the *cause*
of capitalism, or that it is the superstructure, either. It is

merely to say that freedom is all of a piece. Government is necessary, for men, in Madison's phrase, are not angels. But since nonangelic men inevitably become the governors as well as the governed, the liberties of the individual, including the liberty to own, buy and sell, must be protected from the possible cupidity, rapacity and power-lust of office-holders. Capitalism, like any other manifestation of free choice, depends on the ability of a people to discover a political device, or a frame, which, in Professor John W. Burgess's famous phrase, will reconcile government with liberty.

To debate whether capitalism came before or after free government is a hen-egg proposition which can only lead to much scrambled history. All we can say for certain is that capitalism—the free application of energy and property to the making of things for trade in the open market—will grow wherever there is a cranny or a chink in a "planned" or controlled system. Once fairly started, it tends to eventuate in limited government. Venice, the dominant Mediterranean trading community of the later middle ages, was a republic. The free cities of northern Italy and the Hanseatic League operated outside of the lord-and-vassal relational pattern of feudalism, and the feudality was resisted whenever it tried to come inside the city gates. Conversely, when the Roman Republic became the Empire, and the Empire, in turn, started monkeying with fixed prices and a controlled bread-and-circuses economy, the decline came fast. And when the intendants of the French Bourbons tried to consolidate all decision-making, even to the extent of prescribing minutely for the operations of the textile trade, within the reach of government, the great explosion of 1789 was foreshadowed.

It was to get away from the all-encompassing purpose

of king or dictator that colonists of all kinds fled to America. Dimly, they were all seeking the delineation of some realm of individual immunity against governmental power. The Pilgrims and early Puritans came to the shores of Massachusetts Bay to escape the *this*-worldly aegis of Archbishop Laud, who believed that state and church were the divinely ordained co-extensive planners for society or the community. The Quakers journeyed to Penn's Woods on the Delaware because the inner light of their devotions clashed with the outer light of the court. As for the Cavaliers, they too were immunity-seekers once their Stuart patrons were in exile. They flocked to the southern colonies because, in John Milton's own phrase, the Cromwellian presbyter turned out to be "old priest writ large."

It is hardly to be denied that many of the newcomers to America backslid, some of them immediately. Their ideas of the proper boundaries of individual immunity frequently clashed. Some of them set up stringent this-worldly theocracies, persecuting the dissenter, the Quaker, the agnostic or the witch. When the lamp of resolution burned low, they acquiesced in arbitrary rule by colonial governors sent over from England to keep a stern hand on the controls. Nevertheless, despite the backsliding and the cross-purposes, the yeast of voluntary planning and individual choice was at work. America was becoming an open society, not a mere extension of a European state. In the course of a very few generations Puritan and Quaker and Cavalier—yes, and the indentured servants imported by all three—tended to coalesce, accepting the great home-country reconciliation that began with the Restoration of the Stuarts and continued with the Glorious Revolution of 1688, which made limited government its *sine qua non.*

We have seen that the colonists were the heirs of the

thinking of John Locke, the philosopher of inalienable rights. But Locke, after all, was sophisticated stuff: his treatises on toleration and civil government were for the self-chosen leaders of the rebellion against George III. Since there were no Gallup polls at the time it is impossible to know how many colonists actually read Locke save as he happened to be "brokered" for the multitudes by popular pamphleteers. Of one thing, however, we may be sure: colonists of all sorts read the Bible.

As Rose Wilder Lane has pointed out, many of the colonists were children of men and women who had actually risked their necks to interpret the Scriptures for themselves. These sons and daughters of the Dissent didn't read the Bible as a substitute for Aristotle on politics; they were thinking about their immortal souls. But what they imbibed, often unconsciously, was heady political stuff. They read about the God of the shepherd Abraham—a single God who judged a man's rightness in living but made no attempt to force His say on human beings. Man, in the Old Testament, was left to control himself. The Ten Commandments of the God of Abraham were largely negatives: they told man what he should not do. But the negatives presupposed a positive creed.

Charles A. Beard, among others, has emphasized the continuity of Locke's thinking with that of Thomas Hooker, who, in turn, drew upon Thomas Aquinas. But one needs no paraphernalia of scholarship to know that the commandment against murder is simply the other face of Locke's and Jefferson's "unalienable" right to life. "Thou shalt not steal" means that the Bible countenances private property—for if a thing is not owned in the first place it can scarcely be stolen. "Thou shalt not covet" means that it is sinful even to contemplate the seizure of another man's goods—which is something which socialists, whether Christian or other, have never managed to explain away. Furthermore, the prohibitions against false witness and adultery mean that contracts should be honored and double-dealing eschewed. As for the commandment to "honor thy father and thy mother that thy days may be long," this implies that the family, not the state, is the basic continuing unit and constitutive element of society.

By extension, or deduction, the Lockean creed is all here: the right to life, the right to the liberty and property necessary to sustain life, and the importance of the free family unit as the guarantor, through its love and possessions, of "long" days in the land given by the Lord.

The Bible-reading colonists, then, had no actual need for the sophistications of late seventeenth-century political science. They were the children of antiquity, heirs to the oldest wisdom known to Western man. The minds which they brought to the New World were no *tabula rasa:* the slate was colored by a tradition which antedated the medieval world by centuries. Even those deists, the Jeffersonians, who thought of God as a vaguely impersonal Creator, derived their ideas of "natural law" from sources which had been approved by believers in a personal God throughout the ages.

But if the colonists brought with them a tradition, they had managed to shed all those social incrustations of the medieval world—the master-serf relationships of feudalism and a landowning system made static by the device of entailing estates—which had almost caused the tradition to founder. In America there were no incrustations. There was merely an open world. Thus, though many of the colonists were hemmed in at first by the restrictions of Calvinism and its lip-service belief in the predestination of "God's elect," they were in a position to apply the Mosaic—or the Lockean—law *de novo*. They were not *compelled* men. Bound by no master plan, they moved outward from their individual freehold farms to meet their brothers in the marketplace—and capitalism, in its most primitive phases, was the natural result.

In recent years Professor R. H. Tawney (see his *Religion and the Rise of Capitalism*) has tried, at least by implication, to make it appear that capitalism was a mere by-product of the weakening of religious ties, an offshoot of the this-worldly aspects of Calvinism, which regarded a man's prosperity as the visible evidence of election by the Lord. But Tawney's effort to show that true Christianity is incompatible with freedom of choice in the economic sphere is a whopping *non sequitur*. The truth is that morality has no redemptive virtue (and no Christian meaning) when it rests on compulsion. It is utterly incongruous to believe that one can be thrust or pulled into Heaven by a command which is wholly contemptuous of the individual's own will. As Hilaire Belloc, that most Christian man, has said, freedom and the exercise of one's will are aspects of the same thing—and a world which denies to an individual the right to choose the all-important means and methods of his own livelihood is a world without moral content.

Rightly interpreted, what Tawney—and Max Weber before him—actually proves is that Christianity tends to create a capitalistic mode of life whenever siege conditions do not prevail. (This is not to say that capitalism is Christian in and by itself; it is merely to say that capitalism is a material by-product of the Mosaic law.) In the early Middle Ages, which fostered the landholding system which the Puritans, the Quakers and the Cavaliers left behind them when they came to America, Western Europe was palpably under a state of siege. It was the time of the castle, the moat, the walled community. The Saracens had closed out the Mediterranean by seizing its littoral on three sides. The Roman world, retreating into the north, was robbed of its spaciousness and mobility; men gave up city life and huddled close to the "big house" of the armed lord, turning in their titles to freedom in exchange for the protections of the feudal order. As in any armed camp, rights and obligations were made reciprocal. A response to pressures from without, feudalism, with its emphasis on local strength, became the source of anarchistic quarrels between lord and lord within its own European orbit. There were sieges within sieges. The Christian church, growing up in a harsh atmosphere, performed its noble work by softening the rigors of a life that was essentially military; it stressed the spiritual duties of those implicated in a "relational" society and so prevented the feudal lord from becoming a crude caudillo. The church, as the protector of its flock, put a check on temporal government and thus saved each feudal locality from becoming a small totalitarian despotism. Far from being the source and protector of the political and economic institutions of the Middle Ages, the church was the buffer which defended the individual against the more abrasive trends of the times.

Naturally the church took a stand against usury in a period when there was no opportunity for money loans to expand into a fruitfulness that would reward both the borrower and the lender. Because money was quickly "used up" by the small-time medieval borrower, it seemed monstrous to Thomas Aquinas and other Catholic philosophers to compel men to pay interest on what was no longer there. Money as something which had a "rental value," like land, would not readily be understood until the time had come when it could easily be turned into machinery or other capital goods, which had a continuing existence. The church also stood for a "just price" and for the manifold restrictions of the medieval guild because there was little room for adventurous competition in a society of closed manors which strained for protection from Saxon freebooter or Saracen raider, or merely for safety from the lusts of the baron on the other side of the river.

Once the enemy had been pushed back, however, the free will that is at the heart of the Christian order had its impact in the economic sphere. The Venetians, the Ragusans and the Genoans adventured once again on the bosom of the Mediterranean. Freedoms which had flourished in the monotheistic Saracen world seeped back into Europe from the East and South as the frontiers of Christian energy expanded. Moreover, an energy that was capable of building cathedrals was capable of building clock towers to mark a purely mundane time. Even the monasteries themselves became centers of manufacture and trade. The monks made the best liqueurs, as all lovers of benedictine or cointreau can attest to this day.

In all of this, there was a belated continuity with the far past of the Judaic and Greco-Roman civilizations. Actually, the continuity had hardly been submerged even during the most straitened medieval times. Recent revisionists of the Tawney–Max Weber thesis that our economic order grew out of the Calvinistic emphasis on saving and hard work have pointed out that capitalism, including the refinements of credit, first flourished in four-teenth-century Italian cities where Catholicism was at its crest. The Medici of Florence were businessmen. And banking was further elaborated in the Catholic cities of South Germany. This medieval banking escaped the cate-gory of usury for the simple reason that the creditors ad-vanced money to enable people to earn money which blessed both lender and borrower alike.

In line with the revisionism of the Tawney–Max Weber notions, a lively controversy is now going on in the more esoteric economic journals. The Tawney thesis is being turned upside down by economists who argue that the medieval Catholic scholastics were wholly individualist in their approach to economics. The scholastics believed in natural law—and in the inalienable rights that must be deduced therefrom. Unlike the Calvinists of a later day, the scholastics did not believe in the divinity of work. Labor, to them, was the "curse of Adam," a necessary means of making a living. Consequently, they were never bemused into trying to elaborate a labor theory of value. They knew, as all sensible men must know, that value originates in the eye of the beholder. It achieves objective market expression in a price when two or more beholders clamor for the same thing. What the medieval scholastic philosophers stressed was the consumer's sovereignty and the ability of the market to decide value when one thing was offered for another. The medieval "just price," accord-ing to Emil Kauder, Murray Rothbard and other "revi-sionists" of Tawney, was essentially the market price de-cided upon by individuals who were not under the duress of making "necessitous" bargains.

Even on Tawney's own showing, both Calvinism and Lutheranism, far from trying conscientiously to plow a furrow for capitalism, were reactions against the practices of a Christianity that seemed suddenly to let down the bars everywhere, even in its temporal headquarters in Rome. Calvin's own words on usury echo the thirteenth century. In early Calvinistic Massachusetts Puritans were put in the stocks for taking interest or for charging more than the going price. But the pull of the American earth was too strong for Calvinism. Even as in seventeenth-century England, the American Puritans gave up their strictness when it became apparent to the most committed of them that the Western world was no longer living in a state of siege. The defeat of the French and Indian menace on the frontier in the middle of the eighteenth century removed the last block which had kept the Puritan from becoming the Yankee. By the time of the Declaration of Independence Americans everywhere conceived themselves as defending an open society which they regarded as their Christian as well as their English birthright. The Ten Commandments and the natural rights philosophy which Locke took over from the medieval scholastics had had their way.

Obviously, an open society must be guaranteed against the tyranny of an individual, whether he be king or dictator. That, the colonists intended to do when they declared their independence. But the open society must also be made proof against the tyranny of a majority. "Planning," whether it is conducted in the name of a monarch or according to the decree of a mystical "general will" imposed by majority rule, comes in the end to the same thing: the minorities are sacrificed to the requirements of the plan. The colonists had had enough of such sacrifice, and at

Philadelphia, in 1787, they proceeded to fashion themselves a document and a political structure which would, at least as far as they could foresee, be proof against any tyranny, whether of the One or the Many.

At this point it might be asked why, given thirteen state governments which had fought a successful war for the Lockean and Christian rights, a federal government was needed to supplant the existing Articles of Confederation. And, indeed, there is a school of critics and historians which holds that the thirteen states could have gone on managing for themselves. From Randolph Bourne to Professor Van Tyne, this school has insinuated that the Founders, in attempting to create or recover a federal consciousness, were meddling with freedom, not adding to its luster and scope.

Theoretically, of course, rights do not depend on the size of government. But the Founders had fought a war against an Empire, and the fighting, as George Washington could well attest, had been rendered the more difficult because the sovereign American power had had thirteen heads. There had been the money difficulty—what with various state issues, all of them degenerating in value, and with the continental currency "not worth a continental," it had been next to impossible to satisfy the troops on pay day. There had also been the difficulty of getting New Englanders to fight in Jersey, or Jerseymen to carry on as the war moved toward Virginia. The money and enlistment parochialisms might have been fatal if British war office bungling and the French fleet had not come to George Washington's rescue in time.

The Founders sensed that to survive in a world that was still dominated in 1787 by England, France and Spain, all of whom had territory and territorial ambitions in the

New World, a permanent union of states was needed. But how effectively to join the thirteen colonies? Madison sent to Jefferson for books: and the law and the history of confederations which he read about in those books demonstrated nothing but failure. The city states of Greece had perished for want of an enduring principle of freedom-in-federation. Other "leagues" had done no better than the one which had been led by ancient Athens.

What the Founders wanted was a government which could take over the "power of the border" for all thirteen states, with enough sovereignty to conduct a unified diplomacy, to raise a federal army and pay it in good federal currency, and to deal with such matters as tariffs on a uniform basis. A single "power of the border" would keep Britain and Spain, for example, from trying to play off the southern colonies against New England, and both of them against the Middle States. But if the need for a single diplomatic and military power was obvious to the generation of Washington, Hamilton and Madison, the way to get it without sacrificing little Delaware to large Pennsylvania, or without surrendering the rights of the citizens to a possibly imperialist center, was not readily apparent.

Madison's theory, as expounded in No. 10 of *The Federalist,* was that in any great society "there will be rich and poor, creditors and debtors, a landed interest, a monied interest, a mercantile interest, a manufacturing interest." These interests, he continued, "may again be subdivided according to the different productions of different situations and soils . . ." Under pure majoritarian democracy, any combination of fifty-one percent of the people might gang up on "interests" which happened to be in a minority. "A pure democracy," said Madison in elaboration, "can admit no cure for the mischiefs of faction . . . there is nothing to check the inducements to sacrifice the weaker party. Hence it is that democracies have ever been found incompatible with personal security or the rights of property; and have, in general, been as short in their lives as they have been violent in their deaths."

Thus, well in advance of the French Revolution, Madison showed himself to be aware of the totalitarian poisons in Rousseau's theory of popular rule. The Constitution, which sought to set up internal bulwarks against the "passion of majorities," was a "social contract" (to use the French term), but it rejected Rousseau's contractual stipulation that "each of us places in common his person and his powers under the supreme direction of the general will." In common with most of his fellow-Founders, Madison wanted the compulsions of "general will" to be limited to specific, enumerated items.

"The great desideratum in Government is," he wrote, "so to modify the sovereignty as that it may be sufficiently neutral to control one part from invading the rights of another, and at the same time sufficiently controlled itself from setting up an interest adverse to that of the entire Society."

Once that principle had been thoroughly grasped at Philadelphia, the rest was merely architecture. The Convention provided for the continuation of its representative organizing power by providing for ways in which the states or the citizens thereof would have the final say on amendments to the Constitution. As for setting up both state and individual immunities against the power of a federal majority, the Constitution put a whole sheaf of things beyond the reach of legislature and executive alike. There were prohibitions against retroactive law, against double jeopardy of life or limb, against trials not conducted before an impartial jury, against laws designed to curb freedom of speech and the press, and so on. From the economic standpoint three things must interest us here particularly. One is that the states were not permitted to put obstacles in the way of interstate commerce. A second is that the money standard was federalized. And the third was that the Bill of Rights (which should be considered as part of the original Constitution) contained a specific defense of private property. "No person," says the Fifth Amendment, "shall be . . . deprived of life, liberty, or property, without due process of law; nor shall private property be taken for public use, without just compensation."

Finally, to keep the government from exceeding its powers, the Founders saw to it that the various functions of government should be separated, so as to check each other. A Supreme Court was created to keep both the lawmakers and the executive from invading the immunities guaranteed to the states and to individual citizens.

The Founders may have exceeded their authority (which was to "amend" the Articles of Confederation, not to throw everything into the hopper and make an entirely new beginning), but the people of at least eleven of the thirteen states did not object to the loose interpretation of mandate. We have had enough, perhaps, of the crude economic interpretation of the Constitution which stresses the plotting nature of Madison, Hamilton and Company. Charles A. Beard, who fathered the conspiracy theory, himself revolted against it in his old age when he came to Madison's defense in a noble book called *The Republic*. The original Beard thesis—that the Constitution was something put

over by an undemocratic coup at the expense of the farmers and mechanics—does not survive the recent researches
of Professor Robert E. Brown of Michigan State University. Professor Brown has demonstrated both the widespread nature of the franchise in eighteenth-century America (we had a "distributist" republic then, with some ninety
percent of the families owning land) and its broadly honest
representation at the Philadelphia convention and in the
state-ratifying conventions which followed.

The Constitution, on Professor Brown's voluminous evidence, was something which appealed to property holders
of all kinds, the farmers included. And the mechanics, who
possessed the franchise without landownership in many
places, had a hand in voting its acceptance, too. Naturally,
a generation which had fought a revolution for the sanc-
tity of the Lockean triad of life, liberty and property was
interested in the whole scope of the due process guarantees
of the Fifth Amendment. But if the property clause hadn't
been there, the Constitution would hardly have been acceptable to a people that was even then pushing westward
in a scramble to take up land.

The Founding Fathers did not succeed in making their
document foolproof. Professor John W. Burgess of Co-
lumbia University, who makes the "reconciliation of government with liberty" dependent upon the continuing existence of an organizing power behind and antecedent to
government itself, argues that the Founders should not
have permitted either Congress or the state legislatures to
have a hand in the amending process. Men holding political office, so Burgess observes, must be altogether too partial to amendments which serve to increase their power,
not diminish it. To forestall the erosion of liberties through

the aggrandizement of the political officers, amendments should in all circumstances be undertaken in representative convention by the people of the constituent states. They, after all, constitute the sovereign power whose consent made possible the original federal government.

The other flaws in the original Constitution were partly due to deliberate oversight (as in the decision to deny the blessings of liberty to Negro slaves), and partly due to the employment of loose language, as in the general welfare and the commerce clauses. Some one hundred and fifty years after the Founders had completed their labors, it was discovered that virtually anything at all can be done in the name of the general welfare and the right to "regulate commerce among the several states," even to the point of negating other parts of the Constitution. The Founders should have distinguished sharply between the particular welfare of groups and the general welfare, they should have tied the welfare clause to strictly enumerated powers, and they should have made plain that to regulate commerce does not mean to direct it or to control it. Finally, they should have forestalled in perpetuity the possibility of unchecked taxation—which, indeed, they thought they had done when they limited the levying of any *direct* tax to "proportion to the Census." The checks and balances of the federal system, the difficulty of amending the basic law, the fortunate internal division of our political parties and the fact that Senate elections are staggered over a six-year period, all operate to prevent rule in most things by an unchecked majority. But ever since the passage of the income tax amendment in 1912 there has been no constitutional limit on what legislators can do with the people's income. A congressional majority of fifty-one percent could vote *any* expropriation of any income group that it chose, which means that, fiscally speaking, the citizen has no rightful immunity whatsoever in the realm wherein he makes his living.

Given what they knew, however, the Founders did consummately well. While they did not intend to legislate *laissez-faire* (Hamilton had his heart set on the encouragement and protection of infant industries by a system of bounties or tariffs), they began with the individual as a self-controlled and self-directed person. They established a large free trade area under a uniform currency system. True, they imposed no check on the internal fiscal and economic policies of the several states, but the individual's right to move across state lines at will was sufficient of a guarantee against despotic measures in Albany, New York, say, or in Boston, Massachusetts. To this day a Boston citizen can dodge the Massachusetts inheritance laws by moving to Illinois or Florida; and a person who is irked by the New York State income tax can correct the imbalance by migrating for a few miles to Connecticut. Similarly, if a manufacturer doesn't like the labor laws or the business regulations of Michigan, he can move his plant to Indiana.

The Founders were not perfect men, and they certainly did not agree among themselves. Some feared the mob; some loved it. Some believed in paper money, some in a specie-backed central bank. Southerners among them wanted slavery perpetuated forever; some of the Virginians wanted to kill it by degrees; most of the northerners would have liked to get rid of it overnight. The differences were multiple, but on one thing the Founders were agreed: they wanted to set up a republic in such a way that differences—

and even basic inconsistencies—could be accepted and accommodated. The measure of their success is that they provided a framework which would permit lion and lamb, Hamiltonian and Jeffersonian, to go on living together without eating each other up. In all of this they had a big piece of luck: no state among the original thirteen was large enough or powerful enough to become cancerous, as the state of Prussia was to become the cancer in the late nineteenth-century German federation. Moreover, given equal representation in the Senate, it was a foregone conclusion that no Prussia would ever be allowed to develop in the future. Not even Texas is big enough or strong enough to become a Prussia.

The Founders could not foresee what the U.S. would become, economically speaking. Who among them could have prophesied that Eli Whitney's invention of the cotton gin would so strengthen the slaveholding interests as to push the southern states to the folly of civil war? Who among them could foresee that the same Eli Whitney's elaboration of dies to make interchangeable parts would ensure both northern manufacturing supremacy and victory in that civil war? Hamilton thought America would become a manufacturing nation but did not foresee the great westward push beyond the Alleghenies; Jefferson, on the other hand, anticipated the push, but thought the Middle West would remain for a long time a purely agricultural empire. Neither Jefferson nor Hamilton could know that electric power and the fluidity of modern transport would mean that manufacturing could be decentralized to the point where "urban sores" would be wholly unnecessary, thus enabling the Jeffersonian to make the most of the Hamiltonian world, and vice versa.

But if the Founders could not possibly have blueprinted a future America, they knew that freedom would be equal to any contingency. They knew the connections between the great human rights of life, liberty and property and an energy system that would function without impediment. Willy-nilly, they were good economists. Jefferson (who wasn't present in Philadelphia, but who saw to it that Madison got the literature he needed) was a friend and correspondent of J. B. Say, the Frenchman who first demonstrated, in his famous law of markets, that free production generates its own purchasing power. Jefferson knew the Physiocrats, but he was far from being a mere Physiocrat (a believer in simple agrarianism) himself, as his recommendation of Adam Smith's *The Wealth of Nations* as being the "best" book in political economy attests. As Murray Rothbard points out, Jefferson was libertarian to the core, a believer in *laissez-faire* and hard money. (What he objected to in Hamilton's position was its emphasis on tariffs, which would force an *uneconomic* shift of resources from farming and trade into manufacturing.) As for Hamilton, he was, save in the instance of the tariff, a confirmed follower of Adam Smith: many passages in his famous reports on banking, currency and manufacturers are paraphrases or even unacknowledged quotations from *The Wealth of Nations,* as Louis Hacker has recently demonstrated. In the case of Madison himself, though he feared the possible development of plutocracy, it was little Jamie, that "inimitable mixture of boyish fun . . . and sedateness," who thought of property as the great reason for government.

Because the property right was protected in our basic document, free capitalism had the political climate it needed for expansion. Five years after the making of the Constitution, Hamilton's (and Tench Coxe's) famous report on manufactures noted the existence of an American steel industry, a flourishing shipbuilding industry and a copper and brass industry. The textile industry burgeoned quickly on these shores once Samuel Slater had slipped out of Britain with the blueprint of an Arkwright factory committed to memory. Protected by the limitation of government, and with the space of a continent in which to grow, the simple system of natural liberty had found its habitat. It was not to be seriously challenged for a hundred and fifty years.

Chapter Four

Contract—or Capitalism Is Promises

In elaborating their theories of choice and property and the origins of the state whose business it is to protect men in their freedoms, the philosophers of the seventeenth and eighteenth centuries were not satisfied to rest their case on logic as applied to the evolving nature of man. No, they must make an appeal to distant and shadowy origins. In doing this they had little knowledge of prehistory or ancient history to support them. So they guessed.

Adam Smith guessed at an "innate propensity to truck and barter"—which cannot be found, say, among potlatch Indians or Melanesians. And all of them—from Hobbes to Rousseau, and from Locke to Smith himself—guessed at the notion of a grand covenant in the dawn of time which set up a contractual relationship between man and his political overlord, or king. With Hobbes, the contractual trade was one of obedience in all things for the single protection of the right to life; with Locke, the "compact" also included protection of liberty and property. With Rousseau, the contractual trade involved a surrender to the "general will"—which might or might not choose to respect the Rights of Man.*

The truth in all these theories resided in their correct reading of the nature of man as a self-controlled entity: one does not submit even to a potential tyrant (as in the case of Hobbes) or a possibly bloodthirsty majority (as in the case of Rousseau) without inwardly recognizing that a breaking point may come when the contract will be considered invalid. But, if the early "social compact" theorists were psychologically acute in their knowledge of man's political and social nature, they guessed wrong when they thought of man as an individual appropriator and worker of primordial acreage, or as an individual breeder of cattle, goats and sheep. The truth of the matter, as anthropological science began to surmise in the nineteenth century, was that the ancient world knew very little of individuals: Blackstone's romantic picture of a man resting in the shade of a tree and taking the spot for his very own did not reckon with the evidence that individualism belongs to the maturity of the race, not to its beginnings. The original appropriation of land and animals was not by individuals but by families, or by that expanded version of the family—the gens, tribe or clan.

It was Sir Henry Sumner Maine, a professor of civil law at Cambridge University and a member of the Supreme Council of India, who first exposed the unhistorical nature of Locke's and Rousseau's canny savages. Maine's *Ancient*

---

* It may be unfair to saddle Rousseau with the bloodthirsty sins of Robespierre. Rousseau was thinking of the "general will" of small, homogeneous communities, not that of a large, heterogeneous state in which force would be necessary to "conclude" fractious elements within the scope of a "general will."

Law, a magnificently written book which has been gathering library dust for many decades, clearly establishes the origin of property in group, or corporate, ownership. In the beginning the family, the clan, or the larger village community that grew out of family adoption of strangers into the "gens," held title to land and animals as a blood unit. Each member of the clan had his right to share in the product of the land; and each member could give or withhold his consent to the sale or conveyance of productive property to families outside the clan. Even the children were protected in their share of the group property right in the ancient Hindu village communities which Sir Henry studied in India.

The socialists were quick to capitalize upon the blow which Sir Henry's anthropology had seemingly delivered to Locke's theory of the individual's primordial right to property through the working of the law of individual appropriation and prescription. The village community, so the socialists said, was proof of a basic communistic bent in man. Sir Henry Maine, however, had no intention of proving a case for communism in his unearthing of the family origins of the property right. For all through his work there runs a leitmotif: the law of persons (i.e., of individuals) is superior to the law of the tribe, even though it came relatively late in legal evolution. As Sir Henry summed it up in a famous phrase: "We may say that the movement of the progressive societies has hitherto been a movement from status to contract."

The socialists, naturally, have seized upon the "hitherto" in Maine's classic statement as meaning that progress and contract might ultimately be divorced, in which case a new heyday of status—socialist status this time—would return to the benefit of everybody. But Maine, we may be certain, entertained no such delusion. Medieval feudalism he stigmatized as a partial reversion to an unprogressive society of status. Anyway, the village community, historically, was not a socialist or communist enterprise. To use the language of William Graham Sumner and A. G. Keller, it was communalism, not communism. It did not begin as coercive government, as a state; it was a voluntary association of individuals who subscribed, by custom, to the idea of rule by the father of the family.

The prodigal son who wished to abandon his assured place within the family unit was free to go, even to seek adoption by another community. The compulsions of the ancient world were by convention: and filial duty to the father was balanced by a right to family protection. It was not until the idea of conquest grew up as man ceased to be a wanderer and settled the rich river bottoms that the state came into being. As Franz Oppenheimer has shown, political aristocracies evolved when one tribe moved in on another by force of arms, seizing group property and making slaves of the subjugated family units. The aboriginal state—and this is its mark of sin—came into existence as the handmaiden of depredation and pillage, not as the result of a "social compact." But since the pillage-Leviathan is such a hideous thing, man has been driven throughout the ages to try to remake it along fair contractual lines.

Rightly understood, then, the Maine theory of the origin of the property right does not differ in any truly fundamental way from the Locke theory. For, as Maine shows, the original "law for appropriating" and "mixing one's labor" with land was done by a corporation—the family unit—that is very much like the modern corporation, which is a free association of individuals who accept the corporate rules. Unlike individuals, corporations do not die. But they are like individuals in being free, not compelled, agents.

So the property right remains an instrument of freedom no matter whether it originated in family or individual appropriation and prescription. The overriding of the right by state compulsion came, historically, with the rise of usurper warrior clans.

Sir Henry Maine's lasting contribution to economics is his elucidation of the rise of contractual law. It is the idea of contract that alone makes a high capitalism—and a long circuit of productive energy—possible. There can be markets without contracts, but it is obvious that if every trade or exchange or agreement to do something for compensation had to be completed on the spot there could be little forward-planning of production, and little roundaboutness in men's dealings with each other. It is the idea of contract that enables man to subtilize his economic life. "In the beginning was the Word."

If one could not contract to dispose of one's labor and property in a complex world, one could hardly be called a free man. In the modern context contracts are, of course, enforceable by the state: it is the assurance of this, as well as simple trust in the common honesty and common pride of man, that permits thousands of half-completed transactions to take place in business every hour of the day. In ancient law, however, there was nothing to compel the performance of a promise—and "incomplete conveyances" required a religious sanction, ritualized by a solemn ceremonial, to guarantee the fulfillment of an obligation. Man lived up to his promises in those ancient days because the eyes of the gods were upon him!

As Roman society developed, however, the so-called nexum of conveyance tended to pass out of the area where elaborately prescribed religious formalities made the half-completed transaction a cumbrous thing. Contracts, in Rome, eventually took on a modern form—the Verbal, the Literal, the Real and the Consensual, to use lawyers' language. All of them required some form of solemnization, such as a stipulation (the verbal exaction of the promise), or an entry in a ledger, or the simple delivery of something, or a statement that a consensus about a service or a partnership or an agency had been reached. Though Rome, even the Rome of the splendid imperial road system, was always a primarily agricultural society, the idea that men could be bound to complete transactions at some specified future date by the mere giving of a sign was the seed from which the free industrial community and high capitalism were to sprout.

Contract endowed the individual with the dignity of maturity; as Maine put it, it treated man as one who "possessed the faculty of forming a judgment in [his] own interest." Once the world commenced to run by contract and not by status, the individual could deal for himself without begging permission from patriarch or priest or the chief of the village or the tribe. Capsuling two thousand years of history in a sentence, Maine said: "Starting . . . from a condition of society in which all the relations of Persons are summed up in the relations of Family, we seem to have steadily moved towards a phase of social order in which all these relations arise from the free agreement of individuals." Or, as Sir Henry phrased it in another context, contract "is the tie between man and man which replaces by degrees those forms of reciprocity in rights and duties which have their origin in the Family."

Since the idea of contract presumes the maturity of man, it is naturally resented on occasion by the child that lives on in all of us. (Breathes there a man who is so startlingly mature that he has never denounced a bank for levying an extra charge for delinquent interest, or never cursed his landlord for refusing to let the rent go over a month?) But if the eternal child yearns at times for the protective status of immaturity, or even for reversion to the womb, his need to escape the paternal power is even more compulsive. (Taken on balance, Sigmund Freud comes out on the side of contract—and free capitalism.) Even in the status-ridden antiquity the Roman state could hardly have developed its great tribunes, its lawyers, its centurions, its senators, generals and pro-consuls if men in the full plenitude of their adult powers had continued to be bound by the sometimes iron whim of the oldest male member of the tribe.

Picking up from where Sir Henry Maine leaves off, Mr. Harry Scherman has explored the thousand-and-one ways in which contract—i.e., the promise to complete an exchange at some future time—makes possible a rich and variegated life. Significantly, Mr. Scherman calls his book *The Promises Men Live By*. As Mr. Scherman observes, the strange thing about modern wealth is that virtually everything is given away on trust as soon as possible after it has been produced. Even the labor time that is needed to complete an object of trade is donated for a period: normally, a worker does at least a week's—and sometimes a month's—work before he lines up at the cashier's window to collect his wage. The trust that the swap of labor for pay will be completed at a future date belies the notion that corporations are without morals, albeit the morality may be more utilitarian than idealistic. It is not so much that the "law" can enforce the bargain, provided the corporation retains sufficient assets to pay its wage bill. No, the corporation believes that honesty is the best policy for the simple reason that chronic welchers cannot continue to do business in a community which knows them for what they are.

So capitalism is "promises." The promises are everywhere, and it is rarely that one is ever broken. Big deals in cotton futures are made in a gabble which no broker would ever dare say he misunderstood. When an investment banker guarantees the underwriting of a new issue of stock, he normally takes his licking without protest if something happens to go wrong with the prospective market. It is the promise that sheet steel will be paid for once the automobiles are sold, or that the installment on the car will go to the finance company or the bank when it is due, or that the rent will be paid out of the proceeds of the crop, that enables men to gain untold benefits from the "long curcuit of energy" which credit creates. As for the banks, they deal almost wholly in promises—with appropriate forfeits attached for nonperformance of one's trust.

Without credit (and debt) there could still be free capitalism. But it would be the capitalism of the even-up swap— a reversion to the sort of thing that went on at ancient Assuan on the Nile when traders from Ethiopia came to buy and sell, or at a spot on the muddy Tiber when dealers in salt from the Mediterranean coast journeyed up the Via Salerna to haggle with Etruscan farmers. Such a capitalism could hardly drive tunnels through mountains, or uncover iron ore in a Venezuelan jungle, or send great ships to the Persian Gulf for oil, or rear a hundred skyscrapers on an island which once cost twenty-four dollars. It should be axiomatic that without the idea of contract, life, even though it might be lapped in the comfortable "security" of a benign status, would hardly have proliferated in recent decades at a rate which would have caused Malthus to predict universal starvation a hundred and fifty years ago. The starvation hasn't come (the West even undertakes at times to feed the East!), and man, despite his wars, has grown increasingly fat and sassy on his possession of the "faculty of forming a judgment in his own interest."

Why, then, the almost universal popularity of the socialist drive to return us all to a world of status? As we have suggested, it is partly because of the eternal child in all of us. More importantly, however, it is due to a combination of shortsighted cupidity and power lust. The drive toward the "interventionist" state may proceed in the direction of socialism, or totalitarianism, but it has derived its main impetus from those who want to eat their cake (in the form of *their* continued right to contract) and have it (in the form of a specially privileged status) too.

The protective tariff leaves a manufacturer free to contract for the disposition of his own product, but it also gives him a status of exemption from market forces which infringes the voluntary contractual rights of those who might prefer to buy in a foreign market. A subsidy for not planting cotton or wheat leaves a farmer free to dispose of the crops he does actually go to the trouble of raising, but it also provides him with an assured basic income at the expense of those who might choose to keep their tax money for voluntary purposes of their own.

The interventionist or the welfare state, assuming a modern equivalent of the early Roman "patria potestas," or paternal power, is driven by the voting pressure of an ever-increasing number of "me too" leech groups to confer some status on virtually everybody. Thus the area in which free social power is able to contract for itself, whether individually or in the form of voluntary associations, shrinks toward a bare minimum. And still the eternal child in all of us keeps us from hanging our mature heads in shame.

The old theory of property and contract law was that one had a right to "so use one's own as not to injure the property of another." But the U.S. farmer today uses his voting power to injure city labor by cozening from government a support subsidy which very effectively pushes up the price of food. Quite absurdly and idiotically, the taxpayer pays twice for the injury: he pays in the first instance at the grocery store in higher prices, and, in the second instance, when he is taxed to keep the farmer's subsidy going. If we must grant the farmer a special status which no writer, no artist, and no mere business entrepreneur, can aspire to, it would be far more sensible to give him our tax money as a pure gift, without also adding it into the price of everybody's dinner.

In Europe the socialist-oriented labor parties have led the movement away from contract and back toward status. In the United States the most insidious pressure on the right to contract comes not from doctrinaire collectivists (they had their heyday in the thirties) but from a labor movement which still pays lip service to the rights of man. Ever since John L. Lewis, the boss of the United Mine Workers, went all-out in 1941 for the union shop in the captive coal mines belonging to the steel companies, the American labor movement has striven relentlessly for various versions of the closed shop. Nothing fills a modern labor leader with more trepidation than the creeping success in various states of right-to-work laws. What the closed shop, or its union shop variant, does is to violate two basic contractual liberties—the right of a man to work as he wills under his own chosen conditions, and the right of an employer to keep a nonunion man if he is giving satisfactory service. If these two contractual rights cannot be reconciled in a mature contract society, then we are indeed on our way back to a condition of status which denies man the dignity of making decisions on his own.

Historically, the union justification for seeking the abrogation of free contract which goes with the closed shop dates back to the time when employers sought to impose the so-called "yellow-dog" contract on their men. By the terms of a yellow-dog contract, a worker would give a pledge in advance that he would never join a union. This in itself amounted to a coercion: it denied the worker the benefit that might be had from voluntary association with his fellows to seek redress in case the conditions of his employment were to become onerous. But the "wrong" of the yellow-dog contract hardly justified a wild swing to the equal and opposite coercion of the closed or union shop contract. Where the yellow-dog contract effectively froze the union man out of a job, the union shop contract keeps the nonjoiner from making a living at his trade. Actually, neither the yellow-dog contract nor the union shop contract is a contract at all—for it is the essence of the whole idea of contract that it be a voluntary binding of one's self in the "nexum," or chain, which holds men to the completion of partially deferred transactions.

The basic issue is this: can labor—or, rather, a few labor leaders—legitimately aspire to assert monolithic control over the supply of workers available to management to do a given job? In its most objectionable phases, the phases to which the McClellan Committee has paid much recent attention, the right of labor to assert control over the supply of workers assumes all the hideous colors of the racket. The union shop, a milder form of the closed shop which is permitted by the Taft-Hartley legislation, would seem to give management the right to hire whom it pleases, provided that all new nonunion employees join a designated union after a stated period of time. Even so, the union shop is definitely a fetter on management: it can effectively prevent a business enterprise from hiring the type of person who resents compulsion. The wrong done here is that the union shop automatically excludes from employment the very sort of independent human being who might ordinarily forge ahead to the foreman or upper executive class if he is left to work out his own career. Some workers who object to unions may be hopeless examples of pure cussedness. But there are others who come under the heading of "mobile talent." They may happen to be born on the wrong side of the tracks. But they don't feel they must remain part of the labor supply; they may be excoriated by the envious as class traitor in their psychology, but such people have been the essence of middle-class America. If they are to be forced out of our big industries the U.S. will not necessarily be lost. But it won't be the traditional America in which most of us have grown up. It will be a stratified nation, with the classes reduced to fixed and relatively immutable status on the old European order.

There may be certain superficial reasons for thinking the closed or the union shop is not a serious infringement of the right to contract. These reasons are sometimes couched in a form that appeals to management itself. Indeed, when old Henry Ford, listening to the importunities of his wife, granted the union shop and the checkoff of union dues to his River Rouge employees, he did so with the hope of getting both domestic and shop peace. Both he and Mrs. Ford thought that the uproar of open shop contention between union and nonunion men, and between the AFL and CIO, would cease, and that the leaders of an approved CIO bargaining unit would turn their attention to improving shop morale once they no longer had to worry about proselytizing or maintaining membership or collecting dues. But peace may not be the worthiest end in the world if it is achieved by the coercion of the independent workers in a given factory.

Those who prize the value of freedom more than the value of security may well ask if peace is worth taking the pressure off union leaders, who are apt to get fat and smug if they aren't faced with the daily task of proving their worth to the membership of a union. Labor is "vulnerable," so the argument runs, if it lacks the "security" of the closed or the union shop. But maybe labor—or at least labor leaders —should be "vulnerable." A businessman is "vulnerable" to the criticism of his customers, who can always contract to do business elsewhere. Why, by the same standards, shouldn't union leaders be "vulnerable" to the criticism of their followers?

The prime argument against the principle of the closed shop, in fact, is that rank-and-file democracy is retained with difficulty, and at the price of a vigilance that can ruin working efficiency, when a union member lacks the ultimate veto power of resigning or refusing to pay his dues. The argument can be made, and it is frequently made, that such failure of democracy as we have seen in the Teamsters

Union is the individual's own fault. And so it is, abstractly considered. In practice, however, the case is not an open-and-shut matter. Union democracy under the closed shop runs into all the snags that party democracy strikes in the Soviet Union, where power is theoretically passed upward from party units in village and factory to regional committees, and thence onward to the central committee. This "democratic centralism"—whether of the Bolshevik Party or the closed shop union—throws politics into the hands of those who want to make a career of it—i.e., into the hands of those who care ardently about caucusing; who like to sit up after midnight; to neglect their wives and children; and to take time out from productive work to plot tactics and maneuvers and to play the game of parliamentary strategy.

The average human being who wants to do his job by day and relax after dinner just can't keep tabs on the natural-born politician who loves the game of power for its own sake. Maybe this ought not to be so, but it is so. Hence in a one-party state the average citizen finds himself a prisoner of his leadership—a captive of the natural-born politician. And in a closed shop union, by an analogy that is too close for comfort, a person may also find himself a prisoner of the union politicians. Now under the open shop dispensation the individual admittedly runs the risk of allowing himself to be manipulated by the management. Nevertheless, the open shop is the only good, the only certain, guarantee of union democracy. For under the open shop the average union member finds himself cultivated by the natural-born politician. His views are sought out, his wishes are deferred to, his support is courted and solicited. The politician, in the union as in society as a whole, knows what a tremendous veto power the average individual has if he merely chooses to quit the organization or to cease paying dues into its treasury.

The political analogy between the one-party state and the closed shop federation of unions can be pushed even further. Freedom of speech on political issues might itself be the great casualty if union leadership continues to possess the practical power to coerce men under penalty of thrusting them into an outer darkness where they would lose all chance of effectively earning a livelihood. Beyond this, there is the overwhelming fact that the huge vertical unions tend to function as monolithic political entities. Under a universal closed shop dispensation Republican workers, for example, might be robbed of their effectiveness at the polls by means of their own money. A Republican who resents a union gift to the Democratic Party campaign fund must take it and like it, even though a fraction of the gift represents his own dues. If unions are going to play politics as monolithic units, if they are going to use the funds of the minority to promote the national political will of the majority, then it is only fair that members who disagree with the politics of the majority should have the democratic right to withdraw at will.

Since the closed shop inevitably pretends to the prerogatives of a state within a state, with the right to collect taxes from individuals under penalty of taking a man's job away from him, it can only be fitted into the political framework of a republic with the greatest difficulty. Equally difficult is the task of fitting the closed shop into a democratic economic order. If a union is to be part of a free economic order, it must be an open union. From the standpoint of theory the closed shop is compatible with a union open to anybody who cares to join. Nevertheless, the closed shop union is always a shut union to the extent that it can't, by definition, include people who have insuperable objections to unions or who inevitably fall afoul of union discipline.

As a matter of fact, in the more tightly organized craft fields the union almost always tends to become a closed organization, with closed shop principles in the fields in which it works. Having achieved a monopoly of work in a given area, or a given segment of industry, the closed shop craft union, out of "enlightened self-interest," naturally tends to take the next step of limiting membership in order to keep wages at a high level. And the closed shop union in the craft field may tend to arrogate to itself the monopolistic right of using limited membership to put restraints upon the flow of trade. At its worst, the closed shop, or closed employment system, leads to the straight-out racketeering practices which the McClellan Committee has made a byword. But it also leads to simpler forms of the economic holdup. Ever since Mr. Justice Felix Frankfurter ruled, in the *Hutcheson* case, that the Sherman Act did not apply to disputes between labor unions that involved an interstate boycott, the Department of Justice has not been able to stop certain closed trade unions from using their controlled membership to fix prices, control production or freeze the channels of distribution. Whether the Frankfurter decision is good or bad law is beside the point: the fact remains that the Department of Justice's hands have been tied.

And since there is no way, short of bringing the unions back under the antitrust laws, of striking at the closed union that chooses to invoke its control of the labor supply in a given field to gain ends that have nothing to do with legitimate bargaining for higher wages, shorter hours, and more healthful working conditions, the Department of Justice is reduced to listing the weird results of exempting labor from the scope of the Sherman Act. Certain building trades unions have prevented the most efficient use of men and machinery: employers have been kept from contracting for the use of paint spray guns, or even paint brushes that exceed a certain size. Construction workers have refused to permit the use of ready-mix concrete. Such abuses spring from the same motives as the attempt to maintain the closed shop–closed union system as a prerequisite for enforcing the limitation of the labor supply in the interests of higher wages for the chosen few. This world is a far cry indeed from one in which freedom of contract prevails.

The infringement of the right of contract implied in the closed shop means, inevitably, that the state must ultimately make itself responsible for the status of both labor and management under the law. It must eventually lead to the incorporation of unions as well as of business units. It must result in such things as federally certified union accounting and government supervision of union elections and strike votes. It must insist on a tribunal to pass on complaints brought by members that they have been unfairly disciplined. A far simpler and freer way would be for the state to keep its hands off the unions provided labor ceases to press for the universal closed shop. For none of the coercive, undemocratic, racketeering aspects of unionism can last for very long if management in the last analysis can hire whom it pleases and if the rank and file has the privilege of getting out of a bad union.

For a truly free solution of the union problem, we must return to the concept of the mature man who, to quote Sir Henry Maine again, possesses the "faculty of forming a judgment in his own interest." Mature labor leaders must relinquish the idea that their followers are also their captives. And mature men in management must give up trying to lay rude—or even subtle—hands on the consciences of men who are debating whether or not to join a union.

If management should return to the old habit of union baiting, which amounts to an attempted interference with a worker's freedom of contract, or if it refuses to bargain with open unions on an above-board basis, then we shall get the universal closed shop or a condition of chaos and industrial slavery. And so far as democracy goes, the terms may be interchangeable.

In either case the state must walk in. In the case of the closed shop the state must intervene to guarantee protection to both union members and management against racketeering in union leadership. In the case of chaos and industrial slavery the state must intervene to guarantee social security to the underdog. (It must go far beyond such things as minimum wage laws and forced unemployment payments, which are themselves minor and absorbable infringements of free contract.) The state that constitutes itself a warder will soon become a state that is "above" labor and "above" capital—and it will end by ruling with the usual ruthless, unimaginative and bureaucratic hand. It will be a state committed to a return to the ancient concept of status. But status will be applied without the humanity that pertained in antiquity when the patriarch, the father of the family, and not a distant ruler in a bureaucratic capital, regulated the reciprocal rights and duties of individuals who could not be trusted to contract for themselves.

Chapter Five

Gloomy Men and Iron Laws —or Capitalism in a Cage

Nothing is more instructive than to read the long line of British classical economists, from Adam Smith to John Stuart Mill, with an eye to what they regarded as mere footnote material. In the world of Adam Smith all is large and hopeful: the drearier suppositions are stated humorously (as in the famous crack about employers being everywhere in a tacit combination not to raise wages) or elliptically (as in the implied labor theory of value which set up the ninepins for Karl Marx). Taken without hearkening overmuch to parenthetical matter, Adam Smith's economics are open-ended: they leave plenty of room for man's application and ingenuity to pull the human race out of almost any predicament or dilemma. In Smith the accent is on doing, on increasing the "stock," on letting energy flow. If he failed to confront his own contradictions or imprecise formulations about such things as rent and value, it may have been because of an unstated conviction that man is a protean creature. To adapt a phrase from Leslie Stephen, Smith refused to make man an "iron unit"; therefore he was not lured to the unreal precision of "iron laws."

With Adam Smith's successors, however, a darkness sets

in: it is as if the skies of Britain, colored by the smoke from its burgeoning factory towns, had suddenly rained soot on the pages of the economists. With the generation of Malthus and Ricardo, who wrote amid the French Revolutionary and Napoleonic disturbances, the Smithian parenthetical clauses became the main text; and what Smith rightfully regarded as the true body of economics—which is an accounting of the science and art of adding to the wealth and working capital of a nation—is relegated to the footnotes. In the texts of Malthus and Ricardo and their successors, land, labor and capital still play their tripartite role as the factors or agents of production, but instead of following the leading strings which are harmoniously operated by a beneficial "invisible hand," they jerk about in a wild tangle of antagonisms and fated oppositions. The wages of labor are held close to the bare minimum needed to keep a worker, his wife and an average of two children per family alive; the rewards of capital—or of the "abstinence" which creates savings—are only increased by screwing the wage scale down; and the economic rent on land, which increases as corn gets dearer and the population rises, tends to channel all the profits of an advancing society into the greedy paws of the landed squire.

It may be argued that this represents a caricature of the work of Malthus and Ricardo; after all, it was their courageous insistence on the free market that was ultimately to break the grip of the Corn Laws in England and to free the forces of production on a world scale. This is glory enough for anybody. As von Mises has said, nobody has ever refuted Ricardo on the subject of comparative costs as applied to the international trading community. In his insistence on "pseudo-arithmetic," however, Ricardo did an unnatural violence to his own self-adjusting system.* With labor and capital striving (at least on certain of Ricardo's pages) to cut up what appeared to be a definitely limited pie, it seemed as though economics had been forced into a malevolent machine. And this despite the elements in the Ricardian system that allow for the expansion of job-creating capital. Caricature or not, it is scant cause for wonder that a whole generation of socialists, whether utopian, Fabian or Marxian, was to rise up and say "to hell with it."

But what did Ricardo and the other gloomy men actually say, if their hesitancies and footnote material are allowed their proper place in the economic symphony? Was it, indeed, a fated world of poverty and oppression with which Malthus and Ricardo, James Mill, and John Stuart Mill, had to deal? The answer is that these supposedly "logical" and "scientific" men were sometimes the most illogical of reasoners; that they seldom attached sufficient weight to what they themselves perceived as exceptions to the generalizations which the German Ferdinand Lassalle and the Englishman Leslie Stephen were later to call the "iron" or "brazen" laws; and that the qualitative factors—desire, random choice, ingenuity, even genius—which impel men to self-starting action make the effort to confine economics to mathematical statement a footless and puling proposition.

Take the Reverend Thomas Robert Malthus as our first example. Malthus' recently discovered correspondence with

---

* John Maynard Keynes is quite correct when he speaks of the "pseudo-arithmetical" nature of some of Ricardo's formulae. Keynes' own mistake was to substitute pseudo-algebra and pseudo-calculus for the pseudo-arithmetic of Ricardo.

his stockbroker friend, David Ricardo, as well as passages in his *Principles of Political Economy,* shows him to have been very sensible that economics in the practical world is largely a matter of getting production to move off dead center. As John Maynard Keynes has noted, Malthus anticipated all the problems arising from "failure of demand," and from the bad guesses of investors as to the course of future consumption. Like Keynes himself, however, Malthus vastly underestimated the curative role of technological change—though in one of his parenthetical clauses he does admit that there can be causes which can give a great stimulus to production and population for as much as "eight or ten years" at a time.

The great weight of Malthus' work was to exhibit mankind as collectively carrying an albatross that cannot be shucked off. That albatross is Nature's unseemly fecundity, which tends to push animals—including man—into the world in excess of the vegetation that can be raised on finite acres to support them. Or, as Malthus himself put it, "The cause to which I allude is the constant tendency in all animated life to increase beyond the nourishment prepared for it." This was said, mind you, at the very dawn of a century which was to see the population of Britain jump from ten million to thirty-seven million (and all of them, in 1900, considerably better off); and before the vast peopling of the American continent with its multitudes of well-fed citizens had gotten past its beginnings on the eastern slopes of the Appalachian Mountains! What Malthus would have made out of our vast wheat, corn and cotton carryovers is a question. He might, indeed, feel at home in China, India or Indonesia—but these countries, be it noted, have never yet tried the free capitalist system.

Malthus' career as an economist began somewhat haphazardly, with an attempt to shock his father, a semiretired country gentleman, out of an unqualified admiration for the French *philosophes* who thought utopia could be achieved by returning man to a state of nature. The picture is one of a member of a Romantic generation ("Bliss was it in that dawn to be alive," as Wordsworth had said of the very beginnings of the French Revolution) being suddenly confronted by a Young Turk who followed the banner of Grim Realism. Daniel Malthus, the father, and Robert, the son, had been arguing about Condorcet and Godwin, particularly the latter's notion that man could attain perfect happiness if there were no such things as government, private property, and the marriage contract. In his *Enquiry Concerning Political Justice* Godwin had pooh-poohed the idea that community ownership of property would result in a heedless excess of children. Godwin thought there was plenty of room on earth for centuries ahead, and even if there wasn't he believed there was some invisible principle which could be relied upon to keep fecundity and the food supply in proper balance. Agreed, said Robert Malthus to Godwin's mention of a "leveling" force. But the force, far from being a beneficent one, would naturally express itself in a multiplication of vice and misery, and even in actual famine. Thus Godwin's dream of a communist-anarchist utopia could never come to pass.

Malthus has been celebrated as the man who first applied the inductive method to economics. But his "pinking" of Godwin, as he worked it out for his father's edification in his first *Essay on Population* in 1798, began, not with a universal census, but with a couple of self-evident postulates. First, there was the proposition that food is necessary to the existence of man. Second, Malthus took it as axiomatic that "the passion between the sexes is necessary, and will remain in its present state."

The two propositions, so stated, needed no induction to support them. But the next jump made by Malthus was pure assumption of what was to be proved. "Population, when unchecked," he said, "increases in geometrical ratio. Subsistence only increases in arithmetical ratio."

The remainder of the first essay on the "population principle" was pure deduction from premises which Malthus thought too obvious for lengthy exploration. Published anonymously, the first statement of the "Malthusian" doctrine set Malthus' contemporaries by the ears; almost instantaneously he gained a reputation for being an "ogre." Actually, the "monster" was the gentlest of men. A clergyman who was ultimately to become the first professor of political economy at the East India Company's college of Haileybury, he regarded his antagonists in a benevolent light, as cooperators in the great quest for truth. His students, who called him "Pop," held him in great affection; they found his lectures—though delivered with scant regard for the letter L (Malthus had a cleft palate)—far from dull. The controversies that swirled about the "parson's" head left him singularly unperturbed; as he once said, not even the most vicious attack bothered him "after a fortnight." But for all his equanimity he did listen to his critics, and he lived to modify, many times over, the juvenile starkness of his first *Essay*.

At the outset Malthus assumed that there was no way out of the vicious circle created by the clash between animal fecundity and the law of diminishing returns in agriculture save through the callous methods of relying on

Nature's pruning hooks of war, pestilence and starvation. These, said Malthus, were the great natural or positive checks. It followed, therefore, that the English Poor Laws, which subsidized paupers and encouraged them to breed in order to tap higher government allowances, should be abolished forthwith. "Evil," said Malthus, "exists not to create despair, but activity." In place of the "Laws of Settlement," which prevented a pauper from moving from one parish to another in quest of a job, he would restore an active freedom of movement to the "peasantry of England." In a contradictory bit of statism he suggested premiums for turning up "fresh land." And for extreme distress he would allow county workhouses which would serve only the scantiest and hardest of fare.

The doctrine, which was stated in the harshest of terms, was nevertheless sufficiently convincing to turn William Pitt away from the idea of pushing legislation to increase the population of England. But instead of racking up Pitt's conversion as a conclusive victory, Malthus began to have his doubts about his rigorous statement of the Law of Population. In a new edition of his book he argued that "moral restraint," or the "preventive check," could be added to the great "positive" checks of misery, vice and war. To put an "inductive" base under his arguments of the first edition, Malthus toured Europe, visiting Norway and Sweden and (during a pause in the Napoleonic struggles) France and Switzerland. He found the "preventive check" operating in certain Swiss cantons and in Norway, where marriages were undertaken only upon positive evidence that support could be provided for children.

By induction Malthus thus got a glimmering of a counteracting "law" that would become apparent to many in the later stages of the nineteenth century: that as civilization advanced, and as people commenced to put greater value on the amenities of life, the birthrate would tend to level off. Malthus never brought himself to recognize a possible legitimizing of the "preventive check" of artificial birth control; that, to him, would have been to abdicate to "vice." But his recognition that there could be a moral check, or such checks as were imposed by governments when they forced young military conscripts to forgo marriage until their period of army duty was over, took at least some of the "iron" out of the Law of Population.

Even with the operation of the "preventive check," however, there was still enough iron in the Law of Population to give rise to the second of the great "Iron Laws," the Law of Rent. Before the time of Malthus, Adam Smith had been bothered by the spectacle of British landlords who, entrenched in their holdings behind the laws of primogeniture and entail, loved "to reap where they never sowed." Smith surmised that the landlord must always take whatever the "tenant can afford to pay," but he never quite managed to separate what the tenant paid for the use of capital improvements (whose rewards properly come under the heading of interest and profit) and what he paid for the unimproved land itself.

A year after the publication of *The Wealth of Nations,* in 1777, a Scottish colleague of Smith's named James Anderson first hazarded that economic rent represented the difference between the cost of producing a crop on good land and the cost of raising an identical crop at the stony margins of cultivation. Since the price of food would naturally be set by the cost of production on the most refractory acres that squatters could afford to work without paying anything for their use, the landlord who owned fat soil could naturally pocket a big profit on what his own rent-paying tenant raised without undue trouble. But Anderson's perception made little stir. It was not until Malthus conjured up his vision of hungry mouths clamoring for the last bit of available productive acreage that rent came to seem an important category in the fledgling science of economics.

Malthus worked the Law of Rent into his own system some eighteen years after his first discovery of the Law of Population. The price of grain had been rising all through the scarcity period of the Napoleonic wars; in the twenty-year period from 1792 to 1812 wheat went from 43 shillings a quarter to 126 shillings. With the Corn Law of 1815 on the books to prevent cheap importations from overseas, British landlords sat smugly in the driver's seat. If they raised wheat themselves, they could charge plenty for it. If their tenants raised it, they could soak the tenants, particularly when free lands at the margin of cultivation were disappearing. With this plain evidence of the Napoleonic inflation before him, Malthus argued that the Law of Population, which encouraged more births than the land could well support, must operate to the special advantage of the owner of land. There could be no escape: the more food there was produced, the more workers would be born—and even if they found work they would still have to pay higher and higher prices to keep their stomachs full.

Since by 1815 Malthus had grown more cautious in his method of statement, he refrained from putting his own version of the Law of Rent in the crude poster terms of his 1798 Law of Population. There was some elasticity in the situation as he saw it, for with every rise in prices and rents, people must be pushed into experimentation with the poorer soils. Thus "evil," to adapt one of Malthus' earlier statements, was a goad to "action." Even so, the resort to the "inferior machinery" (Malthus' description of poor lands) must add to both costs and prices, thus creating a bigger rent spread for the landlord who owned soil that might be likened to "good machinery."

It did not seem significant to Malthus that experimentation with poorer soils might result in new and more intensive ways of working—or improving—the earth, and that this, in turn, could result in agricultural abundance. This had already happened in the eastern counties of England in the eighteenth century, with the discovery of new ways of draining, new methods of crop rotation, and the like, all of which meant an application of a law of increasing returns to farming.* It was to happen many times over in the nineteenth

---

* It is often objected that there is no "law" of increasing returns. But if there were no conditions under which such a law could operate, no manufacturer would be able to calculate a break-even point on his curve of production; and no farmer would know when to buy a new tractor or pour in a new fertilizer. Whether returns will increase or diminish with the addition of new increments of capital and/or labor is the root question on which business judgment ordinarily turns. Marginal utility may govern all things, and make diminishing returns inescapable at a certain point. But with an open-end technology and a creative soil chemistry keeping pace with the population, increasing returns may bless the individual farmer. As for the businessman, every successful enterprise consists in the outwitting of diminishing returns. These things are, of course, rooted in manners of speaking. The earth is finite: therefore, increasing returns could hardly be pushed to infinity. But to give the phenomena of diminishing returns the status of a "law," while denying the same status to proven ways of getting more return for less effort, seems to me an arbitrary bit of verbal—and mathematical— arrogance.

In this connection the recent comment by John Jewkes, David Sawers and Richard Stillerman (see *The Sources of Invention*, London: Macmillan) is pertinent. Speaking of the impact of technology and invention on produc-

century, as market gardeners learned actually to create new soil out of animal and vegetable waste. Malthus had allowed for some elasticity in his theory of rents, but in his blindness to the ingenuity of man, he put the tenant farmer and the laborer, who must eat the produce of the farms, into the same rigid box in which he had confined the less fortunate members of the human race as a whole. It remained for David Ricardo, Malthus' great and good friend, to pick up the Malthusian leads and to show that the "Iron" Law of Population and the "Iron" Law of Rent meant ultimately diminishing returns for both capital and labor. Malthus had once painted a vivid picture of the Great Feast of Life, from which a certain number of unfortunates were bound to be excluded in the nature of things. This was gloomy enough, but Ricardo, pursuing the image, conjured up a day when the best seats at the feast would be occupied, not by an upper crust of landlords and capitalists, but by the landlord —and the tax collector—alone. As he put it in an "iron" summary of all the "Iron Laws": "There must be an end of accumulation . . . the very low rate of profit will have arrested all accumulation, and almost the whole produce of the country, after paying the labourers, will be the property of the owners of land and the receivers of tithes and taxes."

---

tivity, the authors say: "With the enthusiasm of converts, economists are now crowding into a subject where very little is known precisely because the relevant data are not what they have been concerned to accumulate in the past half-century. It is not, of course, a subject in which they must start entirely from scratch; *economists have not always been so indifferent to the dynamics of their subject as in the present century"* (italics ours). The "dynamics" of economics must reckon with the art, if not the "law," of increasing returns. Personally, I have been unable to locate the economists who, with the "enthusiasm of converts," are "crowding" into the subject which has attracted John Jewkes. But maybe Jewkes and his collaborators will start the needed stampede.

David Ricardo, the son of a Dutch Jew who had migrated
to London, was a man of solid business affairs who prospered by his dealings on the stock exchange. He went to
work at the age of fourteen, he owned his own business by
the time he was twenty-two, and he ran an original capital
of a few hundred pounds into something close to a million
before he died. Marrying an Englishwoman, a Quaker girl,
he made himself an accepted part of English life. He bought
himself a country seat, Gatscombe Park, in Gloucestershire,
which made him a reluctant member of the landlord class,
whose role in society he most particularly distrusted. As a
member of the House of Commons, he refused to let his
landed gentry connections "buy" him: he remained to the
end of his days an enemy of the Corn Laws, and of the
systematic parliamentary corruption by which country gen-
tlemen kept control of the English government. During the
week of Waterloo, he followed his worldly instincts and took
a strong "bull" position. (He even cut his friend Malthus
in for a share, but Malthus, who lacked the stomach for
speculation, urged him to sell his share out before the
results of the battle were known.)

In betting on a successful outcome of Waterloo, Ricardo
was hardly risking his money on purely economic knowledge. He had a strong hunch that the Duke of Wellington's
character would prevail over Napoleon's somewhat shop-
worn star. In short, Ricardo knew that the exchange values
of British stocks depended on more than "labour." He must
have been as good a judge of men as of money—yet, as one
of the fathers of the quantity theory of money, he made
few allowances in his theory for the qualitative use of money
by productive men.

When Ricardo turned to economic writing, the man of

affairs, who could make allowances for exception syncrasies, and the national character, immediately l sure touch with the fluid nature of the workaday world. He began as a commentator on Adam Smith and as a judge (in time a friendly, if still disputatious, judge) of Malthus. He began also at the insistent prodding of James Mill, another great believer in a one-dimensional view of human character. Mill, the advocate of Jeremy Bentham's utilitarianism, thought that all men were governed by the pleasure-pain principle, as if youthful conditioning, inculcated loyalties, inhibitions and revolts, behavioristic tropisms, "drives" and considerations of love, hate, affection, antipathy and propriety (all of which might reck nothing of pain), had little to do with the case. Though Ricardo was not himself a utilitarian philosopher, he assumed that the "economic man" of his *Principles of Political Economy* operated by a crude pleasure-pain calculus. His landlords, for example, must always, if the full logic of Ricardo be followed, be rackrenters, taking the full charge on all occasions from their tenants. Even the very soil which the landlords rented out was something unchanging, something with "indestructible" powers, not a living and breathing envelope which could be ruined by carelessness or revitalized and reshaped by such "boons" of Nature as nitrogen from the air (fixed in the soil by organisms) and carbon filched from the action of the sun.

Ricardo's great concern as a stockbroker was to capitalize on the shattering of equilibrium: in brief, he knew instinctively that the business of business is to disturb the status quo. In his economic writing, however, he dealt with the distribution of the economic product—"who gets what, when"—under conditions which move toward equilibrium.

Everything in his system is hard and fast. Or, at least, everything in his *theorems* is hard and fast. (We will come to the exceptions and the doubts which kept creeping in.)

Value, in Ricardo, is to be understood as use, value and as exchange value, but only exchange value is important to his economics. Leaving out of account rarity items—scarce books, ancient coins, Greek statuary and pictures by Leonardo da Vinci—value in exchange is determined by the equivalents of labor power that go into the manufacture of various products. Since the capitalist contributes stored or accumulated labor (in the form of machines) to manufacture, and since the worker contributes his muscle and brain power to put the capital goods or accumulated labor into motion, there are two labor variables to be accounted for in distributing the rewards for production. These variables, wages on the one side and interest and profit on the other, can only shift at each other's expense: if there is to be more for the capitalist, there must be less for labor.

If this were all that mattered, the Ricardian world would not be such a horrible place: more capital and more labor would simply produce more product, and no one would ever be any the worse for it. In the background, however, there lurks the monster—the landlord, the controller of the food supply, a man who contributes no labor to the productive process save as he acts as his own tenant. What the landlord has to sell, as a collector of economic rent, is the "original and indestructible powers of the soil," which is something he never made. How he operates to put both capital and labor in a cage is Ricardo's own great addition to Malthus' Laws of Population and Rent.

The capitalist is always willing, of course, to pay the laborer his "natural wage," which consists of enough money to keep body and soul together plus a moiety which will allow him to "reproduce" himself. As Ricardo expressed his Law of Wages: "The natural price of labour is that price which is necessary to enable to Labourers, one with another, to subsist and to perpetuate their *race,* without either increase or diminution" (italics ours; it may be significant that Ricardo thought of labor as a race apart). With every hard-won advance in capital accumulation, however, the existing labor supply would become more valuable, at least temporarily. Demand for services must yield better pay, which must tend, in the Ricardian system, to diminish the rate of profit. But, since the demand for labor regulates the production of men (as Adam Smith himself had observed before Malthus), there will soon be more laborers in the market. Meanwhile the price of food will have risen, and more stony acres will have been put to cultivation, thus putting an upward pressure on rents. The capitalist will have to pay his workers enough to cover high-cost food; there will be little left over for profit—and the landlord will remain as the sole beneficiary of economic progress.

Thus reduced to its essentials, the Ricardian system of theorems, which adds the "Iron" Law of Wages to the "Iron" Laws of Rent and Population, resembles an endless treadmill operated for the benefit and amusement of rent collectors. There can be no harmony in a world in which profits must be squeezed out of wages, and in which "the interest of the landlord is always opposed to that of the consumer and manufacturer." Yet in spite of having constructed an economic infernal machine, Ricardo, like Malthus himself, still insisted on the virtues of freedom, on the "let-alone" philosophy. He still insisted that all contracts should be left to free competition. The great wonder is not that Karl Marx, the socialist, and Henry George, the single taxer, were ultimately to ask why there should be freedom for an infernal machine to grind out its perpetual injustices, but that it took a full generation for the implication of the Ricardo system to become plain. Instead of turning to rend Ricardo limb from limb, the reformers of the 1830s and the 1840s concentrated on such things as factory legislation and the repeal of the Corn Laws, which could hardly alter the long-term efficacy of the Ricardian formulae. As for the political economists themselves, they served up Ricardo with further trimmings. McCulloch and Fawcett and James Mill added the concept of the limited wage fund to the Ricardian system. And John Stuart Mill, writing at the midcentury mark, summed up the Ricardian principles in a text that is still notable for its clear, simple and sunny prose style.

Taking Ricardo at his word, that "progress" must feed into the lap of the landlord, leaving the capitalist and the worker to contest the remains, Marx and Engels made the not unnatural assumption that a hard-pressed capitalist would not allow a laborer enough money to reproduce his kind. Indeed, the class war, which is explicitly admitted in Ricardo, must reach such a stage under constricting circumstances if it is truly a class war. True enough, a system which sweats its workers would never have much of a home market to turn to when it comes to getting rid of the product, nor would it have a healthy working force in the second generation. But, as the Marxists saw it, if calicoes could not be sold in Lancashire, they could be sold in India; and if capital could not be employed for lack of workers and purchasers at home, it could be exported to frontier countries where it might earn twenty-five or fifty percent.

Seeking outlets overseas, capitalism would become (in Lenin's imagination) a twin of imperialism; and the world would dissolve in war as the older nations quarreled for the right to exploit the new. The socialists who built on the work of Marx and Engels didn't particularly mind this prospect: anything to get rid of Ricardo's infernal machine.

At this point the reader of these pages must be protesting that Ricardo and the Ricardians—who, after all, helped rescue the world from the cage of eighteenth-century mercantilism—have been travestied and maligned. Whether they have been or not depends on what they themselves understood by their own "iron" laws. (Or maybe it depends on the weight that should be attached to reading the fine print.) In his first edition Malthus was flamboyant and youthfully dogmatic; in rewritten and expanded versions of his original text he admitted that his "law" was a "tendency" —and a tendency that might be counteracted by the rising comfort standards of a progressive society. There were many things to which Malthus was blind: for example, he did not reckon with what an island population might do with the God-given fish of the surrounding seas. (An England with "fish and chips" and "kippers" can never be wholly oppressed by landlords.) Applied to such an area as the Orient, Malthus' doctrine seems all too true even in the mid-twentieth century; and it might eventually become true for a North America with five hundred million people. But we cannot even be certain of Malthus as a long-term prophet when a news story emanating from Hartford, Connecticut, tells of the invention, by the Maxim Silencer Co., of a cheap method of turning sea water into fresh water. Who knows, maybe Nevada, Saudi Arabia and the Sahara Desert, irrigated from the oceans, will yet absorb all of our

excess children, whether white, yellow or brown, for centuries ahead.

As for Ricardo's own basic theorem, the labor theory of
value was ultimately killed by William Stanley Jevons, the
Englishman, and Carl Menger, the Austrian, who rightly
made "value"—a subjective, qualitative notion—a reflex
of marginal desire. Since under competition there can
normally be only one market price for a product, it will be
the last item that can be profitably produced by the worst
machinery which will set the price—and value—of the
whole product. Thus value will be the expression of a meeting of the feeblest "effective demand" and the feeblest will
to produce an item to satisfy that demand. Divorced from
the concept of equivalent labor-units, value ceases to be
a legitimate plaything for Marxian dialectics. True, labor
costs figure in the willingness to produce that "last unit"
for the marginal consumer. But capitalists are always
making bad guesses about the future course of subjective
desire—and where is the "surplus value" (or the "profit"
stolen from labor) when one cleans out the contents of a
store at a white sale, or sacrifices old model automobiles in
late November?

Once capitalism is seen as a profit-and-loss system, with
everyone at the mercy of the sovereign consumer's whims
as he balances one marginal desire against another, the
incidence of anticapitalistic criticism must shift. The only
capitalist who can make money in a consumer-oriented system is the one who shrewdly anticipates the customer's
desires, and under such a dispensation profit—far from
being "surplus value"—becomes the deserved reward for
acumen. (Which is not to say that the reward can't be
shared with both labor and the consumer.) The overall

social penalty for too much bad guessing (with its attendant misapplication and sterilization of capital) is a depression which hits everyone. Thus methods of increasing the gross national product, and of reversing the cycle, will come to seem far more important than any arbitrary "division of the product." Keynesianism (which has its own milder set of fallacies) will come to replace Marxism as the radicalism of a nation which has absorbed the Jevons-Menger subjective theory of value.

Ricardo himself had his many doubts about his own hard-and-fast theorems, and they kept creeping into his supposedly arithmetically exact prose. No sooner had he formulated his Law of Wages—the one which allowed the laborer just enough to subsist and perpetuate his "race"— than he felt constrained to modify his harshness. "It is not to be understood," he said, "that the natural price of labour, estimated even in food and necessaries, is absolutely fixed and constant. It essentially depends on the *habits and customs of the people"* (italics ours). And again: "The power of the labourer to support himself . . . does not depend on the quantity of money which he may receive for wages, but on the quantity of food, necessaries and conveniences *become essential to him from habit, which* that money will purchase." And what changes "habit"? Why, the "progress of society." In other words, even Ricardo allowed for the breach in his Law of Wages long before Lassalle called it the "Iron Law." Since his day virtually everything has poured through that breach—from television sets to Chevrolets, and from washing machines to steak three times a week. When it comes to dissolving "iron," "habit" is a wonderful thing.

Ricardo couldn't hold fast to his idea that the "natural

tendency of profit . . . is to fall." At least "this tendency, this gravitation as it were of profits, is happily checked at repeated intervals by the improvement in machinery, connected with the production of necessaries, as well as by discoveries in the science of agriculture which enable us to relinquish a portion of labour before required . . ." True enough, Ricardo thought of the "repeated intervals" as temporary stays of the executioner's ax, and he never did see that continuing "discoveries in the science of agriculture" (what would he have thought of a binder or a mechanical corn planter?) might extract the sting from the Law of Rent. But did he really believe that there "must be an end of accumulation," with the landlord taking "almost the whole produce of the country?"

Knowing his sanguine character as a stockbroker and, later, as a politician, one doubts it. His attack on the Corn Laws certainly envisioned a long period in which prosperity might bless England once her workers could feed themselves cheaply from overseas. Moreover, Ricardo had a dawning sense of the frontier: "In new settlements," he wrote, "where the arts and knowledge of countries far advanced in refinements are introduced, it is probable that capital has a tendency to increase faster than mankind."

Why, one might ask at this point, did Ricardo insist so on his gloom? Couldn't America absorb England's excess capital if the rate of profit faltered at home? And wasn't it true in the years after Waterloo that what G.M. Trevelyan calls "the Second British Empire"— of "Canada, Australia and New Zealand"—was there to take English villagers who couldn't find work in Manchester? It might even have occurred to Ricardo, the stockbroker, that there were endless frontiers of desire—and of the inventive mind—to be exploited right in his own English backyard.

In the midcentury, John Stuart Mill tried loyally to stick to what Malthus, Ricardo and his own father, James Mill, had taught him about political economy. He repeated the wage-fund theory. But, try as he might, John Stuart Mill couldn't help observing that "subsistence and employment in England have never increased more rapidly than in the last thirty years." Moreover, though the population had risen, too, Malthus' law didn't seem to be working out as predicted, for "every census since 1821 showed a smaller increase of population than that of the period preceding." Perplexed by an obvious increase in well-being, John Stuart Mill bethought himself of a "ladder industry" explanation which might cover a nonrecurring circumstance. "So gigantic has been the progress of the cotton industry since the inventions of Watt and Arkwright," he wrote, "that the capital engaged in it has probably quadrupled in the time which population requires for doubling." Such a circumstance, Mill surmised, must be "rare and transitory."

Again, we might ask why the continuing gloom? John Stuart Mill, who had seen railroads and steamships as well as cotton mills emerge from the spout of James Watt's tea kettle, knew that man, the eternal tinkerer, would in all probability continue to come up with new ideas for ladder industries. What is more, he already had an inkling that Ricardo's Law of Wages, as it had been popularly interpreted, concealed a fallacy. "Instead of saying that profits depend on wages," he wrote, "let us say (what Ricardo really meant) that they depend on the cost of labour . . . What labour brings in to the labourer, and what it costs to the capitalist . . . are ideas quite distinct . . . the cost of labour is frequently at its highest where wages are lowest . . . labour, though cheap, may be inefficient."

There, in a nutshell, is the theory that a high-wage

economy, with its perpetual lures and incentives to efficiency, can be more profitable to the capitalist than a low-
wage economy. Though he publicly recanted his belief in
the wage fund, John Stuart Mill did not pursue the point;
as we shall see, it remained for an American, Francis
Amasa Walker, to work out the theory that profits and the
individual wage can rise together. But Mill had, momentarily, glimpsed a great light.

It is easy to show that the "iron" laws of population and
wages have their rubbery aspects. But what shall be said
finally of the Law of Rent? Innumerable economists have
come to joust with Ricardo (and with his successor, the
American Henry George) over rent, and many of them
have retired with broken lances. Bastiat, the Frenchman,
tried to show that rent, far from being a payment for the
use of the "original and indestructible powers of the soil,"
represented continued interest charges, so to speak, for
work done by the original appropriator in clearing, draining, fencing and improving the land. Henry Carey, the
American, tried to refute Ricardo by proving that the worst
land (on open hillsides) is often cultivated first, leaving the
river bottoms (which are ordinarily encumbered with trees
and subject to periodic flooding) to be brought into sustained use at a later date. Carey also claimed, with considerably more shrewdness, that the law of diminishing returns
applied to farming no more than it applied to other forms
of industry: he argued that everything, from men and rab-
bits to the turnips which can be eaten by both, can increase
in more than arithmetical progression.

Though such objections hardly carried everything before
them, it is obvious to present-day Americans that agriculture has progressively released men to industry as farming

has become more and more mechanized. By substituting the gasoline—or the propane-driven—engine for the horse, the modern farmer has simultaneously rid himself of the need for hired hands and the necessity for keeping much of his acreage in pasturage to feed horses. Food, if we discount the taxation deemed necessary to provide crop subsidies, has become cheaper to produce and to buy.

It is not diminishing returns, then, but increasing returns, that has marked the modern agricultural revolution. If agriculture had not increased its yield per worker, cities would have been impossible. Economic rent should be less onerous today on Ricardo's own showing; and, indeed, it would be if naturally submarginal farms were allowed to go quietly back to the wild state.

One does not have to refute Ricardo utterly in order to perceive that his—and Malthus'—Law of Rent is not an inevitable engine of suffering and economic tyranny. There is, however, something very suspect about Ricardo's own phrasing of the law. He spoke of the "indestructible powers of the soil"   which would assume that incompetent tenants can do nothing to hurt a landlord's acres. Now, as everyone who has looked at eroded, gullied land and sickly, yellowish corn crops knows, the "original" powers of the soil are very destructible indeed. It follows, therefore, that it will pay a landlord to choose his tenant with as much care as he would choose a superintendent if he were to farm the land himself. If the full exaction of economic rent were to be taken, it would hardly pay anyone to rent good land: the living to be scratched on marginal land would yield the tenant just as much as he could gain (in excess of the rent) on the best acres; and he might have the option of being a free man on his own poor (but improvable) soil, to boot.

To lure a good farmer, then, the landlord must permit his tenant something over and above what he could make on stony, or even intermediate, soil. And to encourage good tenants to stay and make improvements, landlords must be prepared to "go shares" on the extra produce that can be wrested from earth by continuous nurture of soil qualities. Malthus himself had observed that "evil" (which certainly includes the evil of soil impoverishment) is a goad to "action." "Action," on the farm, can mean anything from pouring in the nitrates to sound methods of crop rotation. In short, the landlord who wishes to add to the "original and indestructible powers" of his soil will see to it that "economic rent" is no discouragement to his tenants. He will not charge the full toll, ever. Even in case the landlord is the possessor of urban property, it would hardly pay him to rackrent Mr. Tiffany. For the profitability of Tiffany's (or any other progressive or fashionable store) is one reason why land values on Fifth Avenue do not decrease.

There are other contentions about rent to be disposed of as we shall see when we come to Francis Amasa Walker's demonstration that an improvement in industry may increase the demand for labor at a much faster rate than the demand for raw materials and food. But it is, perhaps, enough to say that land is merely another form of capital, which can be added to intensively (by good cultivation), as well as extensively by clearing the wilderness or diking the sea. Taken as capital, it is subject to the same laws of accumulation and the same laws of profit as other capital. It trades even-up with other capital on its ability to earn five or six percent. And besides: there is a purely social justification for rent. As Spencer Heath, another American, has observed in his *Citadel, Market and Altar,* rent is the fee we willingly pay to the landlord for providing us with a nonpolitical method of allocating sites and resources. If we had to go to the politician to gain access to soil and its products—or to a site within reach of our customers—the distribution of sites would become a perpetual nightmare. Favoritism, force and fraud would rule, not the free conditions of the marketplace.

Chapter Six

Premonition of the American System

The excuse which is invariably offered for the misgivings of the gloomy men is "the condition of the times." And, in truth, the post-Napoleonic period in Britain was one in which a prolonged sense of uncertainty preyed upon the nerves of every class. When the price of wheat dropped steadily (as in 1815–16 and in 1822), the landed squire took fright; when the spread of the new textile machinery continued to put more and more country cottagers out of work, the spirit of the Luddites, who had smashed factory equipment all over the north of England in 1811–12, stalked abroad; and when good times came, as in 1824–25, there were strikes which seemed all the more menacing because of the repeal of the anti-trade-union Combination Acts. From 1839 to 1842, there was an unbroken stretch of depression combined with bad harvests; then, after a slight interlude of recovery, the depression settled down again. It often seemed as though good times were lost forever.

The classic statement of conditions in the so-called Hungry Forties was made by Friedrich Engels in his *The Condition of the Working Class in England*. First published in

Germany in 1845, this work made full use of the seamier side of the industrial revolution which had been preserved in the reports of Royal Commissions. Engels, a mill manager himself and the son of a mill owner, knew that the new power-driven machinery of Arkwright, Crompton and the rest of the great textile inventors had called a whole new population into existence, changing Lancashire from "an obscure, ill-cultivated swamp into a busy, lively region." (The description is Engels' own.) He knew, too, that Sir Humphry Davy had applied chemistry to agriculture "with success," which was sufficient earnest that the new industrial population would be fed. Yet despite the plain fact that it was only in the industrial shires that wages stayed above the minimum wage-cum-living-allowance prescribed by the Speenhamland poor relief system, Engels concluded that every advance in the industrial arts must come at the expense of the working class.

Just how he reached this conclusion is not logically or statistically apparent in his frequently eloquent and moving pages; indeed, the inconsistencies are such that even Engels himself, when he came to write a preface in his old age for the English edition of 1892, had drastically to alter the time-scale of his 1845 prophecy of immediate proletarian upheaval. But if Engels had made any real effort to document his thesis as of 1845, he would have had to refute the fact that, after the post-Napoleonic fall in prices, the real wage of the British laborer was considerably higher than it had been in Adam Smith's time. Engels' own description of an Arcadian preindustrial England hardly tallies with the truth of such things as the death rate in the eighteenth-century foundling homes; or even with the fact that foundling homes were necessary in the first place. Nor does it tally with the fact that it was the condition of agricultural labor, not urban labor, which made the decision of the Speenhamland magistrates to "supplement the wage" seem necessary in the light of the new, fast-growing humanitarianism.

In 1845 Engels had dramatically declaimed: "Is this a state of things which can last? It cannot and will not last. The workers, the great majority of the nation, will not endure it." Yet even as Engels was saying that he had "never seen a class so deeply demoralized, so incurably debased by selfishness, so corroded within, so incapable of progress, as the English bourgeoise," this same middle class was busy responding to a whole congeries of humanitarian impulses. The English "bourgeoisie" abolished the slave trade, passed several reform bills, did away with the rotten borough" system of parliamentary representation and considerably modified its own "bloody code" of calling for the death penalty for petty shoplifting; and all without prompting from the socialists.

In 1892 Engels admitted that a new epoch had come in the wake of the repeal of the Corn Laws and the discovery of gold in California and Australia. Employers no longer dealt in "petty thefts"; they had learned to get along with trade unions by "petting and patronizing" them (as Engels put it); they had acquiesced in the factory acts which had put an end to child labor and the sixteen-hour day; they had formed a coalition with the working classes in order to defeat the landlords in Commons. There was no gloom in Engels' words of 1892 when he spoke of the "immense mass of productions of the twenty years from 1850 to 1870."

In the face of all this evidence that his predictions had been hopelessly misguided, Engels still clung to his revolutionary millennialism: the crunch would come, he said, when the overseas lands—the colonies, the U.S.A.—were themselves industrialized. Then, said Engels, the doctrine of free trade would no longer serve to keep British capitalism afloat. Like John Stuart Mill, Engels continued to think of the cotton-spinning revolution as unique and scarcely repeatable; he made no allowance for the inventive mind which was to conjure up a score of similar technological revolutions in transportation (the automobile, the airplane), in chemistry (plastics, cheap fertilizers), in power (electricity, the atom), in steelmaking (the open-hearth process, the continuous strip mill) and in the wholly new science of electronics. Moreover, his failure to foresee the future was matched by his failure to see just how faulty his analysis of the "bleak age" of the 1830s and 40s had been.

The truth is that the "bleak age" (as the Hammonds have described it in a book of that title) owed its depressing atmosphere not so much to the activities of the mill owners as to the failure of the British state to end the repressive laws that kept the new productivity from spreading into the fields of housing and sanitation. The living conditions in Manchester and in the ring of towns around it (Bolton, Rochdale, Oldham, Preston, Ashton and Staleybridge) may have been as deplorable as Engels (or America's own Charles A. Beard) said they were; but, as T. S. Ashton has recently pointed out, the prime reason for the lack of habitation in the 1820s and 30s was the twenty-year cessation of building which had accompanied the Napoleonic struggles. Iron, needed for cannon to defeat "Boney," was unavailable for drain pipe; and wood from Scandinavia could not be had because of the prohibitive war duties. When peace came, the duties on building materials remained, adding a full third to the cost of a cottage; moreover, the old window taxes of the seventeenth century lingered on to make the luxury of light and air too costly for the poor. With the state duties added into the rent, and with builders having to resort for a period to the black market for money because of misplaced usury laws, it is scant cause for wonder that the new industrial towns were largely jerry-built. In addition to state taxes on wood, brick and other building materials, there were the local taxes. The builders themselves earned very little for their pains in putting up even the flimsiest of structures; and most of the blame for the disease that was periodically epidemic in the towns should properly be visited on the state authorities who continued to tax the tile and brick needed for sewage disposal.

Aside from state oppression of the construction industry, there was the eighteenth-century tradition of uncleanliness. Without seeing the import of his words, Engels offered the horrors of the Edinburgh and Dublin slums as examples of capitalist cupidity. Yet both Edinburgh and Dublin had been built before the industrial revolution, and when Engels was writing they were still largely untouched by the quickening industrial processes of the new day. As for London itself, its squalor clearly dated back to the period depicted by Hogarth. Before there was a large new middle class of industrialists and a progressive supporting class of skilled mechanics, the aristocrats used spices and perfumes to hide the plain evidence of their taste buds and nostrils, while the lower elements took to the sodden anesthetics of Gin Lane. It was Engels' despised "bourgeoisie" which refused to put up with the preindustrial conditions: the new middle classes took the lead in wiping out the breeding grounds of cholera epidemics by insisting on municipal sanitation in the latter half of the traduced nineteenth century. It was under Queen Victoria, and not in the time of her wicked Hanoverian uncles, that cleanliness, for the first time in English history, was rated next to godliness.

As for conditions in Manchester and Liverpool, Engels had much to say about the influx of Irish peasants who brought their pigs to live with them in crowded industrial warrens. "The Irishman," so Engels remarked in a characteristic burst of race prejudice, "loves his pig as the Arab his horse . . . he eats with it and sleeps with it." No doubt the Irish did bring considerable "filth and drunkenness" with them into England, but the squalor which Engels noted derived, not from the industrial revolution as such, but from the generations of agricultural poverty that had become the norm in the rackrented Irish land.

That estimable social historian, G. M. Trevelyan, complains that England lost its sense of architectural proportion in the nineteenth century. But since the esthetic blight extended to the habitations of all classes, the rich as well as the poor, the lapse in taste must be attributed to a general decline in sensibilities, not to capitalism as a system of exploitation. Indeed, the rage for the gimcrackery of the neo-Gothic was largely a promotion of the Romantics who yearned for an older, precapitalistic day. When the world eventually recovered from the Victorian penchant for a fake antiquity, it discovered that capitalist builders could be just as accommodating with the "modern" as they had been with turret, tower and gingerbread ornamentation.

If Engels both misread the future and slandered the past and present in his *Conditions of the Working Class in Eng-*

land, a far greater man than he made the same sort of error. Like Engels, Robert Owen was a mill operator who became beguiled by the promises of socialism. But where Engels' socialism paraded itself as "scientific," Robert Owen's millennialism was frankly utopian. Owen's own industrial career spanned the Napoleonic and immediately post-Napoleonic periods in which Engels saw the businessman as a crude trickster who took his profit by practicing innumerable petty larcenies at the expense of the workers. Far from engaging in the sort of sharp practice which Engels regarded as universal, however, Owen proved over the course of a full generation that humane capitalism was eminently profitable. He did this in the depths of the "bleak age," thus demonstrating that the "condition of the times" had nothing whatsoever to do with the viability of good capitalist principles.

Yet Owen had a positive mania for misreading his own genius. He completely lost his sense of direction when he ceased to be a capitalist doer and set himself up as a socialist theoretician and as the self-chosen patron saint of all those who believe the state can do things for people far better than they can do things for themselves.

In every way a paradox, this Welshman—who quit the profitable manufacture of cotton thread to sire such things as labor exchanges and the cooperative movement—betrayed the strangest incapacity to generalize from his own experience. In his business he believed in strict cost accounting, and in all manner of aids to incentive; in his utopian schemes he kept no books and trusted to universal benevolence. As an amateur of educational theory, he preached the gospel that "environment" creates character. Yet he himself was a walking proof that character owes little to surroundings and that it may triumph over the most unlikely circumstances.

As a boy, Owen had left his native mountains to apprentice himself to a linen draper, one James McGuffog of Stamford, in Lincolnshire. Later he worked for a haberdasher on Old London Bridge, getting up at dawn to receive customers at eight and quitting only after arranging and replacing goods on the shelves at one or two in the morning. This "ceremonious slavery" (Owen's son's description) was followed by a meteoric career in Manchester, where Owen became a capitalist at the age of nineteen, in partnership with a cotton-machinery manufacturer. At the age of twenty Owen was a full-fledged mill manager. He had done it all for himself, without benefit of schooling save as he himself had supplied it.

Forgotten at all of the partisan rallies which periodically sing the praises of Owen the collectivist, Owen the labor leader or Owen the Fabian "planner," is the fact of the man's life as a practical businessman. Yet it was as a businessman, one of the best of his time, that he made his only really worthwhile discovery. In the early days of the industrial revolution, at his New Lanark mills at the falls of the Clyde in Scotland, Robert Owen carried out a great experiment—a distinctly capitalist experiment, conducted without recourse to state aid and within a framework of purely voluntary action.

In its own time, the experiment was so successful that it had thousands posting over the muddy roads of England and Scotland to look at what went on in Owen's seven-story brick mills on the wooded banks of the Clyde. As his son, Robert Dale Owen, tells it, the net annual profits from one of Owen's earlier partnerships averaged fifteen percent over a period of ten years; later, under a new partnership, the mills earned a net of fifty percent on the invested capital over a period of four years. But it was not only the money that impressed the 20,000 visitors who signed the guest-books at New Lanark within the space of a decade; it was the tangible proof that money could be made—and in quantity—without grinding the faces of the poor. The Grand Duke Nicholas, son of the Czar of all the Russias, was so entranced with New Lanark that he offered land in Russia on which to settle two million of England's "surplus" population, the sole condition being that Owen himself would come and direct the immigrants at work. (The Grand Duke had presumably been reading Malthus on his way to Scotland.) Quakers praised Owen for his rare "inner light," even though Owen was a vague deist, if not close to an atheist, in his professed religious attitude. And the philosopher Jeremy Bentham, in pursuit of "the greatest happiness of the greatest number," entrusted some of his money to Owen's management as a partner. (Jeremy most emphatically wished to include himself among the "greatest number" when it was a case of distributing the "happiness" of an enterprise around.)

Yet for all of the linked profitability and decency of Owen's experiment, no one seems to have drawn the logical conclusion from it, least of all Owen himself. What Owen had discovered in the years at New Lanark was nothing less than the way to make capitalism work. The discovery was certainly not his alone—other nineteenth-century industrialists, now forgotten, knew as well as Owen that there was no long-term profit in the sheer exploitation of one's help. One of those early industrialists who chose to flout what would soon be called the "iron law of wages" was David Dale, Owen's father-in-law, who had originally built the New Lanark mills. A kindly and religious man who liked on occasion to hold forth in an independent Presbyterian pulpit, Dale followed the custom of his times in utilizing the labor of pauper children from the workhouses. We think this monstrously cruel today, forgetting that in the years before the cotton-mill owners started contracting to take foundling labor, the paupers were left in the workhouses to perish wholesale from disease and starvation. Dale employed 500 children, 200 of them under the age of ten, and he apparently considered himself a humanitarian in doing so. Certainly he did his best to make his factory infinitely preferable to the foundling homes. At a time when other mill owners occasionally beat their child employees into line with leather thongs, Dale was a far more gentle "father." He made a beginning at cleaning up the system of pauper apprenticeship, giving girls and boys different rooms to sleep in, allowing them time off for meals and providing school instruction for anyone who wanted to learn reading, writing and "ciphering" after supper.

Even as early as 1796 a tourist, visiting New Lanark, noted the transformation that had been carried out by David Dale. "The health and happiness depicted on the countenances of these children," he wrote, "show that the proprietor of the Lanark mills has remembered mercy in the midst of gain. The regulations here to preserve health of body and mind present a striking contrast to those of most large manufactories in this kingdom . . . It is a truth that ought to be engraved in letters of gold, to the eternal honor of the founder of New Lanark, that out of three thousand children who have been at work in these mills throughout a period of twelve years, only fourteen have died and not one has suffered criminal punishment." When one of David Dale's buildings was destroyed by fire, Dale reassured his lamenting workmen by saying: "Dinna greet, my children. You've helped me to muckle siller by your labor; and I can well afford to spend some of it in taking care of you till the mill's built up and started . . . I'll pay you all the same wages you've had till now."

The motive of Dale's voluntary "welfarism" need not have been primarily eleemosynary. Though distinctly relative to its time and place, and offensively "paternalistic" to modern ears, it paid off in cash and reputation. The New Lanark mills became known in distant Manchester as something new and better in cotton-mill management. Hearing about it, Robert Owen, the boy wonder of Manchester, leaped at the chance on a visit to the North to see the New Lanark marvel for himself. In Glasgow, he met Dale's daughter Caroline and, in his own cool fashion, fell in love with her. But it was not the girl's hand he asked for on his first visit to the father. What Owen was after was nothing less than the old man's mills.

Mr. Dale's initial response was: "Why, *you* don't want to buy them. You're too young." The young visitor's characteristically beguiling effrontery, however, soon dissolved any reluctance; after all, the old man was dealing with the youth who had had the perceptiveness to buy the first two bags of American Sea Island cotton ever imported into England and to judge that Robert Fulton, the steamboat man, was worthy of a small loan. As soon as Owen had found partners to put up the money for the purchase, Dale yielded up his factory. Later on the brash young man got around to asking for the daughter.

It was characteristic of Owen that he should consider his father-in-law's own startling innovations in the handling of personnel to be inadequate. Owen stopped the importation of pauper apprentices and refused to employ any children under the age of ten. Though the Clydeside workers of the time were a "wretched society" (to use Owen's own description), they responded to the ideas of their new employer once he had convinced them that he did not intend to tamper unduly with their personal lives. Owen won his rude Scots individualists to the idea of a company store when he offered them "pure whisky" for sale as well as cheap food and clothing. He added a second story to the workmen's houses, cleaned up the town's dung-heaps, paved the streets and went into the coal business to keep his employees from being gouged on fuel. He offered medical attention to all, deducting one-sixtieth of a man's wages to make this possible. At the same time he paid good wages and shortened the hours of work. In the mills, over each operative's station, he hung a cube, with black, blue, yellow and white sides. The position of the cube denoted an individual's working behavior, black being turned outward for poor performance, blue for indifferent, yellow for good and white for excellent. Nobody at New Lanark was punished for recalcitrance, nobody was ever spoken to harshly. (The only thing Owen grew visibly angry about was excessive drunkenness.) In the factory the "silent monitor" alone told the story and effected the necessary discipline.

Owen seems to have carried his partners along with him on most of his innovations. Inside the factory he anticipated many of the morale-building discoveries which are now associated with the name of Professor Elton Mayo; and in taking an interest in his workmen's homes as the original breeding grounds of efficiency, he was more than a century ahead of Henry Ford's "sociological department." But when Owen turned his mind to establishing a model school system for the village of New Lanark, he met with indignant protests. Owen had his own ideas about education; he believed in "visual aids," in teaching without the birch rod and in adding dancing and music to the more conventional curriculum of the three R's. In some respects he was an educational "progressive"; in other respects he harked back to the "spirit, mind, body" roundedness of the ancient Greeks. Since he also believed in a measure of vocationalism, he insisted on special instruction for girls in knitting and sewing. And he was adamant about keeping even the ten- and eleven-year-olds out of the factory and in school for part of the day.

These "advanced ideas" led to continual friction, and Owen, in a dramatic showdown, finally offered to buy out his partners or to sell them his own share of New Lanark. This was in 1809, ten years after he had first come to Scotland. When the partners decided they wanted to pull out, Owen offered the sum of 84,000 pounds for the property, or some 24,000 more than he had been paid for it in 1799. When the books were examined, it developed that the business, in addition to paying five percent on the original capital for ten years, had also earned 60,000 pounds. Moreover, New Lanark, in an early version of the "annual wage," had managed to keep its workers on the payroll during a prolonged period of shutdown at a cost of 7,000 pounds. Owen's justification for this was that he wanted to keep his well-trained help in New Lanark.

All the evidence attests to the profitableness of Owen's methods. He raised the 84,000 pounds, entered into a new partnership—and later bought out his new partners at an auction which priced the mills at 114,000 pounds. New Lanark, in the midst of the post-Napoleonic upheavals, continued to be a moneymaking enterprise, and Owen continued to carry out his newfangled notions about education and about luring productivity from workers by providing them with decent surroundings and good wages.

What should have been a valid generalization from all this? Clearly Owen should have deduced from his experience that the most effective way to reform an industrial society would be to persuade mill owners in general to follow the New Lanark prescription. At one point Owen did hit upon the basic postulate of modern "consumer capitalism"; he noted, speaking of the working class, that "these, in consequence of their numbers, are the greatest consumers." (Again, we have the anticipatory echo of Henry Ford.) Yet Owen couldn't see that he had the elements of a universal system at New Lanark. Instead of preaching the gospel of improved unit efficiency via higher wages and shorter hours to the capitalists of Manchester, Owen, at the first hint of post-Napoleonic recession, took flight into the wild blue. He began thinking in socialist terms. He concocted the idea of his famous Villages of Co-operation—a system under which the state, or the county, would buy up land on which to settle the unemployed in government-sponsored enterprises. And instead of offering an increasingly efficient industrial system as the key to employment, he envisaged a "spade agriculture."

Meanwhile, Owen became a money crank as well as a socialist. He suggested that "labor notes" be substituted for money. (This was to have a curious echo in the 1929–33 depression in America, when the Technocrats came up with

the notion of "erg-money" to be based on units of energy.)
Owen also advocated price fixing, with the prices based on
the units of labor power going into specific types of goods.
This, he said, would wipe out "bargaining and speculation."
His ideas were grounded in a pre-Marxian labor theory of
value which can be found in one section of Adam Smith's
Janus-faced discussion of the origins of value. Owen
scarcely noticed that he had himself described "manual
labor, *properly directed*" (italics ours), as the source of
all wealth. (He missed a point which must have been familiar to him as an industrialist, that good management, in
improving the marginal utility of labor in a given factory,
must make mincemeat of the idea that "units of labor
power" can ever be made a static yardstick for a price-and-
money system.) The fact that Owen thought very little of
his own qualifying phrase, "properly directed," was an in-
sult to himself as the "proper director" of manual labor at
the New Lanark mills. After all, the difference between
New Lanark and other United Kingdom mills resided in a
single thing—the superior management provided succes-
sively by David Dale and Robert Owen.

As Owen grew older he became more and more of a fud-
dled utopian. He became bored with New Lanark. Instead
of opening up a showcase branch of his Scottish mills in
Manchester to show the British his superior methods, he
gave up his flourishing business in cotton thread to found
a socialist colony in America, at New Harmony, Indiana.
He did this virtually on a whim when a British agriculturist
named Robert Flower informed him that a socialist community built by the Rappites, a group of Lutheran schis-
matics, on the far edge of American civilization, could be
had for upwards of a hundred thousand dollars. "Well,

Robert, what say you—New Lanark or Harmony?" asked
Owen, turning to his son, young Robert Dale. When the
son answered "Harmony," the die was cast. Within a year,
Owen had arranged for the purchase of the Rappite village
on the Wabash and twenty thousand acres of land. By open
invitation some eight hundred people quickly flocked in to
fill the brick and frame buildings and the log huts constructed by the Rappites. The land around New Harmony
was good enough, for much of it was a rich alluvial soil
above the highest watermark of the Wabash. There were
vineyards, a freestone quarry and a large flour mill. As long
as each inhabitant of New Harmony was paid in accordance with an estimate of the value of his services to the
community, all went well. But Robert Owen, impatient for
the millennium, suddenly decided that, to quote his son,
"the Harmonites . . . should at once form themselves into a
Community of Equality, based on the principle of common
property." A constitution was drawn up, and equal sharing
instituted forthwith.

Five weeks were sufficient to complete a debacle which
necessitated an Owenite dictatorship. Since Robert Owen
disdained force (and, in any event, had no power to hold
people in New Harmony against their will), the dictatorship
solved nothing. Robert Dale Owen, the son, described the
upshot: "Finally, a little more than a year after the Community experiment commenced, came official acknowledge-
ment of its failure . . . Robert Owen ascribed too little influence to the anti-social circumstances that had surrounded
many of the quickly collected inhabitants of New Harmony
before their arrival there. . . ."

The fiasco compelled Owen to inform the "Harmonites,"
who must have been the most glorious collection of dead-

beats ever assembled together in one place, that henceforward they must support themselves or leave town. Some of
the more industrious idealists leased land from Owen and
tried to carry on with smaller agricultural collectives. But
in every instance the collectives failed. The lesson was lost
on Robert Owen. He returned to England from the banks
of the Wabash to put himself at the disposal of the British
labor movement. He became the founder of "Owenism,"
and, as such, he sired practically everything that is debilitat-
ing in modern British society. (The consumer cooperative
movement is an exception: founded by the Rochdale "Ow-
enites," this movement based itself on careful cost accounting, competitive purchases and good store management,
quite in the tradition of Owen's own "company store" at
New Lanark.) Though Thomas Babington Macaulay, the
Whig historian, described the aging Owen as "always a
gentle bore," Owenism eventually carried everything before
it. Far more than Marx, Robert Owen is the creator of
modern British socialism.

The irony of it all is that if Owen had only read and
pondered the histories of the Jamestown and Plymouth colonies, he might have been saved the New Harmony fiasco
and the subsequent plunge into all of his later British aber-
rations. In Jamestown, even though an official ukase declared that "he that will not worke shall not eate except
by sicknesse he be disabled," Captain John Smith could not
keep the earliest Virginia colonists from starving. It was
not until Governor Sir Thomas Dale finally discovered, in
1611, that "martial law did not grow corn," that the incentives of private farming were permitted to save the situation. As Governor Dale learned by trying it out, the colonists, once they were in possession of their own land and

free to work it, "took more pains in a day than they had in a week." Some ten years later, in Plymouth, Governor Bradford, at his wits' end because nobody in the Pilgrim community would work even to forestall starvation, decided in a similar extremity that every man must make provision for himself. Following Dale's example, Bradford assigned every able-bodied person or family a portion of land. "This," so Bradford noted, "had very good success, for it made all hands very industrious, so as much corne was planted than other waise would have bene by any means the Governor or any other could use, and saved him a great deall of trouble, and gave farr better contente. The women now wente willingly into the feild, and tooke their little-ons with them to set corne, which before would aledg weaknes, and inabilitie; whom to have compelled would have bene thought great tiranie and oppression."

As Owenite socialism in England disdained the cumulative lessons of Jamestown, Plymouth, and New Harmony, Indiana, Americans who had probably never heard of the New Lanark experiment moved toward the creation of the very system which Owen himself had abandoned. Instead of calling it "New Lanarkism," they called it "the American system of production." American economists, skeptical of the Iron Law of Wages, began preaching the idea that both wages and profits are paid out of production, and that, as unit efficiency increases and as sales are expanded through lower prices, there must be more and more income for everybody, whether worker, manager or stockholder. A hundred years after New Lanark, Henry Ford, a practical mechanic who didn't know enough about history to know whether it was bunk or not, was to carry New Lanarkism to its ultimate conclusion in high wages and mass selling at low prices.

For those who like to ponder the crazy turns of history, the sobering thing to remember is that the flag of modern "consumer capitalism" could have been nailed to the masthead of the industrialists even at the inception of the industrial system. But Owen, who had seen calicoes sold to Indian peasants for a pittance and who had the principles of consumer capitalism staring him in the face at his own mills, failed to realize the potential of what he had developed. Because of a man who lost his head and couldn't read his own hand, the British Empire was doomed to travel all the way to the brink of ruin. As a final irony the intellectual deposit of Owenism—"Fabianism"—came ultimately to be admired in American universities. So "Owenism" made the bridge to America. But this was not to happen until many years after Fabianism had conquered in England.

Meanwhile the "American system" was to make its own history. Though hobbled by the twentieth-century importation of Owenite ideas, it is still pouring forth its riches.

Chapter Seven

Prometheus Unbound— or the Enterpriser's Function Explained

Americans, almost from the beginning, thought of the "iron laws" as something that pertained to old countries. The "laws" may have been taught in textbooks which were rewritten out of English classical theory, but, as Adam Smith had observed from afar, North America was a land of high wages, a superabundance of food and a voracious appetite for capital. The only problem of the day was this: How long could such conditions last?

Only until there was a full complement of "stock," said Adam Smith, strangely ignoring the fact that "stock" is what increases the productivity of labor. A surfeit of "stock" —meaning factory equipment and machine tools—would drive down the interest rate, eat into profits, and bring the halcyon time to a close. True, Adam Smith never thought of this as overly serious: with him, it simply portended a day when everyone, capitalists included, would have to go to work. With Malthus and Ricardo, as we have seen, it was different: they envisaged a time of endemic and even epidemic starvation for everyone save landlords.

The earliest American economist, Henry Carey, could not believe that the good Lord would be so callous as to set a

Malthusian or Ricardian trap for His children. Nor could Frederic Bastiat in France. These men, who believed in the "economic harmonies," saw nothing inexorable in the laws of wages and rent. They believed that as society grew richer, the share going to labor must increase not only absolutely but relatively to that of the capitalist. (The same "law" that would ultimately make millionaires of Rockefellers would also put gasoline in the tanks of fifty-five million automobiles.) Carey and Bastiat denied the Malthusian predictions of inevitable overpopulation: every new human being, they argued, came into the world with two hands and a directing brain with which to work and feed himself. As to a "possible" monopoly of the soil, Bastiat was emphatic on the queer point that land in itself had no value: the immigrants who cleared a naturally fertile soil in Guiana or Australia, so he insisted, "confirmed" the truth of his theory that value is a purely human creation, and that everyone is free to create it. "They labor," he said of the colonists, "they clear, they exhaust themselves; they are exposed to privations, to sufferings, to diseases; and then if they wish to dispose of the land which they have rendered fit for production, *they cannot obtain for it what it has cost them.*" Rent, so Bastiat explained, was something paid for the use of improvements, not for the "original and indestructible" powers of the earth. And when the improvements diminish in value because of the lack of a market for their products, the landowner must take a loss.

Though this is hardly a respectable refutation of Ricardo (the way to deal with that gloomy man, as we have seen, is to show that agriculture can be made subject to a law of increasing returns), Bastiat was obviously correct in thinking the land problem was really no problem in a country that was still wide open. And Henry Carey, who believed in an increasing return for agriculture, was equally correct in suspecting the relevance of Ricardo, even though his own attempt to show that poor soil is always cultivated before good soil (thus leaving *better* land to be taken up for free by those who can't afford to pay rent on property already cleared) was so laughably undocumented that it fell of its own weight.

Bastiat's general refutation of the iron laws, which he carried out in sparkling fashion in that most sprightly of treatises, the *Harmonies of Political Economy,* was not to receive a practical demonstration on a large scale until Henry Ford came along to give his workers the five-dollar day without raising the price of his car. As we shall see, it was the five-dollar day which knocked at least three of the ancient preconceptions of economics higher than a kite for all to see. After Ford's momentous decision nobody could maintain with a straight face that there was either a static "natural" price, or a natural wage that was cribbed, cabined and confined by an antecedent wage fund, or profits that were in inexorable conflict with the wage scale. If the efficiency of labor and capital in conjunction was high, there could be enough for everybody. Even the Ricardian law of rent suffered from the consequences of the five-dollar day: marginal farm lands all over the Southern Appalachians were deserted by men who had heard the wondrous tales of high factory wages to be had in Detroit. Henry Ford himself, if Charles E. Sorensen's *My Forty Years with Ford* is the last word on the subject, knew nothing of such theorists as Bastiat and Carey. An untutored genius, he had felt his way along in economics precisely as though he were working in the shop on problems of factory layout or on ideas for improving the carburetor. But even if he had known of books like the *Harmonies of Political Economy,* he would not have made much of them, for they were written before the idea of mass production had altered the industrial idiom.

The theory that an enterpriser with the ability to promote a real "union of forces" does proportionately more for society—and the worker—than he does for himself was not fully and comprehensively stated for the American factory age until a Civil War veteran, General Francis Amasa Walker, who taught at the Yale Sheffield Scientific School from 1871 to 1880 before becoming president of the Massachusetts Institute of Technology, applied his fertile mind to the subject of economics. It was Walker who definitely killed what the late Garet Garrett has called the "disastrous foreign theories" by a show of logic that was as beautiful as it was imperious.

What Walker did was to set forth a body of theory in American terms that was eventually to make it impossible for a respectable intellectual opposition to the Ford idea to form. There was, as we shall see, much grumbling in Detroit when Henry Ford decided to share his mounting income with his workers, and so help to get increased marginal efficiency out of them; and there were some predictions, naturally, that ruin would shortly encompass both the automobile industry and the American economic system as a whole. But the predictions lacked fire and cogency—and nobody emerged with the power of persuasion to head Ford off.

Walker, it can be said without much fear of contradiction, was the first really important American economist. He came before John Bates Clark, who worked out the marginal utility theory of prices and wages independently of the Austrians and Englishmen like Jevons and Alfred Marshall. Walker, less meticulous than Clark, was a pioneer in all he touched. He was like Carey in being an optimist. Walker, too, had his doubts that the landlord must inevitably gobble everything by playing a holdup game; as we shall see, he finally got around to stating the Law of Rent in terms that made it seem far less menacing than his contemporary, the single taxer Henry George, thought it must be. But Walker, unlike Henry George or Henry Carey, had a mind that was a steel trap.

With great force, precision and originality Walker exploded one by one the "laws" laid down by England's gloomy men when the science of political economy was largely a series of deductions from premises that had not been sufficiently tested by observation of facts. After Walker had written his articles and books there was no longer any warrant for believing that wages are paid out of a circumscribed wage fund, or that profits are wrung out of the hide of the worker by keeping him close to subsistence levels, or that the entrepreneur "steals" his profits by seizing the laborer's "surplus value," or that every increase in production must eventually go into the pockets of the landlord in the shape of the "unearned increment" of skyrocketing rents or mounting charges for raw materials.

Now, any man who could lay so many hobgoblins to rest ought to be famous for all time. Yet Francis Amasa Walker, save for an appreciative word or two in Garet Garrett's books, is virtually unknown today. Though he headed his department in the Sheffield Scientific School and wrote his most original works while still a resident of New Haven, he gets only one cursory mention in George Wilson Pearson's

history of Yale. The development of "institutional" economics has overshadowed him; ironically, some of his basic
discoveries—such as his theory of the entrepreneur function, which deals with profit as the equivalent of a "rent"
paid for imaginative foresight—have tended to come back
to American shores with other names attached to them. The
Austrian Joseph Schumpeter, for example, is often men-
tioned as the economist who has defined profit as the
temporary reward for innovation, but the definition is
implicit in everything which Walker wrote about the
entrepreneur in a textbook published seventy years ago.

In his own day Walker was a most impressive figure:
those who came into contact with him never forgot him.
Arthur Twining Hadley, who became president of Yale
some years after Walker's departure from the New Haven
scene, once remarked that Walker knew more things worth
knowing than any other man of his acquaintance. On one
occasion, Hadley asked Walker why college students of the
post–Civil War generation had ceased to admire debaters.
Walker's reply was characteristic of both the man's humor
and his large-minded patriotism and sense of duty. "The
answer," he said, "is simple. When the nation had to go to
war for its very existence, and when our college graduates
had the opportunity to serve their country in places of
prominence at peril of their lives, the debaters stayed at
home and left the athletes to go to the front. This is why,
ever since, the country has liked athletes better than
debaters."

Walker, who preferred the athletes himself, was a most
attractive man. Though he was the son of Amasa Walker, a
free trade and hard money economist who taught at Amherst, and though he labored all of his life at intellectual

matters, there was little of the smell of the classroom about him. He came to Yale from the great world, a well-groomed figure who wore a modish and glossy silk hat. When asked to discipline undergraduates for pranks, he declined, saying "I don't propose to be made into a policeman; that's not what I came here for." What seems to have been remarkable about his lectures on economics was their thorough grounding in the American life of the times; Walker knew the United States from many angles, and, though he was a first-rate logician, he was seldom betrayed into insisting on deductive logic at the expense of verifiable facts.

During the Civil War Walker had been an extremely young adjutant general with the Army of the Potomac. He was captured in the late stages of the war near Richmond. After escape and recapture, he was sent to Libby Prison, where his health broke down. Exchanged toward the war's end, he returned to civilian life to become a journalist, a superintendent of the federal census and an authority on the American Indian. In his later life, after his teaching career at Yale, he became a very practical administrator of MIT, rescuing it from the brink of bankruptcy and building it into the strong precursor of the great technological school of today. He served on boards of education in Connecticut and Massachusetts, and continued his work on the census from time to time.

As an optimist Walker was in tune with his era. But he was a humorous optimist with a relish for irony, and he never became fatuous in his hopes. His work on the federal census had impressed him with the protean nature of America and Americans. On this continent he saw "English sense" working hand in hand with "Yankee luck" to produce a constant growth. In a letter to Alfred Marshall, the

English economist, he spoke of the American inheritance of "English sense" as making "a bad law a dead letter almost from its enactment." "Our margin," he wrote Marshall, "is so immense, our recuperative energy so tremendous, that we can do any number of absurd things, yet come out fresh and smiling at the end." In proof of American vitality he cited the Chicago merchant who, "after the great fire, spit upon the ruins, to see if it is yet cool enough to begin rebuilding." When Marshall visited him in Boston, Walker got out a book of photographs of the American Indian. "British economics," he said to Marshall, "has a chief cornerstone in Ricardo's theory of rent; in a sense, that is universal, but the particular developments of it which are of most importance in an old country don't count for much in a land where the nominal owners of a hundred million acres or more are the people whose photographs you have just seen."

The obvious creativity of human energy applied to fresh soil in a land which lacked the incrustations of such medieval relics as entailed property and government-backed monopolies conditioned all the technical ramifications of Walker's economics. The spectacle of unfolding creativity kept Walker from treating his subject as a "closed" system. It kept him from taking economics as something which strained for equilibrium instead of giving way to the constantly disruptive dynamism which he found productive life to be. The only limiting factor which Walker recognized was the overall ceiling on productivity imposed by scarce natural means. Within the given natural means, Walker had a keen sense that creative ingenuity could push a four-part division of the product between land, labor, capital and entrepreneurial imagination upward in a way that would benefit everybody on a broad front.

One could begin a discussion of Walker's fluid system by cutting into it anywhere. In point of time, however, Walker made his first attack on the rigidity of orthodox British economics by questioning the validity of the Iron Law of Wages. He did this in a lecture delivered before the Alexandria and Athenae Societies of Amherst College, his father's old college and his own alma mater, in July of 1874. Six months later he expanded the lecture into a *North American Review* article for January 1875, on "The Wage-Fund Theory." The article was the equivalent, in economics, of Emerson's famous declaration of independence for the American scholar which had appeared a generation or so before. As Garet Garrett has said, the line of reasoning displayed in Walker's paper rescued Americans from the compulsions of "the European Book of Doom." The repercussions of Walker's foray were startling, both on this side of the Atlantic and in Europe itself. But the Walker arguments came too late to head off the developments of Marxism in Europe, which continued to take the "iron laws" formulated by Malthus, Ricardo and James Mill at face value.

Economists today take the dependence of wages on productivity for granted. Accepting the tools, the fixed capital, as given, it is obvious that there will be more to go around for everybody if the tools are handled well. When Walker started teaching economics, however, the libraries were full of treatises which argued that at any given moment there was a fixed sum of circulating capital constituting a "wage fund," and that this sum couldn't be violated no matter what the productivity of labor in any given year. The wage fund could be increased for the future out of savings, but that would affect future wages, not present. J. R.

McCulloch, H. Fawcett and James Mill, the father of the eminent John Stuart Mill, had worked it out arithmetically. The average wage, they said, must be the quotient obtained by dividing the sum in the wage fund by the number of workers employed in industry. Enlarging on the Mill and McCulloch arithmetical formula, an American, A. L. Perry, had said: "The question of wages is a question of division. It is complained that the quotient is too small. Well, then, how many ways are there to make a quotient larger? Two ways. Enlarge your dividend, the divisor remaining the same, and the quotient will be larger; lessen your divisor, the dividend remaining the same, and the quotient will be larger."

For fifty years the "inexorable" nature of this Iron Law of Wages had been accepted in England without serious question. Every time a body of workers went on strike for higher wages, the "iron law" was duly trotted out to prove that the strikers could only get more by stealing from the "wage fund" an amount of money that was due other workers.

The first attack on the wage-fund theory came in 1866 from a lawyer, not an economist. The lawyer, a Londoner named Francis D. Longe, argued in a pamphlet that it was ridiculous to suppose there was any fixed fund for wages that could be distinguished from the fund of general wealth, upon which levies for wages could be as elastic as specific circumstances permitted. Obviously, said Longe, if an employer could get a worker for less than his due share of any "fund," he would do so. The employer might have to pay more or less for a worker, depending on the competitive situation in a given line of industry, and his ability to do so would be governed by the amount of money in his own till, not the money in a "general" fund. How, asked Longe with a flourish, could shoemakers compete with tailors, or blacksmiths with glassblowers? Shoemakers competed with other shoemakers—and there was no way in which the proprietor of a cobbler shop could get his hands on the circulating capital of a master tailor to pay his own workers their proper arithmetical proportion of a predetermined amount of money set aside for labor in general.

Three years after Longe's pamphlet had appeared, Mr. W. T. Thornton, a writer on population problems and a close friend of John Stuart Mill, paid his own respects to the Iron Law of Wages theory. Some of his arguments paralleled those of Longe. The Thornton foray had an electrifying effect on John Stuart Mill, who announced in the *Fortnightly Review* for May 1869 that he was abandoning his father's old doctrine without reservations. Thornton, said Mill, had shown that the "barrier" of the Iron Law of Wages is "but a shadow which will vanish if we go boldly up to it."

Francis Walker was the first economist to accept the Mill challenge and move boldly up to the barrier. He dismissed some of the Longe and Thornton arguments as inadmissible; Thornton in particular, he said, argued too much from the individual, not the average, and hence missed the point of wage-fund theory. But Walker found one truly significant passage in the Longe pamphlet. "The amount of money . . . which the farmer is able to pay, or contract to pay, as wages," said Longe, "is limited only by the amount of money for which his crops and stock *will sell*" (italics ours).

This seemed to Walker to be the crux of the matter. It accorded squarely with his own experience of American life. As a young man in Massachusetts Walker had seen farmers paying their workers out of the proceeds of the harvest *after it had been marketed*. In Connecticut, when tobacco culture was started, payment out of the harvest was general. Walker was willing to concede that in Britain it had long been the custom for employers to lay down the whole of the wages to be paid as soon as the service was rendered, even before the products were sold. But in frontier America, during the time when the wage-fund theory was being elaborated in England, "employers were paying their laborers by the year, giving them their wages, in full, only when the crops were harvested or the goods marketed, making meanwhile such advances as their means allowed." The practice had continued to the late nineteenth century in the American South and West.

Thus, by his own observation as well as by going to the account books of farmers, Walker confirmed the theoretical insight of lawyer Longe. But where Longe had merely thrown out a few stray gleams, Walker developed the theory that labor is paid out of current production with a logical coherence that carried everything before it. His own contribution was to attack the wage-fund theory roundly on the score of motivation. "An employer," he said, "pays wages to purchase labor, not to expend a fund of which he may be in possession. He purchases labor, not because he wishes to keep it employed, but as a means to the production of wealth. He produces wealth, not for the sake of producing it, but with a view to a profit to himself, individually, in that production . . . If a person have wealth, that, of itself, constitutes no reason why he should expend any portion of it on labor, on machinery, or on materials. It is only as he sees that he can increase that wealth through production, that the impulse to employ it in those directions is felt. But for the profits by which he hopes thus to increase his store, it would be alike easier and safer for him to keep his wealth at rest than to put it in motion for the benefit of others. The mere fact that the employer has capital at his command, no more constitutes a reason why he should use it in production, when he can get no profits, than the fact that the laborer has arms and legs constitutes a reason why he should work when he can get no wages."

Though the logic of this seems very simple today, its explosive effect on the science of economics was revolutionary at the time. It turned economics into a dynamic, future-oriented thing. Elaborating his theory, Walker observed that the more labor a man can employ with the agencies at his command at a profit, and the more profit he can get out of an individual man, the more he can afford to pay in wages. "Wages," said Walker, "bear a clear and direct relationship to the product." The more profit that could be had out of the product, the higher the individual wage could be.

This, of course, directly contradicted Ricardo's idea that profits and wages were in perpetual conflict with each other. It also made mincemeat of Marx's theory of the inevitable class war, which presupposed that profits could only be maintained in an advanced capitalistic society by progressively cutting the individual's wages.

The process of disproving the wage-fund theory naturally involved Walker in prolonged consideration of the "industrial quality of the laboring class." In studying the question of quality, he opened up the whole characteristically American study of unit productivity. The level of productivity, he noted, depends not only on tools and money capital but on the industrial aptitude of people, their intelligence, sobriety and thrift. It also depends on the added element of teamwork. As for individual workers, they manifestly differ among themselves. Having seen New England Yankees at work with machinery and contrasted them with immigrants who were "all thumbs," Walker was not at all willing to concede that a proper "divisor" could be made out of the mere sum total of workers available. The arithmetic of James Mill, which arrived at the average wage by dividing a wage fund by the number of available workers, was silly because it tried to combine qualitatively different things.

"Suppose," said Walker, in attacking James Mill's arithmetical formula from the "divisor" end, "suppose [the laborers] to be East Indians." In this case there would be one sort of annual product. But "if we suppose Russian peasants to be substituted for East Indians, we shall have twice or three times that product; if we suppose Englishmen to be substituted for Russians, we shall have the product again multiplied two or three fold. An Englishman will do from three to thirty times as much work in a day as a Bengalee, according as the nature of the work makes smaller or larger demands upon the skill and strength of the laborer. By the wage-fund theory, the rate of wages would remain the same through these changes." In point of practice, however, a man who could do thirty times what another man did would certainly be paid far more for his work, as the wage scales of various countries showed. A preponderance of good men would raise the average wage of a whole community.

With his eye on the quality of what James Mill regarded as the natural "divisor" in the wage equation, Walker reached the not illogical conclusion that an increase of population, far from lowering the wage scale, might be the very agency leading to a general wage increase. For with more people available to work in accomplished teams, the qualitative aspect of each might be multiplied many times under many circumstances. Production would rise at a faster rate than the population increase wherever two men could join to do the work of three, four or five. This, as Walker knew, had happened again and again on the American frontier as the land filled up; it was demonstrated anew at every barnraising, at every husking bee; and whenever a farm family had more able-bodied sons to work land that had not reached the point of diminishing returns.

With qualitative factors destroying the very possibility of "describing the unit" which goes to make up James Mill's "divisor," and with quantitative changes in the "dividend"— the amount available for wages—resulting from every shift in the "divisor" quality, the old formula for obtaining the average wage naturally became completely inoperable. The refutation of the "iron law" was implicit, of course, in Adam Smith's celebration of the advantages to be derived from the division of labor. Walker, by combining the classical idea of the division of labor with his own observation of the benefits deriving from the "union of forces in production," arrived at a seemingly startling conclusion: that the "average" wage was not a product of division at all. A far more complex mathematics would have to be devised to account for the effect of quality times quantity of workers on productivity—and on the average wage. And the fixed capital, too, must be figured in the secret of productivity; as tools become better, either by themselves or in arrangement with other tools, there would be more product—and more for the worker out of the product.

Since his refutation of the Iron Law of Wages had been accomplished so easily, carrying economists in England and Ireland as well as in America with him, Walker was inclined to make light of his success as he grew older. In his textbook, published in 1887, he remarked that "it would be brutal to inflict further blows upon a body so exanimate as the theory of the wage fund." But the elasticity which destruction of the wage-fund theory afforded was felt in all aspects of Walker's economics. Having slain one dragon, Walker went looking for others which stood in the way of thinking there could be a wide dissemination of the benefits of increased unit production. For one thing, there was the dragon interposed by the Law of Rent as formulated by Malthus and Ricardo; for another, there was the theory that the entrepreneur was an excrescence on production, a leech who stole his profits by taking money which the worker should properly have received for putting "labor value" into the product. With the same logical clarity and command of the facts of American life which he had brought to the destruction of the wage-fund doctrine, Walker soon took the "iron" out of these theories as well.

Following Ricardo, Walker defined economic rent simply as "the surplus of the produce over the cost of cultivation on the poorest lands actually contributing to the supply of the market at the time." Walker did not deny the relevance of Ricardo's law, nor did he try to argue against John Stuart Mill's feeling that the "unearned increment" of increasing land valuation due to general social progress often gave the landlord what seemed like an unfair advantage over other people. But he differed radically with those who saw nothing but disaster ensuing from the "take" of the landlord in a complex modern society.

To begin with, he doubted the universal relevance of the Malthusian idea that population tends everywhere to increase faster than subsistence, driving people to scratch the barest sort of livings on the scantiest soils. Where people had become demoralized, as in large parts of the Orient, it might seem that the "constant tendency in all animal life to increase beyond the nourishment prepared for it" applied to humanity as well as to fish and tigers. But it seemed to Walker that there was an almost inevitable lessening of the "procreative force" of human beings whenever there was a multiplication and diversification of economic wants in society. When once men got their heads above the poverty line, they found ways of regulating births in order to make further gain in decencies, in variety of diet, in luxuries and so on. Walker noted that in France "even the peasants" were alive to the inexpediency of rapid multiplication; they did not wish to have to divide their lands among too many sons. And in New England, in Walker's own time, the rise in the standard of living had checked the growth of population. With a lower birthrate, the pressure on land was neutralized to the point where increasing knowledge, better tools and better fertilizers could keep pace with the need for more food to take care of a slowly expanding population.

The landlord, then, did not necessarily have society by the throat. True, he could exact full economic rent for his property, if he chose to be a rackrenter. But in a society where land was a form of capital, competing with industrial capital and hence tending toward a common rate of return, rent was no hardship. Certainly it did not follow that the landlord was in position to take every increase in the productivity of industry for himself, as Henry George was preaching at the time when Walker was considering the land question. In his *Progress and Poverty* George had said that "land being necessary to labor, and being reduced to private ownership, every increase in the productive power of labor but increases rent—the price that labor must pay for the opportunity to utilize its powers; and thus *all the advantages* gained by the march of progress *go to the owners of land and wages do not increase.*" This, said Walker, was "blunder piled on blunder, to reach a conclusion so monstrous."

The Henry George proposition offended Walker's common sense—but even more it offended his feeling for statistics and his keen sense of logic. At a time when George was writing about an alleged increase in poverty in America because of the inflexible nature of the Law of Rent, Walker himself was noting that "the dietary of an American farmer, cultivating his own land and with the aid of his growing sons, would amaze a peasant from any portion of Europe. An abundance of nutritious food is and has been, ever since the revolutionary period, the sure condition of the life of the agriculturist in the United States. It was not with our fathers, even in New England, a struggle for the necessaries of life, but for social decencies and what, in any old country, would have been called luxuries. . . . With an abundance of cheap land . . . few able-bodied men are likely to be drawn into factories and shops on terms which imply a meaner subsistence than that secured in the cultivation of the soil . . . if, then, the farmer will have services performed, he must admit those who perform them to share his own abundance. . . . Hence we find the mason, the blacksmith, the plumber, the carpenter, the house painter, the cobbler, in every part of the United States, receiving wages which bear no relation whatever to the wages paid for the same class of services in other countries. . . ."

So much for Walker's commentary on Henry George's ability to observe American life. But even in old countries where land was closely held by aristocrats it could be demonstrated that the landlord had not monopolized the gains achieved by increased labor productivity. Walker, a born statistician, noted that the English laborer worked five days in 1770 to pay for a bushel of wheat, four days in 1840, and only two and one-half days in 1870. In 1840 probably not a third of the British population had meat more than once a week; in 1870, however, virtually the whole population had meat, cheese or butter once a day.

The statistics proved also that the value of capital engaged in industrial enterprise exceeded that of land itself. Profits and interests took more of the total value of what labor produced than the increase of rent over the years.

The reason why the landlord couldn't "take all" was inherent in the fact that improvements in machinery naturally increased the demand for labor, as well as for raw materials and for food to support labor. Moreover, the demand for labor often multiplied many times over without any corresponding demand for the products of the soil. Walker let a pound of raw cotton stand for the landowner's contribution to the industrial process. This cotton might, in a crude state of society, be turned into rough cloth in half an hour by a single worker. But, with progress in the textile arts, the same cotton might necessitate five hours of work in order to turn it into a really fine fabric. The landowner, selling the same cotton for cheap shirts and expensive fabrics, would be in no position to take more for his cotton than the sum offered by the producer of cheap shirts. The value added by manufacture in the fine fabric shop would go to the worker, the entrepreneur, and the capitalist who put up the money for the textile machinery.

Walker applied his reasoning to meat which goes into a laborer's corned beef and cabbage dinner on the one hand, and into a Delmonico steak on the other, and to wood which goes into cheap and into expensive furniture. The "draught upon the essences of the soil" was the same whether the steer wound up in a cheap hash house or at a Fifth Avenue restaurant. Similarly with iron going onto a cheap scythe or into fine surgical instruments. Surveying the field, Walker concluded that the enhancement of the demand for land fell far short of the increased demand for labor as civilization advanced. Indeed, many inventions actually reduced the demand for land. For instance, cheap transportation which enabled Dakota farmers to sell their wheat in Liverpool tended to throw the poorer English soils out of cultivation. Inasmuch as rent is defined as "the surplus of the produce over the cost of cultivation on the poorest lands actually contributing to the supply of the market at the time," this naturally tended to reduce rents in England.

Like the Marxists, who cling desperately to the theory that wages and profits are locked in mortal combat, Henry George's disciples have never relinquished the notion that the landlord must gobble everything in sight. Yet just as Walker had refuted the "iron laws" which the Marxists depend on even before Marx's *Das Kapital* had converted Europe to socialism, so he disposed of Henry George's contentions four years after *Progress and Poverty* was written and before the single-tax movement was well under way. Walker objected to the single tax at its ideological inception in America because he felt, quite rightly, that it would put the allocation of sites and resources into the hands of politicians; better let the landlord collect his rent than turn over the control of the soil to a political master class with no direct interest either in freedom or in production. But beyond this objection to Henry George's panacea, Walker had a better reason for rejecting George: the man's diagnosis was wrong in the first place. The Ricardo Law of Rent, though it does operate as a tendency mitigated by custom, inertia and a sensible prejudice against rackrenting, cannot foster a monopoly of profits or keep the worker from getting more of the product of industry for the simple reason that the landlord isn't in position to scoop up every "value added by manufacture." The laborer, the capitalist—and the entrepreneur—must get theirs when competition is on, even as the landlord himself. And when the demand for labor increases at a faster pace than the demand for raw materials— the "essences of the soil"—labor will get more than anybody else.

In his writings on wages and rents Walker appeared in the guise of the Great Unstiffener. He carried on his role in his consideration of profits.

It is a commonplace that one can find forty different definitions of profit in as many books on economics. To the businessman, a profit is what is left when he has paid his costs; it is the difference between red ink and black. To the economist who believes that an economic system strains toward equilibrium, profit is a temporary thing which is destined to disappear whenever competition in a given field of endeavor has reached the point of saturation. To a Marxist, profit is wrung from the poor by taking from the worker the "surplus value" he creates over and above the cost of his subsistence. And to believers in an illusory "perfect competition," profit is a monopolistic charge which the proprietor of a patent or the possessor of some temporary secret piles on top of the "natural" price which is compounded of costs plus the "wage" of management and the interest paid out for the loan of capital.

To Walker, most of these definitions seemed sterile; they tended to miss the point of motivation, and they ignored the social function of profit, which is to guide production and provide the wherewithal for new investment. They also missed the point that some men have special aptitudes, a special faculty for seeing where labor can be most creatively employed. To state the matter in the more rounded terms of John Bates Clark, the man of entrepreneurial skill will know what to risk in payment for the relative productivity of "last units" of land, labor and capital, and will make a profit if his calculations are correct. But it was Walker who first accented the "where" as well as the "how." In order to clarify his theory, Walker considered profit as something more than the remuneration for the use of capital, something more than a "reward for abstinence" or for taking the risk of loss. Such remunerations, such rewards, were covered adequately by the term "interest." Beyond the concept of interest there was another thing—the entrepreneur's share of the product of industry, which could be great or small depending on the ability of a special breed of man.

By limiting his idea of profit to the share which is due the man who exercises the "entrepreneurial function," Walker directed the attention of economists to a fourth species of reward in the distribution cycle. Schumpeter and others have tended to accept this idea of a "fourth" reward in addition to wages, rent and interest—but they have tried to circumscribe it by defining it as a "payment for innovation," as something which one willingly gives to an inventor for enlarging the productive horizons of man. To Walker, innovation was indeed a part of the entrepreneurial function. But there was considerably more to it than that.

During Walker's lifetime, the consumer cooperative movement in England had had considerable success. But nearly all the attempts of labor to form producer cooperatives had come to grief. Surveying the wreckage of these attempts, Walker concluded that the entrepreneur, far from being an excrescence on production, was really the heart of it. An imaginative entrepreneur, with a good grasp of market possibilities and internal shop economies, was worth more to the working classes than fine gold. It was the entrepreneur who brought jobs into being in the first place, and who enabled the worker to use his talents in the most marketably worthwhile manner in the second.

Concentrating upon the entrepreneur's special talents, Walker concluded that profits bore more than a superficial resemblance to rent. For, just as there were no-rent lands which produced for the market at the bottom margin of cultivation, so there were no-profit industries which somehow staggered along, consuming savings or proceeding from bankruptcy to bankruptcy. The capitalist received his interest from no-profit industries willy-nilly; either that, or he took over as receiver. In the no-profit company, the entrepreneur could gain no recompense beyond a salary for putting in his time and efforts; he was like a landlord who had to be satisfied with barely enough income from property to pay the taxes. But as a company "measured up" from the no-profit margin, there was more and more to spare for the enterpriser who could devise the ways of improving unit productivity, or of increasing the sales.

Walker observed that profits, like rent, do not figure in

selling price under properly competitive conditions. For, just as the price of wheat is set at the margin by the wheat grown on no-rent lands, so is the price of an industrial product set at the margin by the output of the no-profit company. Profits, then, are the special creation of the ability, the know-how, the inventiveness, the foresight, the imagination, of the superior executive. They are, in effect, not added into price but *taken out of the cost*. Walker doubted that the entrepreneur could take all of the increased wealth he brought into being by cutting costs and enlarging the market. For every time an entrepreneur improved a given company's position, he made it harder for incompetent companies at the no-profit margin. Some of these companies would be forced out of business by the successful entrepreneur's action. By "leveling up," then, the competent employers who were both willing and able to pay more in order to raise the standards of efficiency would be left to dominate a given field. Society would be better off all around, for the efficient company, in addition to paying more in wages as an efficiency lure, is obviously in a better position to charge less for its product and to plow more funds back into research.

By keeping his eye on the specific contribution of the entrepreneur, Walker isolated profit as the driving force of industrial progress. Theoretically, an equilibristic economic system might outgrow the need for the enterpriser's special abilities. But Walker, with his eye on what was happening around him in America, knew that the good enterpriser is always able to turn equilibrium (another word for stagnation) into dynamic change. He doubted that the world would ever reach a stage in which all secrets have been discovered, all potential wants plumbed and all opportunities exploited to the uttermost limits of human ingenuity and human energy. Such a state might be imaginable, but only at the close of the evolutionary cycle. Obviously the human race had not reached that point in Walker's lifetime. Indeed, the possibilities of American technological ingenuity, spurred onward by the entrepreneur with the vision to see its market applications, had just begun to unfold in the days when Walker was establishing a specifically American economics to explain the du Ponts, the Sears Roebucks, the Fords and the Bethlehem Steels which would emerge in the post-Walker generation.

Walker, of course, lived before the dynamics of mass production had become the distinguishing feature of the American economic landscape. When he was writing, people still believed in Adam Smith's more or less static "natural price." Smith had defined the natural price as the sum of the cost of production (labor, etc.) which had gone into the article, plus the going rate of profit on capital in the neighborhood. But this simple definition did not reckon with the dynamic effect of the good entrepreneur on cost of production *and* profit.

By separating the two concepts of interest and profit, and by showing that profit was something saved on cost, Walker had destroyed the possibility of considering "natural" price as a simple sum. The natural price was whatever the enterpriser could make it: if he could perform the seeming miracle of expanding production and sales by rearranging his tools and simultaneously raising the wage and lowering the price, the "natural" basis for price could be changed overnight. This is essentially what Henry Ford did, and it has been done over and over again since his day.

The Ford system of pushing the use of labor-saving machinery way past the "break-even point" of clearing expenses on the tooling was still in the womb of time when Walker lived. But by removing the blocks which had prevented economists from seeing that wages and profits—and the price—were dependent on the entrepreneur's imagination in a dynamically interrelated way, Walker cleared the theoretical ground for Henry Ford in particular and for the American system in general. In our national emphasis on doing, on action, on the method of cut-and-try, Walker has been overlooked in the history of our thought. But generations at the Yale Sheffield Scientific School and the Massachusetts Institute of Technology listened to him—and the seed must have sprouted in industry in a myriad uncelebrated ways.

Chapter Eight

"Contrived Fecundity"— the Ford System and the "Margin"

There are two ways of following the course of American economics after Francis Amasa Walker. One is to read the economists themselves. The other is to study Americans as doers, to look at the evolution of American shop practice and merchandising techniques as businessmen, emulating the Romans of old, went ahead without benefit of the academy.

If one takes the first road, that of studying the economists, one eventually arrives at something called "institutionalism." But, curiously enough, one learns little about "institutions"—i.e., the corporations themselves as workaday units—from the "institutionalists." "Institutionalism" leads us to Thorstein Veblen, who looked at American life through the lenses of a satiric social anthropologist; to Wesley Mitchell, who changed the interpretation of statistics from a crude to a sophisticated art; to the prophets of the "national income" approach, who subordinate the "microeconomics" of the individual, the family and the "firm" to the "macroeconomics" of the Gross National Product; to J. Kenneth Galbraith, the analyst of the "countervailing power" of politicalized pressure groups; and to a thousand-

and-one foundations and bureaus which turn out excellent monographic material on topics ranging from Automation to the Geographical Distribution of Zirconium. (The first road also leads, by a fork, to the theorists of monopolistic competition, which is something we will come to later.)

The "institutionalists" should not be disparaged, for by keeping their eyes on statistical aggregates, they have done much to reduce the hazards attendant upon the projection of economic trends. Nevertheless, it is sobering to read the judgment pronounced by the Englishman Lionel Robbins on the works of the institutional and the "historical" schools. Says Professor Robbins: "But of 'concrete laws,' substantial uniformities of 'economic behavior,' [they have produced] not one—all the really interesting applications of modern statistical technique to economic inquiry have been carried through, not by the Institutionalists, but by men who have been themselves adept in the intricacies of the 'orthodox' theoretical analysis."

The second road, that of investigating American shop and merchandising practice as it developed without the benefit of any theory or *a priori* commitment, leads us to striking evidence of "substantial uniformities of behavior." Americans have always been cost cutters more than they have been price maintainers. The American businessman may have known very little about the Englishman William Stanley Jevons or about the Austrian "marginalists" or John Bates Clark, the American, who reached conclusions similar to those of Jevons about value and price. Articles, said Jevons, must vary in utility according as we already possess more or less of the same article. It follows that value will diminish for subjective reasons as abundance of a commodity or service increases. But the uniform price will always tend to be the one charged for the "last unit" to clear the market from the worst factory or the least efficient purveyor of a service that manages to continue in business. The American businessman may not have been able to trace this line of reasoning to its intellectual fount, but he has always understood the concept of the "margin" instinctively. And he has usually reacted by trying to improve the marginal efficiency of labor and so change the margin itself.

Indeed, ever since Oliver Evans patented an automatic flour mill in 1790 Americans have labored mightily to junk the oldest, most creaking "marginal" machinery. To cut something out of cost and to attract the weak marginal buyer by lowering the price—that has been the American way. The "marginal pair" of bargainers whose weakly fluctuating desires set the value of the "last pound" of flour to clear the market from the most inefficient mill of Oliver Evans' day must surely have affected the price of postcolonial bread in the way described a century or so later by the Vienna school. It is not description, however, but motivation, that has interested Americans. From the standpoint of motivation, of dynamics, the man who was really important to the price of bread in the post-Evans period was not the marginal buyer but the man with the idea for a still better mill than Evans himself had invented. By improving the conditions prevailing in the better mills, the margin itself could be moved to a more efficient point by undercutting and by knocking out the most antiquated machinery which Oliver Evans himself had not succeeded in killing. The price, therefore, though it is set *at* the margin, is not set *by* the margin. The place of the margin itself—and the price charged thereat—is the resultant of ingenuity elsewhere.

The concept of beating down the cost of effort in a way to shift the margin dates back, of course, to the Stone Age savage who first taught his fellows to improvise hatchets for use on their prey. Presumably the savage "broke even" on the effort expended on making the hatchet when he had killed his tenth rabbit. Every rabbit after that contained an element of pure gravy. But the pursuit of marginal efficiency as a conscious industrial dynamic had to wait upon a machine-tool industry capable of turning out devices to produce identical parts in a continuous stream with a minimal amount of labor. In America, the machine-tool industry has one progenitor so great that he looms above all others. The giant was Eli Whitney of New Haven, Connecticut.

There is a story in New Haven that Eli Whitney derived the idea of mass production of interchangeable parts from watching his friend, Abel Buel, stamp out identical coins at a local mint. Whether apocryphal or not, the story is apt: for with the proper dies, jigs and fixtures of his own devising Whitney was soon "coining" identical parts for the rifles he had contracted to deliver in quantity to the government of Thomas Jefferson. This was a far greater invention than Whitney's first brainchild, the cotton gin. (The gin, it might be said parenthetically, may have started the Civil War by making slave labor seem profitable, but it was mass production in northern gun factories which ended the war with the Union triumphant.)

Eli Whitney did not have to know anything about the theory of the marginal efficiency of labor to run a successful shop. Nor did he have to know anything about the theory of "break-even" points beyond which the profit would mount dizzily. It was from Whitney's "felt necessities" that the theory later developed. From Whitney's first employment of the mass principle in the arms industry to Henry M. Leland's domestication of the efficacy of interchangeable parts manufacture in the Detroit area, there runs a straight line. Leland, who had worked at the Springfield Arsenal and at the Colt Arms Co. in Hartford, where the Whitney idea was in force, took his New England memories of precision concepts to the Middle West, where he adapted them to the making of Cadillacs. In 1906 Leland shipped three Cadillacs to England, where he disassembled them and, after thoroughly scrambling the parts, reconstructed three new cars to the astonishment of his audience.

This was not, however, evidence of the real "union of the forces of production" which Bastiat and Francis Amasa Walker had made integral parts of their economic systems. Nor was it the ultimate to which the specialization of Adam Smith's pin factory could be pushed. Still another ingredient was needed to make the marginal efficiency of labor, as applied in conjunction with Eli Whitney's tools, the amazing thing it was to become. This ingredient was supplied by Frederick W. Taylor, the apostle of "scientific management," who thought of the worker himself as a "multiple-purpose" machine tool whose motions in any given sequence could be studied and simplified—and recombined with the motions of collaborators—in a way which would permit a simultaneous achievement of lower costs, lower selling prices, and higher wages. Putting Eli Whitney and Frederick W. Taylor together, one penetrates to the truth of John Stuart Mill's amendment of Ricardo: that profits depend, not on wages, but on the cost of labor, which may actually be lower when the individual wage is high.

Significantly enough, Taylor began his career as an athlete. As a kid pitcher for the baseball team at Exeter Academy in New Hampshire, he was the first person in America to employ an overarm motion on the mound. The umpires complained that the motion wasn't in the rule books, but Taylor stoutly maintained that it was a more efficient way of throwing the ball. In 1881, Taylor teamed up with Clark to win the National Doubles Championship in tennis, using a spoon-handled racket of his own design to produce an improved stroke of his own. He made his own golf clubs, introducing a filed mashie, a fork-handled putter and a long-shafted driver which were outlawed by the convention-bound authorities for tournament play.

Taylor's father was a Quaker lawyer; his mother was the daughter of a hard-driving New Bedford whaling skipper. In himself the young Frederick Taylor combined an intense "inner light" with a most Puritanical hatred of waste. He carried the light and the zeal to his first job with the Midvale Steel Company, where he rose from day laborer to become a technical adviser. At Bethlehem Steel he made his first famous experiments in the production of pig iron, teaching workers to handle forty-seven tons a day instead of twelve. His innovations were simple yet effective: they consisted of such things as matching shovels to men, of putting stopwatches on comparative motions and of insisting that men be of the right height and weight for a given task. Older workers who were set in their methods and rhythms hated Taylor for his brusque insistence that there was only one right way for a man of given endowments to do a thing. But over the course of the years even some union leaders were convinced that labor's rewards might be higher if marginal efficiency were higher.

At Midvale, Taylor amazed everybody by turning a

straight chimney stack into a corkscrew to achieve a more effective "pull" for flue gases. As a consultant to woodpulp manufacturers, he reduced the cost of production from $20 a ton to $8.58. His work with cutting steels was monomaniacal and went on for fourteen years: "The best measure of the value of a tool," he pronounced, "lies in the exact cutting speed at which it is completely ruined at the end of twenty minutes."

Taylor made many enemies in his efforts to turn men into what the public took to be an approximation of machines. But his driving urge was not to produce automatons, but to free the worker for leisure and the hobbies which he himself so prized—and he insisted that labor should be paid enough to enjoy the leisure when it came. His effort at Bethlehem to reward men in proportion to the increased efficiency of their work was ahead of his time, and in 1901 he was fired for his pugnacious obtrusiveness about it. For fourteen years thereafter, or until he died in 1915, he functioned as an industrial consultant without fee, intent only on spreading his gospel of "the one right way to do a thing."

The date of Taylor's death was virtually coeval with Henry Ford's decision to pay his workers, even the sweepers, a minimum of $5 a day, partly as a reward for increasing efficiency, and partly to lure the most efficient workers from other automobile plants. Yet for all that Taylor was his contemporary, Henry Ford seems to have been utterly oblivious to the widespread literature on "scientific management." What Ford did at his Highland Park plant in Detroit was to put Eli Whitney and Taylor together to prove Francis Amasa Walker's point about wages being limited only by production. But he did it without benefit of any knowledge of the past (to Ford, history was "bunk"), and what

he learned from others he took on the fly, out of the surrounding atmosphere.

The heart of the Ford adaptation of cost-cutting ideas to
automobile manufacture was the moving beltline, which has
become our greatest industrial commonplace. Although
Ford himself said, in his later life, that he got the idea of
the moving assembly line from watching the moving *disas-
sembly* of hogs and steers in the stockyards, Charles E. Sorensen, who was Ford's Man Friday for many years, denies
that any such immaculate conception ever occurred. According to Sorensen, it was a wild man named Walter Flanders, a boisterous, forceful and irreverent fellow who lasted
with Ford less than two years, who first pointed the Ford
shop toward mass production in the modern sense. Flanders recombined the Ford machines in such a way that men
ceased to lose time going from place to place in the factory
for parts. He might be described as the first industrial chore-
ographer, doing for the machines what the producer of a
dance does to blend the various human motions learned at
the ballet bar into a significant moving pattern. The Flanders dance-of-the-machines led finally to the moving assembly line and the subjoined parts-delivery lines, with stationary men fastening cylinder blocks, carburetors and doors to
the car chassis frame as it moved slowly past them. Sorensen
experimented with the moving line for six years before its
final installation at Highland Park. Its intellectual kinship
to the dismemberment of hogs in Chicago was purely an
afterthought.

Since Walter Flanders and Sorensen presided over the
industrial choreography which so vastly increased marginal
efficiency in the Ford factory, it might be argued that the

rewards of the efficiency should have gone primarily to them. But that would be to take a short view of the matter. If the whole reward had been apportioned to the men who first devised the new pattern of the machines, jealousy would quickly have intervened to render the pattern virtually useless.

In his *Capitalism the Creator*—a book which argues that the average wage is a "conditioned reflex" of the average product per worker (which, in turn, is determined by the amount and type of capital employed in an industry)—Carl Snyder tells the story of a Ford factory conference at which it was decided that a wage boost might draw the best workmen away from the other factories in the Detroit area. Snyder's own account of what happened after the wage boost went into effect proves that worker attitude may be fully as important as the amount and type of capital in use. Since the automobile industry was booming at the time and Ford was having trouble filling his orders, he needed an especially agile and willing labor force to speed the production of the existing Highland Park assembly equipment. Worker attitude had become an all-important item to what Henry Hazlitt calls "labor-capital productivity," or the efficiency of the "man-machine hour."

The plan, as Sorensen picks up the tale in his *My Forty Years with Ford,* was worked out one Sunday morning in January of 1914. Sorensen had already provided Henry Ford with production figures: 34,000 cars in 1910–11; 78,000 in 1911–12; 168,000 for 1912–13. The profits on this doubled and redoubled production were soaring beyond belief, for as volume increased unit costs went down and down. Ford had taken a preliminary look at Sorensen's figures and said: "That's enough, Charlie. I have the smell of it now. I don't need any more figures. Just keep them available."

At the famous Sunday meeting Ford got Sorensen to put his figures on a blackboard. In 1913 there had been dividends of $15,000,000 plus a $28,000,000 surplus—the fruits of lowered production costs resulting from the new parts-conveyor systems. By transferring a mere $4,000,000 from the surplus to the labor cost column, Sorensen showed how the daily wage could be increased from $2 to $3. And so forth and so on, until Ford said: "Stop it, Charlie; it's all settled. Five dollars a day minimum pay and at once."

Although Ford's own administrative assistants and stockholders protested that "the crazy scheme will wreck the company," it did nothing of the sort. (Here history echoed what had taken place at Robert Owen's New Lanark Mills in Scotland a century before.) What the $5 decision did, according to Carl Snyder's account, was to increase the output of the given machinery by some twenty percent. The higher wage, by virtue of its "leverage" on worker attitude, thus paid for itself.

The social dividends were, of course, tremendous: with a $5 wage—the equivalent of a $20 minimum today—a Ford worker could afford to get rid of his bicycle and make an investment in a Tin Lizzy of his own. Here was consumer capitalism at last. Later on Ford came to see that his 1914 idea had set off a chain reaction. But it was a dozen years before he truly realized the full impact of his idea.

Previous to 1914, so Sorensen says, "American business had operated on the principle that prices should be kept at the highest point at which people would buy. That is still the operating principle of much French and British industry." This traduces the inventors from Eli Whitney on; they were always interested in low prices. After 1914, however, the American idea was to look for profits *in volume* at low prices. With Ford's action, 1914 became the watershed year in the history of capitalism. The American system prophesied by Francis Amasa Walker was a reality.

In the 1920s, there were intellectuals in America who grasped the significance of all this. Those were the years in which Garet Garrett talked of the "American Omen," and Winston Churchill, the son of an American mother, echoed Garrett by quoting him in London. But the vocal partisans of the Ford idea never got very far. To most of the writers of the twenties (and to virtually every self-styled intellectual in the depression-ridden epoch which followed), Henry Ford, the man who had first demonstrated the tremendous "leverage" possibilities of high-wage, low-price, long-line-of-production capitalism, was a menace. He was an enemy of craftsmanship, the epitome of mass production vulgarity. He didn't believe in history. He was naive enough to think you could stop a great imperialist war with a gesture (*vide* the notorious "peace ship" expedition to Oslo) and an appeal to the McGuffey Reader type of morality. He made absurd remarks about the bankers, or about Wall Street or about the "international Jew." He had crackpot ideas about the therapeutic value of folk dancing and the dietetic magic of soybeans; he was a monomaniac on the subject of the twin evils of tobacco and alcohol. Finally, he believed in Hitler tactics in his own shop, for he hired a goon, Harry Bennett, to ride herd on his son Edsel and to keep labor from organizing by establishing a widespread company espionage system backed by force.

In short, a crotchety, queer, sometimes malevolent character—and clearly not one to be trusted as an aspirant to political office (he once stood in Michigan for the U.S. Senate, and he had followers who boomed him periodically for President). One can hardly deny the crotchets, nor can one discover any valid excuses for the excesses of Harry Bennett, or for the period in which Henry Ford swallowed the fake Protocols of the Elders of Zion. But, in spite of his many crotchets, Henry Ford will go down in history as the practical genius who exposed the pretensions of Karl Marx (and all the subsequent Marxists of whatever school) to the status and title of intellectual. Ford may not have been a master of syllogistic reasoning, but after he had lived and worked nobody could claim that Karl Marx was anything else but a fool.

As we have seen, Marx's foolishness was far from being his own; it stemmed from assumptions made by the classical economists whom he read with no eye for tautology or for the logical howlers that had become sacrosanct by virtue of incessant repetition. Out of the classical mishmash of the wage fund and the labor theory of value and the idea that wages and profits were in inexorable conflict, it was perhaps inevitable that Marx should arrive at the theory of stolen surplus value and the idea of the class war. If it was the amount of crude labor time, and not the coordinated impulses of marginal buyers and sellers to exchange goods and services, that accounted for value, then it was obvious that profits were a "theft" of part of the worker's labor hours. And the drive to keep the rate of profit from falling must be at the sole expense of labor.

Though, as we have seen, the wage-fund theory had been exploded by the British pamphleteers and by Francis Amasa Walker long before Ford came on the scene, employers in

1914 still invoked its ghost in setting rates of pay. Ford walked boldly up to the ghost and proved its insubstantiality. To repeat: it was Henry Ford's decision to pay $5 a day without raising the price of his car that proved the wage fund and the other preconceptions of British economics had little to do with industrial realities in a dynamic world.

The chief thing to fall with the advent of the Henry Ford system of production and pricing was Adam Smith's old doctrine of the "natural price." In prowling around his famous pin factory, Adam Smith had correctly observed that a proper division of labor vastly increased the number of pins that could be made during a given number of labor hours. But the implications of this were lost upon him when he came to evolve his doctrine of the "natural price." The "natural price," he assumed, was a "norm" which included the cost of production, plus the ordinary rate of profit in the neighborhood. At any given moment the market value could be above or below the "natural price," and given certain circumstances it might tend to stay there for a long period. But, assuming both competition and sanity, the "norm" must in the long run prevail.

So far, so good: we can grant that there is a "natural" point to which prices will tend to return. (Nobody stays in business for long at a loss, and nobody can charge egregious prices without attracting a competition that undercuts them.) But since a "natural" price represents a point of movement in itself, and since there can be no perfect foreknowledge of what a moving figure will be at any given moment, the whole conception of "naturalness" in price can be shot through with misunderstanding.

What, for example, was the "natural price" for automobiles when Ford came on the scene? If Ransom Olds, say, thought he knew, he was most definitely mistaken. For the "natural price" of the Oldsmobile was not sacrosanct to Henry Ford when Walter Flanders was· teaching him the new way of laying out a factory to achieve mass economies once the production of cars had passed a certain point. The moment that Henry Ford discovered how to knock down the cost—and the price—of a car by pushing production past the break-even point that paid for the production line, the going "natural" price was outmoded. Thus, under a dynamic technology, Adam Smith's description has no value. The "natural price" is always disappearing into the past. Under high technology what Adam Smith thought of as "particular accidents" have become commonplace—and "monopoly secrets" have become the harbingers, not of "maintained prices," but of lower and lower costs to the ultimate consumer.

Naturally, not all of the benefits need be passed on to the consumer; some may be distributed to the worker in the form of wage increases, some may be distributed to the stockholder, and some may be retained in industry as a fund to pay for research and development. (Or so it used to be before government began to cut in on the deal with its taxes which now account for about a third of the retail cost of a new car.) Thus technology, when it is unfettered, crashes through all the rigidities of the old economics, whether it be Ricardian or Marxist in its orientation.

John Stuart Mill, who believed in "iron" laws of production, came eventually to doubt that there were "laws" of distribution. But Henry Ford proved that distribution does have a "law": lower the price, increase the volume, distribute costs over a longer mill run and you make a lot more money than you made before. Adam Smith had thought of industrial "masters" everywhere as being in a "tacit" conspiracy not to raise wages. But Henry Ford adhered to no such "conspiracy" or combination, whether "tacit" or other. He was a disturber of the peace, a man who thought of economics as the eternal disruption of "equilibrium." When he took a temporary loss in 1920–21 on material which he had bought at inflated wartime and postwar highs, he was accused of "disturbing conditions." But this, he said, "is exactly what we were trying to do." For a long time he lost $20 per car. With each car he sold, however, he tossed in $40 worth of parts at no reduction—and the profit on the parts did much toward canceling the loss. Though Ford could not stop the 1920–21 depression by himself, he weathered it and came out of it more quickly than some of his less nimble competitors. That was Henry Ford, a genius who considered that one way to force costs down was, in Sorensen's words, "to name a price so low that everybody in the shop would be forced to higher efficiency."

Today the automobile companies do their pricing by assuming a "standard volume of production" (say, the volume which will be turned out if the plant is worked at eighty percent of capacity). They set the price at a figure which will return a certain percentage of profit on the overall operation if the standard volume is reached. If the "informed guess" as to future sales probabilities is good, a company will have money for dividends, for future research and for additions to plant and equipment. If the guess is bad, the company may lose money.

It was Henry Ford's pioneering that first permitted a departure from the idea that the cost of production must be covered on the sale of every unit as it left the factory, regardless of what "standard volume" might be assumed to be. As we shall see, a company may not be able to hold to the "standard volume" price in adverse market conditions; and, because the "standard volume" price is vulnerable, it is no true "administered price." But "administered" or not, the dynamic conception of "profit-at-a-volume price, which Henry Ford first opposed to Adam Smith's static "cost-of-production-plus-average-profit" price, has paid off for both consumers and workers. Would *anyone* want to go back to the "natural price" of 1914, when "standard volume" was an unheard-of thing?

Eli Whitney, Frederick W. Taylor and Henry Ford do not quite span the reaches of the "American system," though they were incontestably the geniuses of its first phases of development. What this trio did was to attempt to engineer the job for maximum efficiency. This is a fecund approach up to a point. But with Whitney, the approach led to an ultimately one-sided concentration on tools—and tools with which to make tools. With Taylor, it led to a narrowing concentration on human motion in time and space. And with Ford, it led to the assembly line, which dictated a uniform and impersonal rhythm to the motions of men.

The Ford ideal, naturally, points to the completely automated line which the Cross brothers, Milton and Ralph, were finally to develop after World War II to machine the automobile cylinder block. As befits the grandson of a pioneer, it was Henry Ford II who lured the Cross brothers into making their ingenious contraption—"as long as a football field"—which carries the cylinder block from its first stage as a hunk of raw metal to its finished state as a polished and purposeful thing—all without the intervention of a human hand. (The only concession to humanity on the floor of a Cross-machine plant is the presence of tool watchers who set the gauges, watch for the emergence of mechanical defects and change the drills and reamers when they wear out.)

Henry Ford himself knew a great deal about the motivation needed to *integrate* the work of a human team; he was not merely an apostle of mechanizing the work, even though he pointed to the coming of the Crosses. But it was the money incentive for integration that came to dominate the Ford organization in Henry Ford's later days. The money incentive is admittedly a big one, but, as Elton Mayo was to prove in his famous Hawthorne experiments of the late 1920s, human beings work best when they are interested in what they are doing. They may do better work for less money if a job offers variety, or if there is a reinvigorating change of pace or if, like soldiers in a platoon, they don't want to let each other down. Quaker chocolate makers in England, inaugurating a switch on the Ford and Taylor methods, demonstrated that production can be increased by training individuals for several jobs and by rotating them from task to task throughout the working day. But such devices for luring efficiency are variations on a central theme. They have to do with the art of management—which is essentially different for every type of industry, every type of factory production.

What is lost sight of is that what Henry Ford *did* somehow runs away from what he *was*. Most of Ford's biographers have dwelt upon the supposedly schizophrenic aspects of his character. He took men out of the quiet countryside and piled them up in urban and suburban warrens, yet he had a nostalgic hankering for the days of square dances, homemade rhubarb pies, wayside inns and McGuffey's First

Reader. He built the intimidating bulk of the sprawling River Rouge plant—and close to it he plunked down the quaint anachronism of Greenfield Village. He believed in soybeans—but what he sowed primarily was miles of asphalt and concrete. Obviously, such a man is easy to dismiss as a split personality.

But was he so "split," after all? Burrowing into the mind of the youthful Henry Ford, before the day of the "peace ship" fiasco and the crotchety fears that he must hire a Harry Bennett to keep the Detroit "underworld" from kidnapping his grandsons, one comes upon a man who had a whole view of life. The young Ford—it may seem comic to say it, but it is nonetheless true—was a Distributist very much in the manner of England's Gilbert Chesterton and Hilaire Belloc. He wanted to make every man in his employ a capitalist-farmer. The early Ford idea was that a workman might own his own small acres on which he could grow crops, part time, for his own personal use, or even for sale to industry. The Ford experiments in soybean culture were undertaken with a view to providing a crop which a part-time farmer could sell to industry for important oils.

Ford's notion was that the part-time farmer would also hold a job in a factory for high wages. He would earn a lot in good times, and he would put away a sustaining sum for the bad times that must come periodically. In bad times the part-time farmer could comfortably outwait depression on his small acres, stepping up his food production and conserving his savings thereby. The whole double life of city and country, of transportation to work in good times and transportation for fun in bad, was to be made secure forever by a car that could be bought at mass prices.

Thus, in the mind of Henry Ford the old and the new

were blended. There would be the leisurely tempo of country life plus the quickened pace of mass production. There would be the morality of the McGuffey Readers, the fun of skating and square dancing, the charm of the seasons, and of carefully preserved heirlooms, plus the conquest of time and distance. City and country, the man with the Tin Lizzy would have the best of both.

The irony of Henry Ford's life—and of the American System generally—is that human beings in the 1920s refused the Ford gambit. Where they might have used the cheap Ford car to bridge distances and to help them finance the old, leisurely life, they insisted on an upgraded quality product—at a vastly increased cost—for purposes of keeping up with the Joneses in the city.

But things go in cycles. Looking beyond irony, what we see in the distance is the Ford ideal coming true. The automated factory releases men for a hundred more pleasant occupations, from running motels in Florida to exercising scientific ingenuity in programing the work for automated equipment. The four-day week will not come by *force majeure* at Walter Reuther's behest, and it is hardly the time to think of it with the Russians breathing down our necks. But in the nature of things it will come— if people really want that much leisure—when the machine is ready for it and when we don't need $40 billion worth of annual labor time to produce for war. If men don't choose to use their leisure in raising soybeans on part-time farms, they will have it for other jobs of a secondary nature. We have "moonlighting"—the practice of holding an additional job—now. If a man likes the variety, the income and the comfortable "insurance" security of two jobs, there is nothing to be condemned in moonlighting. What is to be condemned is the drive for a third source of security or income: taking something from the government as a handout at someone else's expense.

Always, before Eli Whitney and Frederick Taylor and Henry Ford, the world struggled with scarcity. And when economics ceased to be wholly a matter of the deployment of scarce means, it was perhaps natural for habit-ridden manufacturers to devise cartel methods for inducting a "contrived scarcity," the better to keep prices at a point where the inefficient marginal producer could still remain in business. With Whitney and Taylor and Ford, however, there was the courage to dare the new. What these men wanted was "contrived fecundity." They wanted to put the marginal producer out of business—knowing, of course, that in a fecund economy he could always find something better to do.

They were, in brief, *upsetting* men. But the American system strains away from equilibrium, not toward it. Out of free choice comes innovation, the unexpected, the qualitative decision that provokes the unknown quantity. Value does not depend on the past, on time units of labor power frozen into an article. Value depends on the present psychological rating of effort against effort—with a view to satisfaction in the future. The advertiser can add to value or take away from it; he can ply his silvery-tongued trade for good or evil, depending on what he places and displaces. The American system is everywhere and always a *chancy* system. But it has never known a famine, and it has always managed to push marginal efficiency higher.

If mankind isn't up to meeting the efficiency imperative, is that the capitalist's fault?

Chapter Nine

The True Perfection
of Competition

In chapter two we spoke of the market, where buyers and sellers meet to compare and evaluate what they have to exchange, as the characteristic institution of capitalism. The governor of this institution is competition. In a system that operates without compulsion, fraud or government interference, competition provides the social control by which the customer can call the turn. The opportunity to compare and reflect upon alternative choices before making a decision to buy, rent or lease is obviously at the heart of any free system of production and exchange. All the customer has a legitimate right to ask of government is that it prevent misrepresentation of goods and make sure that contracts are honored.

But modern competition, so one hears from every side, is vitiated by the growth of the mammoth corporation which, in tacit conjunction with its fellows, can put fetters on the competitive process. The theory of modern permutations of monopoly is all in the books written by economists who speak in ominous or cynical tones of the "administered price." The term was invented by Dr. Gardiner C. Means, who has used it on occasion as a synonym for an "established" price—meaning that a quotation is offered well in advance of supplying goods and services in the market. Quoted prices are, of course, as old as the hills and, as Roger Blough of the U.S. Steel Corporation has remarked, can be found everywhere, from the corner newsstand to Macy's basement. It is only when a firm has the "market power" to make the "established" or the "quoted" price stick through periods of declining sales and unused manufacturing capacity that competition ceases to be the governor of market transactions.

Despite Dr. Means' insistence that "administered prices" often lead to "greater efficiency and higher standards of living," the dog has a bad name. An "administered" price is usually interpreted to mean a price set and maintained without regard to the old-fashioned forces of supply and demand. Not only politicians but economists from onetime presidential adviser Edwin G. Nourse on the Right to Harvard Professor J. Kenneth Galbraith on the Left assume it in its more sinister sense to be a fact of life. It dominates the textbooks used in more than half the colleges and it was clearly the starting point for Walter Reuther's suggestion that the automobile companies lop $100 off the price of cars even before his union's wage demands for 1958 could be known.

The persistence of the idea that, in a modern economy, markets conform to prices, and not vice versa, is a tribute to the ability of a few intellectuals to set a fashion and make it prevail without subjecting it to periodic analysis and check.

Since there is a time lag in intellectual fashions as they circulate through society, certain key members of Senator Kefauver's congressional committee still accepted the "administered price" stereotype when they started their 1957–58 investigation of the relation of prices to inflation. Nevertheless, despite the archaic flavor of some of the congressional questioning, the hold of the stereotype seems to be weakening with the general public. We are now at a peculiar turn in our attitude toward economic bigness, with the questions it raises about a competitive market system. Troubled by a spate of mergers, public officials seem more and more inclined toward the idea of throttling bigness before it comes into being. The general public, on the other hand, is demonstrably more friendly toward bigness than it was throughout the 1930s and 40s.

In 1920, the law of the land about bigness and its relations to monopoly was supposedly settled. In the United States Steel decision, the Supreme Court handed down its verdict that the government had no case against the U.S. Steel Corporation as long as it behaved itself and desisted from restraint of trade. Mere size was not evidence of wrongdoing; and to punish a man—or a corporation—because of a possible *expectancy* of wrongdoing was in itself a lawless construction of the law.

This was a far cry from the attitude of the Supreme Court in 1904, when the men behind the Northern Securities holding company were effectively informed by the Court that they couldn't combine two railroads, the Great Northern and the Northern Pacific, lest they "menace" the economic freedom of the Northwest in the future. Since railroads, in the days before trucks and airplanes became important, constituted a "natural monopoly," there was some excuse in 1904 for thinking that a combination of two parallel rights of way would be inevitable death to competition. But today, without any mitigating excuse, the government has often seemed intent on overthrowing the decision of 1920 *in re* U.S. Steel. We are in danger of returning to the early days of the century and rejecting, once again, the old English common-law idea that the punishment must fit the crime. The prevalent idea in antitrust circles these days is that punishment should anticipate the crime.

To pick the outstanding current example, the Bethlehem Steel Co. and the Youngstown Sheet and Tube Co. were virtually ordered some years ago *not* to merge lest they be tempted to restrain steel competition in the Middle West, where Youngstown has its plants. This attempt to apply justice in advance of an overt criminal act is scarcely in accordance with the laws of evidence or the presumption that men are innocent until they are proven guilty. It is "government by injunction." The unspoken assumption here is that bigness *must* result in illegal activity—which is a bit like branding a man a murderer because he has a receding skull or a twitch under his right eye. It ignores the fact that there are a lot of other steel companies in the Chicago and Youngstown areas which might make it impossible for a Bethlehem-Youngstown combination to achieve a monopoly even if it wanted one.

How do the American people stand on this idea of a prejudgment of cases? Possibly the average newspaper reader who is puzzled by the clamor about mergers hasn't thought things through. Nevertheless, it can be demonstrated that Americans have little desire to throttle bigness merely on the ground that it is big. A great majority—some eighty percent, according to recent public opinion tests—think "big business" has been a good thing for the nation. This sizable majority doesn't think big companies should be broken up—or, presumably, kept from growing by legitimate means, including mergers for mutual cost-cutting advantages. The public is, however, quite definitely in favor of watching big companies and cracking down on them if they do indulge in monopolistic practices. Many survey respondents are convinced that big business pays off for everybody by expanding job opportunities and by lowering prices through the application of its special "know-how" in the techniques of mass production and modern marketing.

In a word, the common idea is that competition, like gold and good behavior generally, is where you find it. It can be absent in a small town where one man owns both newspapers and the radio station or where the barber or the hardware store proprietor has a local monopoly. It can be present among automotive giants when they are engaged in a dingdong battle for sales leadership. Whether it is present or absent is a matter of an objective test. All the customer— or the Department of Justice investigator—need do is to ask himself two questions. The first is: "Do the customers have bargaining leverage vis-à-vis the suppliers?" And the second (which assumes a negative answer to the first) is: "If not, what alternatives in the form of substitute products are available?" If the customer has a way of controlling the supplier, or if he can readily turn from a metal, say, to a plastic, or from wood to concrete blocks, or from the railroad to the airplane or barge, then the whole question of whether prices are "administratively" established becomes academic. It is the presence or absence of alternatives in reasonably viable form that provides the litmus paper for arriving at a proper antitrust decision.

To keep alternatives open, sixty-seven percent of the people responding to a recent survey question feel that

"enforcing present laws is enough." The "present laws"—
including the 1920 Supreme Court decision in the U.S.
Steel case—go back a long way in the life of English-
speaking communities—all the way, in fact, to the provision
in Magna Charta (1215) that merchants should have the
right "to move about as well by land as by water, for buying
and selling by the ancient and right customs, quit from all
evil tolls."

Though the state continued to grant monopolies and
trading privileges up to the very time of the publication of
Adam Smith's *Wealth of Nations* in 1776 and beyond, there
was always a tendency on the part of judges to disallow the
practice of such favoritism. In Queen Elizabeth's day a
tailor's guild ordinance "confining" half the cloth dressing
work in London to guild members was judged illegal. So
too was the attempt of the queen to give a monopoly of the
sale of playing cards to a court favorite. In the time of the
Stuart kings, the struggle against royal monopolies culmi-
nated in the Statute of Monopolies of 1624—a law which
voided "all monopolies and all commissions, grants, li-
censes, charters and letters patent heretofore made or
granted to any person or persons, bodies politick or
corporate whatsoever, of or for the sole buying, selling,
making, working or using of anything. . . ."

This animus against monopoly was part of the common-
law attitude of the American colonies. Chartered though
they were as the handmaidens of monopolistic trading companies, the colonies had thoroughly repudiated their origins.
The Sherman Antitrust Act, adopted in the United States in
a time of worry about "trusts" and "corners" and "robber
barons," elevated the common-law tradition to federal dignity. But other laws which have been piled on top of the

Sherman Act have tended to obscure the original intent of antitrust legislation. Some of the laws—those permitting "fair trade" price maintenance, for example—apply an entirely different set of criteria to market practices. In the NRA period, the Sherman Act was virtually suspended: companies were invited to draw up Blue Eagle codes for what amounted to market sharing at fixed prices. A whole sector of the economy—that of agriculture—has been exempted from the natural laws of the marketplace. And, as we have seen, the laws designed to restrain mergers are tending to make presumptive future behavior the test of contemporary retribution.

So puzzlement is here—and the puzzlement is reflected on every side, even in court decisions which apply the antitrust laws to professional football while exempting professional baseball clubs on the excuse that they are engaged not in business but in a "game."

During the thirties and the forties, an intellectual fashion had it that the only cure for bigness (assumed to be monopolistic *per se*) was more bigness—with the socialistic state stepping in to take over with its monopoly of force. Today the intellectuals aren't so sure that big government is good. (They have arrived a half-century late at Hilaire Belloc's position as set forth in *The Servile State*.) Nevertheless, out of laziness or despair, practically everybody is for the "mixed economy," with the state in the picture at control points with a mixture of ownership and "countervailing force." Few there are among them who think the present system could be trusted to engender sufficient competition in and of itself to take care of things without the intervention of Big Brother state.

If the people as a whole combine acceptance of government intervention with a feeling toward big business that is less hostile than the attitude current in the thirties and the forties, it cannot be said that some teachers of economics have relaxed their distrust of the big corporation. (Oddly, two ex–New Dealers, Adolf Berle and David Lilienthal, are far more friendly to big industrial units than are most of the members of college economics faculties.) As recently as 1955, over seventy percent of the teacher-respondents to a questionnaire answered yes to the question, "Do you see any important flaws in our antitrust laws and their adminis-tration?" Some of the economics teachers cited the ambi-guity of the laws. But a full quarter of them argued that existing antitrust legislation is not sufficiently rigid, and a fifth of them complained of poor enforcement of the laws we do have. The teacher-respondents lagged far behind edi-torial writers and the general public in willingness to grant that big business has, on balance, been a good thing for the nation.

So the hostility stereotype regarding bigness still holds sway in the academic community, which is so important an element in setting the intellectual fashions of the country. It appears in the important college textbooks—those by Paul A. Samuelson and George Leland Bach, for example—books which swathe the topic of modern competition be-tween big units with such a prejudicial aura that the stu-dent is bound to go away with the notion that contempo-rary business life is a complex tissue of quite artificial re-straints on production. Both Samuelson and Bach tend to accept the idea that if there are only a few big producers in a given field—the five-dollar Greek-compound word for this phenomenon of a market dominated by a Big Three or a Big Five is "oligopoly," which is a word businessmen must learn to reckon with—then some sort of tacit price-fixing and market-sharing skulduggery is inevitable.

The teachers' prevailing tendency to see monopoly in its "oligopolistic"—or "few to sell"—form behind every bush and tree in a big enterprise system completely mystifies the average businessman. If this businessman is, say, a Du Pont executive, he points to the host of new products which his company has sponsored at lower and lower prices and asks plaintively wherein he could possibly be at fault. If the businessman works for Sears Roebuck, he offers his company's astoundingly protean catalogue as *prima facie* evidence that he is a competitor par excellence. To the businessman, the hostility stereotype is rooted in a false analysis of actual economic conditions. The businessman's claim is that bigness, instead of creating monopoly, has actually widened the areas of competition, leading to a constantly accelerating presentation of more and more alternatives at progressively lower prices as figured in constant, or pre-World War I, dollars. And the businessman has one important book to back him up in his contentions—the Brookings Institution study carried out by Professor A.D.H. Kaplan called *Big Enterprise in a Competitive System*.

The theory that big business is by nature monopolistic—or oligopolistic, which is an approach to the same thing—gained enormous impetus in the later days of the New Deal, when the Temporary National Economic Committee was busy with its investigations into American business practices. The TNEC monographs tell a varied story, but what the public got out of it all was the notion that big business abhorred classical price competition as a cat abhors getting its paws wet. Behind the TNEC, providing a number of starting points for its studies, was a body of theory. The patron saint of the investigation was a Cambridge University Englishwoman, Joan Robinson, whose book on "imperfect" competition (*The Economics of Imperfect Competition*) had vastly impressed an influential government economist, Mr. Leon Henderson. More widely known to the public as the lively and combative head of the wartime OPA, Henderson was instrumental in getting the TNEC corps of investigators organized.

It was Professor Joan Robinson's theory that a large business unit must appreciably affect price by its behavior, holding it above what it would naturally be in a "perfect" market of small, evenly matched competitors. The large unit could use the threat of price discrimination to make its smaller competitors stick to a posted price; it could, in perhaps tacit collusion with other big fellows, limit its output in order to keep the market price well above the point where it would naturally be if production were unrestrained.

While Mrs. Robinson was working out the implications of this theory in England, Professor Edward Chamberlin in America was pursuing a somewhat parallel course—and also having his affect on a number of younger economists who went to work for the TNEC. Where Robinson spoke of "imperfect competition," Chamberlin used the phrase "monopolistic competition." Although they have their differences (Professor Robinson is far to the left of Chamberlin), between them they captured the field of thinking about competition (or its lack) in a world of big producers of durable goods. The general idea accepted by Robinson-Chamberlin followers is that industries dominated by a Big One (monopoly), a Big Two (duopoly), or a Big Three or Four or Five (oligopoly) can "administer" their prices in such a way that the classic "higgling" of the market is inhibited, if not entirely suppressed. The result is a world of price stiffnesses that is not as rich in production as it might otherwise be. Corporations maximize their profits by not competing in price—and the customer, in making the corporations richer than they should be, gets less than he deserves. The customer is usually beguiled by the offer of a differentiated product (a Ford is not quite like a Chevrolet or a Plymouth), but the monopoly which each big unit has in its own brand names and distinctive styling or gadgetry makes it all the easier for it to keep the price higher than it would be if a lot of smaller companies were making undifferentiated units. Thus, the "theory of monopolistic competition" in a world of giants. (Whether it is a description based on factual evidence is, as we shall see, quite another story. It should be enough to observe here that even if a few big companies were to "go easy" about price competition, they still might charge a lot less for their products than a score of inefficient small companies engaged in a savage fight for survival.)

By using such adjectives as "imperfect" and "monopolistic" to qualify the noun "competition," Robinson and Chamberlin have left people with the idea that the world has declined from a time in the nineteenth century when "perfection" of competition was the rule. To do justice to Professor Chamberlin, however, this was not part of his intention. It is obvious to close readers of the totality of Chamberlin's work that he attaches no nasty or prejudicial or disparaging connotation to phrases like "monopolistic competition." He is not talking of a "decline," or of a state of lost innocence, or of an exile from Eden. He merely had to start somewhere in order to get his book written, so he began with what had been handed to him by way of word usage. To Chamberlin, "monopolistic competition" is merely a tag, a technical tool in the economist's analytical kit. (Professor Robinson might take refuge in the same theory of word neutrality.) What Chamberlin has been after is to establish differences without condemnations. It is the Chamberlin idea that "workable" competition is good enough for him. But if Chamberlin didn't mean to be invidious or pejorative, his practice of modifying a noun with an adjective derived from its opposite has certainly served to intensify an invidious atmosphere. The followers of Joan Robinson and Chamberlin, unwitting victims of a verbal snarl, picked up the words and employed them in a wholly prejudicial sense to imply moral condemnation. "Imperfect?" "Monopolistic?" Why, common sense, the dictionary and common English usage all decree them to be bad.

The verbal snarl has been wished upon us by a trick of fate. In the days of the classical economists "monopoly" had a clear and simple reference: it was what happened when the state gave an individual or a trading company the sole right to exploit a given market. Monopoly was a grant of privilege by a government. It was assumed commonsensically that in the free market no two competitors were precisely alike, that individual differences made for advantages and disadvantages. One man had better muscles or brains or skills than another; one man had a better shop location than another; one, owning his own mine, could command better ore. The differences were accepted as the economic equivalent of a difference in muscular reflexes in racehorses or prizefighters. So what if one man—or one business—had an edge over another? That was to be expected. After all, it is a difference in muscular reflexes that makes horse races.

As the nineteenth century gave way to the twentieth, however, the bluff common sense of the classical school was forgotten. Beguiled by the idea of formulating mathematically exact "representational" theories of "pure" or "perfect" competition, economists constructed a model of perfect competition. Quite in the spirit of Robert Owen, who saw no sense in ordinary athletic competition because all it usually proves is that one person *begins* a race or a game with better reflexes than another, these economists decided that true, or pure, or perfect, competition demands an identical or uniform product. It hardly mattered to the model makers that people in the real world shop for difference even more than for sameness, or that nature very seldom runs to absolute identity of product anyway.

Compounding the trick of fate that saddled us with a mathematician's "representational" plaything in place of a workable theory of competition, there was the natural emphasis of nineteenth-century history. In the early and middle parts of the century the dynamic new "facts" about economic life were the growing international trade in staples (wheat, cotton) and the rise of the textile business which followed the invention of the spinning jenny and the waterframe. Price competition in wheat and textiles tended to be instantaneous and keen. Blinded by the preeminence of international staples and cotton cloth, the model makers hastily jumped to the conclusion that these represented "perfection."

The second step of the model makers was to analyze "perfection" for its "constants." The first "constant" was the "undifferentiated" nature of wheat and cotton cloth: every grain of wheat or bolt of calico was like any other grain or bolt. In the wheat and textile markets, moreover, there were many suppliers and many customers, no one of whom could appreciably coerce the price by his own behavior. There was also an absence of trade secrets. (In the case of textiles the big break came when Samuel Slater "stole" the secret of the Arkwright mill and fled to America.) Absence of secrets meant that information making for "perfect foresight" in the market was available to all. And anybody with a little capital could get in on the game of raising wheat or erecting a small textile mill.

These, then, were the characteristics of the so-called perfect market: An undifferentiated product, many buyers and sellers, no trade secrets, no great difficulties about entering the business.

So the model of perfect competition was built on the economics of the wheat market. All of this was very fine, but it made no connection with vast portions of actual economic life. To make contact with the real world, the theorist of perfect competition had to admit, *sotto voce,* that even wheat growers differed among themselves. One might have superior storage facilities—which would mean that he could hold his grain for a rise in the market. One might have better soil, another might hold a lease from a landlord with a liberal or lazy interpretation of the Law of Rent. Still another might have capital to tide him over bad patches. (The behavior of a number of exceptionably situated growers might indeed "appreciably" affect the price of wheat futures.) Finally, there were all the differences in levels of know-how and experience, not to mention closeness to the marketplace and skill and speed in reaching the customer.

In order to get their theory off the ground, the makers of the perfect model were prepared to grant certain minor concessions to realism. (Ricardo made the same type of concession when he exempted diamonds and Rembrandts from his labor theory of value.) But the model makers were not at all prepared to extend their concessions to the world of big business. Obviously, the characteristics of the wheat market do not apply to the Chevrolet division of General Motors, which tries to put out a distinctive ("differentiated") product, maintains its own dealer service, quotes its prices well in advance of sale and is part of an industry which a newcomer finds it expensive to enter.

If General Motors were a wholly new phenomenon, it might plausibly be maintained that the modern world had departed from the "norms" of "perfect competition." But the curious thing about it is that even in the mid-nineteenth century the wheat and cotton markets were merely one type of economic activity.

Long before there was a Chevrolet division of GM there were coach makers who made "differentiated" gigs and barouches and quoted prices on them. Long before there was a General Electric Co., the firm of Boulton and Watt relied on an established price for its steam engines, not on the higgling and haggling of an auction market.

Moreover, even in the case of wheat, the moment wheat flour passed into the hands of a pastry shop proprietor the characteristics of the "perfect" market ceased to apply. "Differentiation," the "trade secrets" of varying flavors, the "monopoly" of a good pastry cook, the site "monopoly" of a corner building in a good neighborhood—all worked to destroy the "perfection" of the wheat market in its secondary stage. As for textiles, the market for fine fabrics differed entirely from the market for cheap calicoes designed for export to the masses of Asia.

It is worth laboring these points to show that the con-cocters of the perfect model were guilty of abstracting the characteristics of merely one form of competition and making them do duty for the whole.

If they had started with the idea that "perfection" should be based on a competitor's ability to change and improve his product every year or so to get an edge over his fellows in appealing to the public taste, they might well have made the coach-making industry, not the wheat market, their idea of the "norm." In which case, present-day competition among Chevrolets, Plymouths, Fords, Ramblers—yes, and Volkswagens—would seem "perfect"—and the market for wheat or cabbages would loom up as a departure from the rule.

Had the theorists of competition kept it clearly in mind from the beginning that there are many types of market, each with certain distinguishing characteristics which have as much claim to the name of "perfection" as any other, they would not have been beguiled into creating their prejudicial formula.

The irony of the whole intellectual bemusement over the idea of "perfection" in competition is that the model itself becomes a monstrosity the moment the test of consistency is applied to it. If the model makers had not bootlegged some elements of "imperfection" (the "natural monopolies" of differences in skill, wisdom, experience, know-how, luck or location) into their theory, their model would have ended competition forthwith by grinding it to a halt. In a "perfectly" competitive world, with every buyer and seller fore-armed ("absence of trade secrets") with perfect knowledge of market conditions, and with perfect mobility pertaining across the board, each promising field of endeavor would soon be filled to the point where nobody could make a profit. The customer, like the donkey standing an equal distance between two equally appealing carrots, would have only whim to guide him—unless, by chance, he took his custom to a friend, which in itself would be destructive of "perfect" competition. The attainment of perfect equilibrium would be close to paralysis; certainly it would make a Sargasso Sea of economic life. So far as I am aware, the only economist to have commented on the logical absurdity of the perfect model is F. A. Hayek, who has derived considerable wry amusement in pointing out that "imperfections" are to real competition what gasoline is to an automobile. It is the "imperfections"—the special advantages in skill, resources or know-how which some men have over others—which make the thing go.

The theorists of perfect competition were ill-prepared for the rise of modern big industry, with its Big Twos and Threes, its subtle distinctions in brand-name products, its accent on innovation, and the constant remaking of markets, and its ability to quote prices which, if the "educated guess" happens to be right, manage to hold for a full year of the calendar. Caught short by events, they could hardly make a switch without disrupting the continuity of economic thought. But science is forever being faced with the necessity of discarding old hypothetical models, and the economists should not have minded a little basic reconstruction. They could have stressed the continuity, not of their textbook writing, but of human nature in the marketplace. They could have demonstrated that different markets have always had their own distinctive characteristics. They could have argued that competition is a many-faceted thing, each facet being as legitimate—as "perfect"—as any other.

There is competition in price—both fast and slow competition, with all sorts of elasticities complicating the subject. But there is also competition to get something which your business rival hasn't got—a difference in brand, say, or an improved style or design, or a unique skill, or a new patent. The seekers for a perfect model could have done what Einstein did when confronted by the odd behavior of light (sometimes it was a wave, sometimes it wasn't); they could have invoked a "unified field theory" to explain all the various facets of competitive behavior.

By changing the model, or by throwing it away and doing without any "representational" system, the economists could have tied the world of the eighteenth century to that of the twentieth and still made allowances for the behavior of international staples like wheat. They could have acknowledged that the whole world of differentiation—and the competition to achieve something better or at least more acceptable to the customer—existed long before Chevrolets, Fords and Plymouths, with their distinctions in line, fabric and engineering, had ever come into being. No economist who has read Jane Austen's novel *Northanger Abbey*, with its remarks about the difference between the coaches used by visitors to fashionable Bath ("Oh! these odious gigs," said Isabella, who wanted something more on the Edsel or Chrysler Imperial style), could ever assume the world had changed very much. Products have always been differentiated, in violation of Rule One for perfect competition—and therefore what the Robinson-Chamberlin school calls an "imperfect" or "monopolistic" element has always been present in most economic life.

If it is an error to think that economic life as a whole once conformed to the perfect model, it is equally a mistake to entertain the converse supposition that price competition necessarily disappears when model conditions no longer hold. There is Professor John Kenneth Galbraith's chapter "The Abandonment of the Model" in his *American Capitalism: The Theory of Countervailing Power,* for example. Says Galbraith: "A convention against price competition is inevitable under oligopoly." The alternative, says Galbraith, is self-destruction.

There is a whole tissue of unwarranted assumptions lurking behind this type of hard-and-fast "either-or." First of all, it is not true that "pristine"—Galbraith's word for suicidal—competition has ever predominated for long periods in any industry which involves the possession of unique skills or competitive differentiation. Did the coach makers of old England characteristically seek bankruptcy? Did the sellers of fine linens get rid of the contents of their shelves at a loss? When Robert Owen went to work for his first employer, Mr. McGuffog, at the end of the eighteenth century, he encountered a queer phenomenon: rich widows would turn down fine Irish linens at eight shillings a yard and ask to see something at ten shillings. The more expensive fabrics were not worth anything more "intrinsically"—to use the word chosen by Mr. Owen. They merely had an added cachet. The incident described by Robert Owen happened in a trade that was open to anybody with a little capital— and it may be accepted as something that has always been inherent in human psychology. What it demonstrates is that destructive price wars have never been an inevitable result of competition in any field which offers distinction of product.

Yet it should also be observed that Mr. McGuffog—who, incidentally, refused to mulct the widow—could not have departed very far from the "natural" fine-linen price, or at the "natural area of price," for very long in any direction, whether up or down. Even the well-heeled customer resents a shopkeeper who gets a reputation for price-gouging. And even the most aggressive price competitor must refrain from "chiseling" to the point of putting himself out of business.

Mr. Galbraith assumes that "crypto-monopoly" in businesses such as the automobile business means that "the old goals of social efficiency cannot be realized through the operation of the market. But the automobile business, while it is demonstrably a Big Three "oligopoly," is hardly a "few to sell" affair when it comes to its dealer-cum-customer ramifications.

Looking outward at the market, how does the "oligopolistic" position look to a vice president of the General Motors Corporation? Surveying the general car market, the GM executive finds he has considerably more than the Ford and Chrysler companies to reckon with. There are upwards of some fifty million cars on the roads of the U.S. Each one of the fifty million is in the hands not only of a buyer *but also of a potential seller*. The fifty million potential sellers, barring a fringe with old rattletraps, can hold on to their cars or get rid of them at choice.

If the price of a new car is right in terms of the factory quotation minus the turn-in allowance minus the dealer's discount, the seller will sell and buy in the same motion. Otherwise, he will wait for a more favorable deal, which will come along one way or another, particularly in a bad year. True, the manufacturer can "administer" the price to the dealer. But it must be within the dealer's "area of cost," or the dealer will quit and go into the beer business or take a job selling corsets. The manufacturer cannot set the factory price without long and sober consideration of its probable impact on the loyalty and energy of a dealer organization.

So who "administers" the price over the long run? The producer? Or the dealer who must allow for the trade-in? Or the buyer in the used car market? Or the consumer of the new car? Or is it a combination of all four? And if it is a combination of all four isn't this the normal higgling of the market? Actually, when Madman Muntz ("Nobody, but nobody, outtrades him") gets into a dicker with a man who has a three-year-old Cadillac which has gone only 20,000 miles, the conversation resembles nothing so much as a couple of Orientals bargaining over the disposition of a fancy rug. Following through on this line of thought, the lay reader may be considerably perplexed by Galbraith's insistence that a "convention against price competition is inevitable under oligopoly."

Galbraith's assumptions must seem nonsense to the businessman, who knows that price must ultimately conform to the world of choice, not to the internal dictates of company management. Even if there is no immediate competitor breathing fire down his neck, the businessman knows that the consumer's dollar can only be cut so many ways. If the price of a car is too high, the consumer may elect to buy a new television set and take his amusement at home. In this sense every price is competitive with every other price— and the seller must take heed if he wants to stay alive.

To judge by the example of Professor Galbraith, it is obvious that when an economist speaks of "perfection" in competition he is referring to price competition alone. Economic life could remain static in every other branch of competition, with no improvement whatsoever in quality or type of product, and to the Galbraith school it would still be "perfection" as long as the auctioneer system of pricing prevails.

Such a notion of "perfection" must seem high-handed and arbitrary to the businessman. For in the real world, "perfection" in competition must necessarily imply a struggle to surmount a whole series of problems across the board.

The General Motors executive, for example, must compete with Ford, Chrysler, a scattering of independents and foreign manufacturers in the effort to give his products such ramified things as style, horsepower, engineering precision, new and attractive gadgets, new and distinctive features. One year it is power steering, another year it is Madison Avenue color matching, the year after that it is special carburetors for stock-car racing. Mistakes—such as the "pregnant Buick"—have to be lived down. And no one can afford to repeat a mistake—witness Chrysler's narrow escape when it shifted just in time from cars which gave the impression of stubbiness on a short wheelbase to the long, sleek lines of the "forward look."

To competition in innovation—which is the driving force, the real competitive "perfection," of the American economy—the GM executive must add the competition to achieve economics of production. If Ford does some pioneering on automation, building a long production line to machine the cylinder block without the intervention of a human hand, GM must counter by buying some of the Cross Co.'s intricate "transfermatic" devices on its own. And Chrysler must join the procession or die.

This by no means exhausts the across-the-board competitive list. There is competition to build up and service the best possible dealer organization; to do the best job of persuasion (public relations, advertising); to borrow money for new equipment if necessary; to conduct the most profitable research; to do the best job of market prediction. Finally, there is the competition in price—still a very clear and present thing even though prices are quoted "administratively" in advance. Though car prices change officially within narrow ranges these days, no one of the Big Three can charge much more than a competitor for a given class of car, even though its own car may have a demonstrable edge in styling, in horsepower or in accessories. And if cars don't sell at the quoted price, they must eventually be moved at bargain rates in order to clear the showrooms for next years' models. Many a person has gotten a real bargain by waiting until November or December to buy a new car.

Living and breathing this sort of "total" competition, with the possibility of a bad car year always lurking in the crevices that remain unaccounted for in the statistics of expectancy (rate of obsolescence, new family formation, creation of two- and three-car families, "disposable income," etc.), the GM executive would very likely snort if the classic criteria for "perfect competition" were called to his attention. He couldn't very well bring GM within the classic rules by breaking his company up into separate Buick, Chevy and Cadillac companies, for the resulting autonomous firms would still remain oligopolistic, or "few to sell," in their own separate car classes. (Even the Pontiac and the Oldsmobile would be "few to sell" against the Mercury and the Dodge.) But there are other things the GM man might try to do to come within the scope of the model. He could conform to rule one of perfect competition by making a Chevy in the

exact image of the Ford. And he could follow classical pricing concepts by setting up auction markets on corner lots
everywhere in the land.

Would this actually be an approach to "perfection"? It
could be, but under its terms there would be very little improvement in cars (barring collusion between the designers)
from year to year. As for the auctioneers, would they be
required to go into the business of servicing the cars they
sold? And who would handle the turn-in problem? Would
the auctioneer have to be a buyer of cars, as well? Even to
pose these questions is to expose the silliness of the attempt
to justify the perfect model as something pertaining to economic life as a whole. The model describes the commodity
markets—or it did in the days before the government
stepped in to put support-price floors under such things as
agriculture, oil and mining operations. It describes very
little else in the modern world.

Chapter Ten

The Consumers' Plebiscite

The test of an economic system lies in the choices it offers, the alternatives that are open to the people living under it. When choices are limited by coercion of one sort or another, the system must fall short of meeting the test in greater or less degree. The virtue of a free system i.e., competitive capitalism—is that it allows energy to flow uncoerced into a thousand-and-one different forms, expanding goods, services and jobs in a myriad, unpredictable ways. Every day, under such a system, a consumer's plebiscite (the phrase is von Mises') is held, the vote being counted in whatever money unit is the handiest. With his votes the consumer directs production, forcing or luring energy, brains and capital to obey his will.

It might be supposed, if one were to take the critics of modern "oligopolistic" society seriously, that the consumer's choices have been progressively narrowed since economists constructed the perfect model of competition. But have they?

Is a smaller percentage of the U.S. population eating steaks, wearing good clothes, living in decent homes and sending their children to school? Are people taking fewer vacations, reading fewer books, spending less time on amusements? Are good jobs harder to come by, and have all the positions at the top been preempted by the sons of the rich? Does it cost more to cure a man of pneumonia— or to keep him from getting it in the first place?

If the answers to such questions are yes, then "oligopoly" stands damned. But if they are no, then there is at least a presumption that "oligopoly" is offering a richer, far more varied life than would have been possible under the old so-called perfect competition. There is, of course, the possibility that life has expanded but not at a pace commensurate with the technological possibilities of the modern industrial machine. But this is not a question that can be answered one way or another with any scientific assurance. The "controlled experiment" necessary to yield an answer here would have demanded laboratory conditions—and whatever economic life may be, it is not a laboratory.

The best we can do is to make forays into such things as the price behavior of big companies, to study their reactions to increased competition, to investigate the job possibilities of this generation in comparison to the last. Moreover, we must always be aware that possible failures of expansiveness in parts of the system may be due, not to anything industry itself has done, but to the actions of government in inflating the currency and in taking a third of the people's income away from them to devote to its own uses, including a vast amount of paper pushing that adds nothing, net, to the product of the economic machine as a whole.

If we are looking for clarification of the nature of contemporary choices, the alternatives open to modern man under the competition of the so-called oligopolies, we will find very few people devoting their energies to field work in this realm. There are plenty of armchair studies which assume the problem *must* be thus and so because theory is inexorable. But there are only two readily available book texts which reject the *a priori* certainty that big industry is a system of "contrived scarcities" in favor of doing a factual study on big industry's actual behavior. One of the texts is A. D. H. Kaplan's *Big Enterprise in a Competitive System,* a study carried out under the auspices of the Brookings Institution; the other is a book by a *Fortune* magazine writer, Herrymon Maurer, called *Great Enterprise.* A third study, by Warner and Abegglan, canvasses the whole subject of job possibilities in contemporary America; statistically it demonstrates that there are comparatively more positions "open at the top" in the 1950s than there were a generation ago, and that there has been no relative contraction in the possibility that a boy from the wrong side of the tracks will some day be a member of the corporate high command.

Professor Kaplan begins by asking a simple question: What do we want an economic system to do? His assumptions are that the American people want a wide choice of goods and services available in a "workably" free market; that they want room for individual opportunity and initiative to seek the rewards of competitive effort (either on their own or working for an employer); that they expect to raise "the plane of living (which requires the pooling of big capital aggregates and an intricate organization of personnel). They also want all these things within a climate where "business rivalry is tempered by social ethics," and they depart from a general libertarian philosophy by seeking social benefits and protections "administered by or under regulations of government."

Whether more or less of the technological cream, the annual increment from improved efficiency, should be passed on to the consumer by way of lowered prices or higher wages and/or increased dividends, or by taxing it away for redistribution by government, is, of course, the burning question for contemporary politics. To judge by public opinion surveys, a majority of Americans are not averse to using taxation to favor small business and to cut back the scope of the big corporation. Only a minority, however, is in favor of direct meddling with big enterprise, or "managerial enterprise." Doubtless the majority would agree with Kaplan when he says "a large measure of regulation need not weaken the essential drives of a competitive society, if the existing forms of enterprise, private or public, provide the consumer with a number of choices and if, for the bulk of our economic wants and satisfactions, the market remains the final arbiter."

Waddill Catchings, in a brilliant piece of pamphleteering called *Do Economists Understand Business?* says it is "currently being taught in every school and college throughout the U.S." that bigness has destroyed competition. The statement may be extreme, but it is true that the texts in use in a large number of colleges (Samuelson, Bach) do slant things that way. The statistical underpinning for this slant goes back to the 1930s, when Adolf Berle and Gardiner Means were arguing that in thirty or forty years, at the then-current rate of growth, all corporate activity would be in the hands of 200 corporations. The presumption piled on top of the Berle-Means curves is that 200 corporations could not be trusted to satisfy the wants of the American people at progressively lowered prices for an ever-increasing output.

Waiving the question of whether it would be to the

interest of 200 corporations to limit their production to an amount that could be sold at high prices, Kaplan quite effectively demolishes the long-term applicability of the Berle-Means study. Between 1929 and 1948, the annual national income rose from $87 billion to $223 billion. But in this same span of time the profits of the large corporations dropped from 6.1 percent of the national income to 5.7 percent. While this was happening, the profits of smaller corporations rose from 5.4 percent of the national income to 8.1 percent, and the profits of unincorporated business jumped from 15.9 percent of national income to 17.8 percent.

Farming as an individual occupation has fallen off in the past quarter-century: in 1929 there were 5.6 million proprietors, while in 1950 the number had declined to 4.4 million. The drop represented a decrease of farm proprietors from 12.2 percent of total employment to 7.4 percent. But meanwhile the active proprietors of business firms increased from 4.1 to 5.4 millions, of from 8.9 percent of total employment to 9.3 percent. So, as Kaplan says, "on balance, the number of self-employed kept pace with the growth of population."

It is apparent, then, that the big corporations are not in process of taking America over. Adolf Berle himself, who never argues with statistics even though he is sometimes guilty of extrapolating curves in an all-cats-grow-up-to-be-tigers manner, has agreed that his fears of the thirties have not been borne out. Little business has even been gaining on big business. So Kaplan's question, "Does the American economy provide room for individual opportunity and initiative to seek the rewards of competitive effort?" must be answered affirmatively.

Even though the big haven't been eating up the little, it might be argued that America is no longer a place where the little can aspire to become big. But here, again, Kaplan proves the case for opportunity. He does this by comparing lists of the 100 largest corporations for 1909, 1919, 1929, 1935 and 1948. What the comparative lists go to prove is that the top, as Kaplan says, is an extremely slippery place. The list has changed continuously and only thirty-six of the 1909 giants were still in the first 100 in 1948. Two companies which considerably improved their positions over the years—General Electric and Du Pont—did so by changing the entire nature of their product mixes.

Entirely new arrivals in the 1948 list included Dow Chemical, International Business Machines Corp., Coca-Cola, Curtiss-Wright, Allied Stores, J. P. Stevens and Co., Twentieth Century–Fox Film, Skelly Oil, Burlington Mills, Monsanto Chemical, Owens–Illinois Glass, Weyerhaeuser Timber, American Cyanamid, General Foods, American Viscose, Standard Oil of Ohio, Celanese, Distillers Corp.–Seagrams, Schenley Industries. Some of these represented new industries, some of them were the result of mergers, some were old companies which had suddenly become galvanic. Over the years some companies fell out of the first hundred and climbed back. Some of those which dropped out, possibly for good, continued to expand, but were outstripped by other companies in the more dynamic sectors of the economy.

What the comparative lists demonstrate is that competition continually winnows the field, forcing ceaseless change. The lists even manage to bear out the sardonic dictum of the old trustbuster Thurman Arnold, that the easiest way to make money is to invade a supposedly "monopolized" field.

For example, in 1909 Standard Oil of New Jersey had assets greater than those of all the other members of the oil industry combined. Although the parent Standard Oil Company has grown greatly since 1909, notwithstanding the separation of its subsidiaries, its percentage in petroleum now represents a minor fraction of the expanded industry's total. In 1948, Standard of New Jersey had to share its place of leadership with its former subsidiaries, now independent, and with eleven other oil companies, only two of which were on the list in 1909.

Steel is another case in point. In 1909, the U.S. Steel Corp., which had over two-thirds of the business in its field at the time of its formation, was still the country's number one behemoth. There were, however, thirteen other steel firms represented among the first hundred companies. In 1948, there were nine steel companies remaining among the hundred largest corporations. Of this nine, only four were survivors from 1909. Five of the 1948 steel giants were newcomers who had bucked their way upwards in a supposedly monopolistic area. In the order of their size, they were National Steel, Armco Steel, Youngstown Sheet & Tube, Inland Steel, and Wheeling Steel. These had displaced such companies as Colorado Fuel & Iron, Crucible, and Sloss Sheffield from the list. (Challenged by the relative newcomers and by the prodigious growth of Bethlehem, Republic, and Jones & Laughlin, U.S. Steel itself now does only one-third of the business in steel.)

The modern competitiveness of steel has waxed over the years because the industry itself, far from making the same old products, has been engaged in providing more and more alternatives, more and more effective choices, for the consumer. Where the industry once sold carbon steel, in the form of rails, structural shapes and plate, it now takes color from the chemical industry, becoming a vast proliferation of special steels, with plenty of room at the bottom for small companies with electric furnaces and new alloying formulas. And the products of steel compete with wood, plastics and all the other metals.

Only in the sense that a new "monopolist" is created when a steel company hits upon a new alloying or a new steel-use formula, can the diversification of steel be called an infringement of competition. But such temporary "monopolies" as vanadium steel have served only to increase the range of consumer alternatives and provide a new challenge to established products. U.S. Steel, for example, may be the only supplier at the moment of all-steel prefabricated homes. Yet this "monopoly" acts as a competitive whip to such prefabricators in wood as National Homes, and the U.S. Steel house, in turn, may be challenged by the maker of an aluminum house.

Steel, though it is obviously basic to the economy, no longer bulks as large investmentwise as it did in the early years of the century. This is an index to the plain fact that there are many substitutes for steel in plastics, in wood products, in glass and in aluminum, and other nonferrous metals. To meet substitute competition, Republic Steel, the third-ranking producer in the nation, has even gone in for manufacturing plastic pipe. Other steel companies are interesting themselves in titanium, and in zinc and aluminum coated steel.

In England and pre–World War II Germany, the big corporation, when faced with the prospect of diminishing returns on its products, characteristically sought refuge in market-sharing and price-fixing agreements with its competitors. This live-and-let-live urge produced the cartel, a device for mulcting the consumer by offering him only "contrived scarcities." The impulse to cartelize in America had a brief run for its money in the 1880s and 90s, but it soon ran afoul of the national temperament, as expressed in the Sherman Act. To solve the problem of diminishing returns, the American corporation turned from the philosophy of "contrived scarcity" to the opposite philosophy of "contrived fecundity."

This fecundity has been expressed in the continuous process of remaking the market by altering the nature of the product from year to year. The "remade market" in steel has substituted light automobile sheets for heavy sheets, stainless for ordinary hard steels in cutlery, coated plate for old-fashioned tin plate. In aluminum, next to nickel the most traditionally "monopolistic" of the metal industries, market saturation has been avoided by pushing outward from the household utensil market, where the competition with copper and heat-resistant glass is fierce, into the electrical transmission, building, automotive and aviation fields. As Professor Kaplan shows, the agile company always supplies its sales force with new products, or drastically restyled old products, whenever a given product mix appears to be approaching the point of no-profit return.

The competition in innovation—which is the American idea of the perfect model of competition—has been carried to the point where, far from seeking market-sharing agreements, virtually everybody is now playing in everybody else's backyard. Management advisory companies now make lush livings in offering consultation on the art of "planned diversification." It was considered a joke when Aaron Burr's water company, the Manhattan Company, established a bank called the Bank of the Manhattan Co. But this is nothing in comparison with some of the strange amalgams of recent history. Today we see an Olin-Matthieson engaged in making firearms, shells, paper, cellophane and caustic soda, and even taking a flyer in aluminum. We see a Clevite going from automobile parts to electronics; a Thompson Products shifting all its emphases; and H. K. Porter Co. raying out from switching locomotives to steel, firebrick, rubber and electrical devices; a General Mills adding a mechanical division (precision gearing, electronic systems) to its old business of making flour; a W. R. Grace & Co. expanding from steamships into fertilizer, plastics, airlines, outdoor advertising, coffee and paint; a General Tire & Rubber Co. making rocket motors and plastics; and a Rockwell Manufacturing Co. developing a line of products that includes gas meters, power tools, valves and electrical conduit fittings. Oil companies, deep in the new applied science of petrochemicals, have developed synthetic glycerine processes (bringing them into competition with soapmakers); and have produced toluene, hitherto a coke-oven product. As for the old-line chemical companies which once reigned supreme in the nitrogen field, they are faced with competition with a dozen oil and gas companies which have invaded this territory.

All of this makes price fixing and market limitation and the other devices of cartelization a practical impossibility in the U.S. How could Allied Chemical & Dye and American Cyanamid, for example, ever hope to come to an agreement on nitrogen fertilizers when a new nitrogen manufacturer is appearing on the horizon every other month? And what will the chemical and oil companies now deep in the fertilizer business do if the new process of shaking nitric acid out of the atmosphere by pushing air through wind tunnels at high speeds ever comes to something? They will find ways of meeting the competition or, if they can't, they will turn to other products. And in either case the consumer will win.

Competition in innovation is, to be sure, not the same thing as competition in price. *But—and here is where the theorists of perfect competition missed the boat—it amounts to the same thing in the American economic climate.* As Herrymon Maurer has said, the big corporation puts its emphasis on production of a constantly improved or restyled entity rather than on price. But, in the course of centering on production, the big corporation aims at covering its costs and making a profit on penny savings at some far point along the sales curve. The price, inevitably, comes down as the market expands.

The idea is so familiar in Detroit that nobody bothers to mention it as a justification for outlining a hypothetical "area of price" for months or years ahead. Detroit simply talks of going beyond the "break-even point" to a volume of sales (say at eighty percent of operating capacity) that will enable a company to prosper and pay for new innovations and newer and newer machinery. Because there is no body of theory to explain the relation of "price administration" to the practice of keeping the price at a figure which will wring near-optimum use out of a production line that is obsolescent every time a model is changed, some popular textbook authors still talk of the automobile market as one of "restricted" competition and "contrived scarcity." But to anyone who has watched the battle between Ford and Chevrolet for first place in 1955 and later, such talk is nonsense.

The big company, with its resources, can afford the planning and the technology which enable it to increase the number of units produced per manhour and machine and so decrease unit costs. Thus the big company can afford to lower prices where a small producer cannot. Low prices increase consumption, and the increased consumption in turn leads to more production on a gamble that the market is virtually insatiable—which sometimes happens to be the case. The dynamic increase in earnings out of penny savings at volume sales justifies more investment in plant, still more production at higher wages, and still lower prices. Meanwhile, society becomes more and more consumer-oriented. With such a dynamic process at work, it would be sheer idiocy for an "oligopolist," or even a monopolist, to stick to the price policies of small-scale industry; sheer insanity to "charge all the traffic will bear" for the first items off the production line.

Neither Herrymon Maurer nor Kaplan rests his case for the price-competitiveness of big industry on the mere assertion of principle. Kaplan shows how the rubber tire industry (an "oligopoly" dominated by a Big Four which accounts for seventy-five percent of output) has kept its prices low in terms of constant dollars and satisfied itself with a very small margin of profit. Here the fact that fifty million consumers have tires which are continually coming into the recap and retread market introduces a competitive element that cannot be lightly dismissed. But beyond this, the tire manufacturer, like the automobile manufacturer, must set his price at a point which will keep a high-capacity plant operating somewhere near its peak. The tire manufacturer has not sacrificed quality to the demand for cheapness, for tire mileage, in general, has more than doubled in the past twenty-five years.

In aluminum, the nearest thing to a "monopoly" that exists in the U.S. (International Nickel is a Canadian company), prices have actually been set in the fiercest sort of competition for the consumer's dollar. Aluminum prices have had to battle copper prices in the electrical-wiring market. They have had to fight galvanized-iron prices in the roofing market, steel prices in the automotive market and copper and glass prices in the kitchenware market. The only place where aluminum has had things much to itself is in the airplane field. Yet here again the growing capacity of the aluminum industry means that the price of primary aluminum must be kept low enough to insure optimum use of plant and quick clearance of the market.

Even though long-run considerations dominate the setting of prices in big companies, the problem of retaining the loyalty of the customer is Consideration Number One. To woo that customer, big industry has put on a dazzling show of price reduction over the years. The comparative figures set forth in Herrymon Maurer's *Great Enterprise* are conclusive. International Harvester's six-foot twine-binder sold to farmers in 1880 for $325; by 1929, its price had dropped to $120. In 1882 the price of aluminum stood at $8 a pound. The electrolytic process cut the price to $2 in one swoop. And between 1913 and 1937, when prices in general doubled, aluminum prices declined by fifteen percent. In constant dollar terms, aluminum in 1953 was 9.6 cents a pound. Rubber tires sold in constant dollars in 1937 at about 13 percent of 1913 prices; gasoline at 19 percent; automobiles at 30 percent. Cellophane, priced at $2.65 in 1924, sold at 58 cents a pound in 1955. Nylon was cut in half in a decade's time. So the declining price record unrolls in the "oligopolistic" industries. As Kaplan sums it up, "when compared with secular reductions in the prices of rayon, or dyestuffs, or compared with the improvement in performance that a consumer's dollar has been able to buy in tires and gasoline, in sound-reproducing machines, or in 'miracle' drugs, the downward price pressure of atomistic competition appears relatively feeble."

Indeed, so keen is the competition in some areas that Congress, taking alarm, has sought to offset its own anti-trust legislation in certain "fair trade" fields. But the rise of the discount house and the ubiquity of the under-the-counter deal, make "fair trade" laws a dead letter. On the other hand, the Sherman Antitrust Act continues to work its over-all watchdog magic. As Waddill Catchings has indicated, the effectiveness of the Sherman Act does not reside in its positive enforcement by the Department of Justice. Its effec-tiveness derives from a simpler consideration: as long as it is on the books, cartel agreements in America are not sus-stainable in law.

This means that the maverick can go his own way, cutting a price here, invading the Detroit area with a steel mill there. There can be no retribution as long as the law is on his side.

Chapter Eleven

Labor Had
the Right Idea

S ince it is a fact that wages in America have risen just as
fast in periods of declining union activity as they have
in periods when unions have been gaining momentum—
wages doubled in actual purchasing power from 1865 to
1900, when unions were negligible   it is an arguable inference that "collective bargaining" has had little to do with
the wage scale. The point, however, is scarcely worth making a political issue at this stage of history: the union movement is here to stay. In any event, men voluntarily join
unions not solely because they think they are effective; they
join them because they feel happier and more dignified in
free association with their fellows. It is perfectly true that
wages rise with productivity per worker, and that, in bidding
for good workers, companies would raise wages out of increased production anyway. But some method must be
found to make and register bargains between worker and
employer, and the diffident man may feel more comfortable
if an agent helps perform the service for him.

The essence of a free society, however, is that no man
should be coerced into taking a bargaining agent if he pre-
fers to bargain for himself. Nor should the state be called

in to force an issue between man and man: it can only do
this by denying to individuals the right and the power to
compare services. Such engines of coercion as the closed
shop and compulsory arbitration are incompatible with the
market mechanism, which, as Frederic Bastiat says, is
merely another name for letting men live by their own wills
and intelligence.

Historically, American labor has tried to gain its ends
without reliance on the state: that was the essence of Gompersism, as formulated by Samuel Gompers, Founding
Father of the American Federation of Labor. "Pure and
simple trade unionism," designed to the end of getting
"more" without the compulsions of politics—that was the
Gompers way. Even today, a large segment of the labor
movement feels uneasy about becoming either a ward or an
organizing arm of the state. And though the "one big union"
idea has made some progress (witness the merger of the
AFL and CIO), the American labor picture is still one of
diversity, with industrial unions and craft unions pursuing
different objectives, and with many people rejecting the
idea of unionization *in toto*. American life still falls neatly
into the pattern of checks and balances within checks and
balances; and diversity is still an organizational sign of
health. If men can afford the luxury of difference, it argues
something about basic satisfactions.

Diversity does not, of course, imply that the American
labor movement is incapable of acting as a reasonably
united force for certain ends. But what ends, and under
what general philosophy of society? What are labor's ideas
of a good civilization? Ever since the New Deal, the movement has been tempered in an atmosphere of combat. Will it
continue to exalt a warfare psychology at the expense of

possible agreements with a mellowed managerial class? Will it eventually push for a labor party, a class party and a government created in its image? Does it have a hidden and still formless urge to swallow the state? Or is it content to remain a force within a state that includes other estates, other groups, other classes?

These ultimate questions, abstruse and alien though they may seem to both the pragmatic labor organizer and the practical shop manager, will nonetheless prove to be root questions in the years ahead. In Europe, the theoreticians of labor have tried to answer them one way. Regardless of "immediate aims," the European labor parties—the parties of social democracy—have been committed to the theory of the ultimate eclipse of the democratic capitalist pattern of society. Social democracy has had no faith in a society founded on the theory of free contractual relationships.

In its fundamental premise, social democracy proposes ultimately to swallow the state. Not immediately, not by the exercise of naked force. "Gradualism" has been the word for the followers of the Kautskys, the Blums, the Laskis, the Webbs, the Henri de Mans. The social democratic leaders have been civilized human beings; they have withstood the illegalism of bolshevism; they have been dignified in the face of fascism; they have refused to fight with barbaric weapons. But their root premise—the premise that the democratic capitalist state, which presupposes a dynamic balance of conflicting and cooperating forces in society, is destined everywhere to be swallowed by a single majoritarian force—has proved disastrous to an entire continent.

Where "labor" swallowed the state, as in Soviet Russia, the result has been a single-party dictatorship over trade unions and citizens alike. In the Germany of Hitler and the

Italy of Mussolini, the fear that labor might eventually monopolize the state led directly to the creation of a different type of social python, a monster with wider jaws. The social python, fascism, was hatched from the egg of "scientific socialism's" fundamental political premise. Marx, even a watered-down Marx, stands in relation to Hitler and Mussolini as "condition" to "reflex."

In the U.S. the theory of the triumph of any single social force over all the others has never taken real psychological root. This is the nation where everyone thinks of himself as a member of the middle class. The notion of a "final conflict," implicit in the combat psychology of industrywide strike and lockout, has yet to be made official doctrine by the CIO on the one hand, or the National Association of Manufacturers on the other. We still hold to the theory of society as a dynamic balance of autonomous forces; we still believe in the free individual as the constitutive unit that is anterior to any force. American society, for all its "gimme" tactics devised to mulct one's neighbor by way of pressure-group seizure of his substance, still hungers for free patterns. But, if the patterns are to remain free, organized labor must consciously refuse the social democratic gambit. It must forgo the idea of the monolithic labor party.

The American labor movement is hardly likely at this date to be impressed by Communist sectarians, even though Communists still retain their ability to cause a lot of trouble behind so-called transmission-belt and innocent-front screens. But the Marxism of social democracy, so reasonable in its "immediate" demands, so tolerant in its practical workings, can easily act as a corrosive on the American axiom that the good society is an expression of divergent and various group interests competing and cooperating under law.

Is *any* important part of the labor movement in danger of accepting the answer of statism? Labor has, indeed, accepted many favors from government, and has had many of the breaks. But the competition for favors has not been a *reasoned* philosophy. At the very outset American labor decided against Marx. Back in the yeasty 1840s, when all America was seeking the millennium, a printer named George Henry Evans broke with the ideas of his fellow labor leader Thomas Skidmore on the subject of private as against state-manipulated property. Skidmore, an early "Share the Wealth-er," had been arguing for an equitable "division" of both land and capital goods among the citizens of the republic. But Evans, who had a correct theory of the biological nature of man, argued against any "natural" right to a share in capital equipment. Man must breathe, drink and eat, said Evans; therefore, if it be granted that a human being has a basic right to life, he must also possess a natural right to air, water and soil. Other rights—to capital, to education, to "freedom from want"—are necessarily derivative and dependent, since they come into being as a result of applying energy to the working of the earth's surface. They belong to men as they can get them, by using intelligence and muscle. According to Evans's logic, the modern theory that the state owes every citizen a minimum of subsistence is a false notion; all that organized society can properly do is to see that the human being is given access to the earth's surface on the easy terms that must exist in countries that have abolished the laws of entail and primogeniture and refused subsidies and tariff benefits to big ownership.

The reasoning of George Henry Evans led straight to the Homestead Act, by which thousands of Americans acquired title in fee simple to quarter sections of western earth. In popularizing his land policy ("vote yourself a farm"), Evans had the aid of Herman Kriege, a German who had helped organize a European secret society known as the League of the Just. In the 1840s the League of the Just was controlled by Karl Marx, who was even then arguing that the very stars had decreed the universal destruction of private property in the means of production. When Marx heard of Kriege's "rightist deviation," his practical abandonment of communism, the always formidable wrath of the founder of "scientific socialism" exploded. Herman Kriege was unceremoniously and summarily expelled from the League of the Just.

The whole episode, which might have been forgotten if Herbert Harris had not resurrected it in his *American Labor,* is prophetic. For the history of European labor theory has been the history of the triumph of Karl Marx's attitude toward private ownership of productive property. The history of American labor, on the other hand, has followed an equivocal course even in its theoretical aspects; the pull of the doctrine of natural rights—to "life, liberty and property"—has torn more than one George Henry Evans into the "rightist deviation," which has kept American labor from organizing under European philosophy and along European lines. Hooked to the millennial aspirations of socialism, these European lines have differed only in the approach to the problems of tempo, of methods, of immediate versus long-term demands. Bebel, Kautsky, Bernstein, the Liebknechts and Rosa Luxemburg in Germany; Jaurès in France; Hyndman, the Webbs, Laski and Bernard Shaw in England—all of them have had a vision of mankind eventually organized by and through a friendly bureaucracy. The dominant parties of the social democratic

tradition have been steeped in the thinking of these Marxist actionists, infiltrationists, "gradualists," and "open con-
spirators"—steeped, in brief, in the doctrine that the state as
possessor or manipulator of the productive acreage and
machinery must assume primary responsibility for the activities of man, both economic and social.

Yet, since the tradition of Western Christendom has always assumed the right of the individual to regard himself
as an end and not as a means, there has lingered in European labor thinking the notion that a state-subjected man
can somehow remain free. But how to maintain individual
freedom if it is divorced from the ultimate right to an individual physical base on the earth's surface? Such a right is
the precondition of a number of free employers—and many
such competing employers are needed to guarantee alternatives in society for the landless. European labor theory has
always remained more or less transcendentalist in its idea
of man; by implication it has denied that freedom must exist
through the body and on a physical base. The "natural
right" to individual productive property, inalienable even
in the face of state power, has been regarded as romantic
nonsense by the whole long line of European socialist and
social democratic theoreticians, from Marx on down to La-
borite Aneurin Bevan in our own confused time.

Denying the existence of inalienable rights, Marxist history becomes a study of the struggle for state power to sup-
press one's class antagonist. As the Marxists put it, "All history is the history of class struggles." There is, however, a
history of social power that exists independently of the
history of political power. In the really spacious times of
human development men have simply gone ahead with
pioneering, sowing, reaping, building, inventing, writing,

painting and thinking without worrying unduly about politics. No politician bothered Willard Gibbs in New Haven as
he played with the formulas of thc laws of thermodynamics.
No politician bothered Thomas Edison, Henry Ford or the
Wright brothers as they tinkered in their shops with machinery. When social power is freest, men rise to productive
heights—provided, of course, that monopolists have not
previously succeeded in engrossing the wealth by use of
the political means. We look back with wonder on the heyday of the Greek city state, the early Roman Republic, the
free cities of the Middle Ages, the rise of Venetian, Dutch
and American republics, simply because in these separate
instances the political power was subordinated to the social
power of the individual.

In point of fact, political power is correctly to be defined as interference with social power. Some such interference may be necessary, since the earth's surface is limited and the traffic on the main roads is crowded. But since
production cannot be fostered best by interference with production, political power is uncreative. At best it achieves
the creativeness of slave labor. Policemen, bureaucrats and
policymakers must alike be fed out of produce that is
brought into being by social power. Although some political
"overhead" is productively necessary, just as block signals
are needed on a railroad, a point can easily be reached
where it constitutes a confiscatory tax on social power, a
net burden on those who work.

When the interference with social power is at a minimum,
when it is fixed on custom and law and follows predictable
channels, when the toll it takes for the support of the state
apparatus is not an overbearing percentage of the national
income, men can work without fear. But when it becomes
unpredictable and arbitrary, when it works through admin-

istrative agencies or palace functionaries whose scope of activity is not defined and circumscribed, men cease to work at the top of their bent. This remains true whether the interference is in behalf of Big Ownership in search of tariffs, subsidies and the use of police power against labor, or whether it is designed to help the Little Man by assisting him out of taxes or the unions in an organizing drive. Whenever state activity becomes an unpredictable dynamic element whose direction and rate of speed vary from month to month in response to pressure-group campaigning, then social power tends to take less responsibility on its own shoulders.

Social democratic theory, following Marx, has assumed that no class can resist trying to use the political power against all other classes. And, in truth, it has had considerable excuse for its attitude. In Germany, the country of the first great social democratic organization, a business class that had scarcely had time to forget the social patterns of feudalism tried almost from the start to limit production and allocate markets through the interference of the political arm. The land policy of the German East, a policy that favored the creation and continuance of great estates by the political means, prevented a free play on the margin for human beings who might otherwise have escaped the fate of being a drug on the labor market. In England, the policy of land entails forced men into the cities, whence a few escaped by emigration overseas. Coming to birth in a society that frequently used the political power to trench upon social power, labor quite naturally imitated its elders. Disaster was avoided in Europe only just so long as America, the land of social power, existed to serve as a safety valve for the caged energies of the Old World.

In contesting the doctrine of "natural rights," in denying

the patent fact that the inner principle of Western and Christian civilization has been the urge to individual, as against "class," freedom, the social democratic theoreticians have neatly deprived themselves of a moral base along with a material base. For if there are no properly inalienable rights to which each and every individual may lay claim, surely the rule of force cannot be contested. If "all history is the history of class struggles," and not a struggle for the rights of the individual under God, then history is deprived of its moral meaning and there is no reason why Fascists or Communists should not have possession of the state if they can exercise superior force. If the right to life, for instance, is not inalienable up to the point of collision with the right to self-defense, then no one has a moral base from which to object if a majority should vote the extinction of a minority.

The social democratic theoreticians did not, of course, suspect they were depriving history—and life itself—of its moral meaning when they adopted the Marxian view of history as a struggle for class possession of the state apparatus. But some dim perception of the individually suicidal nature of Marxist theory saved many trade unionists in the Latin lands, which had a heritage of the laws of Rome and of the historic freewill beliefs of the Catholic church. Latin peoples in modern times have never deified the state; they accept dictators cynically or they rise passionately against them from time to time.* It is hardly accidental that anarchosyndicalism has been an effective labor doctrine in France, Italy and Spain. The theory that the labor struggle should be fought on the economic front,

---

* As Willmoore Kendall has wittily put it, "Not even the Spaniards can occupy Spain."

against the employer and without recourse to the state, is an appealing one, for it is rooted in a knowledge that only social power can lead to a high order of productivity. But syndicalism is defective in logic, even though it springs from a love of freedom. It is defective because it ignores the twofold nature of economic life, which is a matter of production *and exchange*. In the early 1920s, the Italian syndicalist trade unions seized the factories. But there followed a sitdown strike of the salesmen, the commercial agents, the factors, the middlemen. Syndicalism had no way of entering the world of commerce, the world of *connection,* which must go either by the law of contract or by administrative fiat. When no provision is made for the world of commerce, a vacuum exists outside of the factories. A state is needed to enforce the freely accepted terms of contracts or to staff an administrative apparatus. If there is no state, gangsters step in to do the job, as the histories of Italy and Volstead-era Chicago both go to prove.

Administrative law, the handling of exchange matters by bureaucratic fiat, is, of course, what old-style social democracy is driven to when it enters the world of commerce and connection. By degrees the social democrats of Europe were driven to accept the imperatives of top-down planning and a regimented economic world, for one administered sector of an economy begets the necessity for another. Top-down planning in economic life must be done in terms of an estimated volume at a fixed price in relation to a defined amount of purchasing power; else it is merely an attempt to guess the market, which is familiar capitalist technique. It ends with an attempt to control all the sectors of production as the prerequisite for controlling one, two or ten. And so, of course, it ends in a fixed, slave world—in fascism, communism, the "corporative state," the Fabian administrative bureaucracy or whatever.

The alternative to administrative law in productive matters is contract law, under which production can rise as high as the free wishes of men can push it. Policing contracts is quite different from policing energies that go into creating goods and services. The policing of contracts provides human beings with a framework of certainty. But the policing of energies introduces the element of fear into economic life, for no single individual can be sure what the next "due process of administration" may do to the present day's decision.

Since there has been no social democratic recognition of the property and contract bases of individual freedom, the European labor movement has never been able to reconcile its theory with its practice. For in practice a union must strive with all its might to get a contract with the management. And a group contract should differ in no way from an individual contract; it is an agreement that counts on the philosophy of "rights" for its enforcement. The theory of rights, which is invoked to protect the stockholder, is also used to protect the agreed-upon wage scales of the miners. Even the existence of union property depends on a right that must have a sanction beyond that of "class expression." What would become of union strike and welfare funds if the same law that protects a stock operator's brokerage account did not protect them?

Even in England the general criticism of social democratic theory applies quite as much as in Germany and elsewhere. Between G. D. H. Cole, Harold Laski, Aneurin Bevan, Léon Blum, Edward Bernstein and Karl Kautsky the differences have been negligible; all have believed in the triumph of socialism, which denies the freedom to own and to sell what one owns in the free marketplace. In England and Scandinavia, however, the union movement has kept itself fairly clean from the corrosion of cynicism simply by remaining oblivious to official Labor Party gabble. The English unions have never made a fetish of anything verbal, such as the "closed shop" or the "triumph of socialism." They have simply gone ahead with bargaining, getting contracts, living their life within the context of a system that is based on the law of contract. For a few years prior to World War I anarchosyndicalism had a brief flurry in England. Then guild socialism, which believed in "encroaching control" of shop property, had a short-lived day. But the English union man has always returned to his Ernie Bevin, who is not to be confused with Aneurin Bevan. The Crippses and the Bevans have talked the language of the European continent; the English worker has lived in the tradition of John Locke and the Cromwellian and "Glorious" revolutions. Possibly the willingness to compromise that has characterized English and Swedish big ownership has enabled labor in the two enlightened North European countries to have faith in the possibilities of the contractual way. But whatever the reason for it, England and Sweden have been saved from at least some of the devastation of "history as class struggle" by the common sense of human beings who refuse to listen to theory when it bears no relation to practice and continuing tradition.

In America, the land of George Henry Evans, Marxism never took deep root. Some philosophers have ascribed the persistence of the "American dream," which is based on property consciousness, to the presence of the beckoning trans-Appalachian land. But almost certainly the thinking of Jefferson and Madison has had as much to do with it. Jefferson persuaded Virginia to abolish the laws of entail and primogeniture, with the result that a landed family in the British sense has for a long time been an anachronism in American life. And, since even factories in a nonagrarian culture must stand on the earth's surface, the result has been opportunity for the little businessman as well as for the farmer. No one is likely to hoard land in America, for the laws do not favor the continued existence of uneconomic estates. As for Madison's contribution, the federal framework of the American Republic, it distributes stresses and strains and leaves a large area of rights to individuals who can count on the check-and-balance system to preserve those rights against the jealousy of a transient majority. The federal framework and the protection of individual and minority rights mean that human beings do not have to fritter away energy in political activity. Americans haven't had to waste themselves in "party" life on the European model. Government has been their agent, entrusted with certain powers; the rights have remained with the individual. There are those who say the Bill of Rights should be balanced by a Bill of Duties, but no one has ever explained how one can owe a duty to his agent beyond supporting him as long as he is living up to his contract. The agent is supposed to do what he is told to do; the citizen's duty is to himself, his family, his church, his lodge, his association, his community as the constitutive unit that delegates power to the state agent. Even in time of war the citizen ought, ideally, to do his duty voluntarily, as something that he owes to himself and to a tradition that allows him to dispense with that "sense of the state" which has ruined much of Europe.

Those who have tried to domesticate Marx in America have first had to make the attempt to arouse state consciousness. That is why social democrats have been prolific with ideas for the invasion of local rights; that is why they have talked about the "obsolescence of federalism." Marxism demands a centralization of power, it demands the encroachment of political upon social power. To make any intellectual headway it must accustom people to thinking in terms of fighting for control of state leverage, even though their rights may still leave them theoretically immune to the reach of that leverage.

Before World War I, the American Socialist Party was officially Marxist. Yet Eugene Debs, the perennial Socialist candidate for President, cared little for theory. He was, in point of fact, a folksy, warmhearted Indiana Populist, a person who hated to look upon distress and suffering. Daniel de Leon, the leader of the Socialist Labor Party, who called for the "unconditional surrender of capitalism," was something else again. But de Leon, it is important to note, got his education in Germany. It was de Leon who, in the words of Lenin, "first formulated the idea of a soviet government." But if Lenin took the idea, America ignored it. The ordinary American workingman has never heard of de Leon, never heard of the Socialist Labor Party.

Anarchosyndicalism, the theorizing of Bakunin and Sorel, has been exemplified on these shores by the IWW, which won many important strikes before World War I. But anarchosyndicalism has died here as it died in Britain and Sweden. The European philosophies, although they made a great deal of noise and attracted more than one American intellectual who never bothered to study Madison, have not had a tithe of the influence of old Samuel

Gompers on the American labor movement. Gompers has been reviled of late years; his "pure and simple trade unionism" has been called "the philosophy of no philosophy." Yet it fitted neatly into the Madisonian structure of the American political system. The American Federation of Labor left union rights in the hands of the separate constitutive unions; and it did not arrogate to itself the power to decide for the worker in his larger role as citizen. In politics the AFL followed a policy of rewarding its friends and punishing its enemies. It did not seek to create a political party of its own, one that would be compelled by the logic of political representation to have opinions on foreign affairs, sumptuary legislation and a whole host of problems that more properly belongs to man as citizen. As a result of Gompers' superior insight into the conditions of American life, the AFL flourished where Terence V. Powderly's Knights of Labor died. The Knights of Labor believed in industrial unionism as against the AFL's craft unionism; but they also tried to substitute the union for the community in enlisting the complete identification of the worker's personality. It was the grandiose aim of the Knights that led to their eclipse quite as much as the attempt to build industrial unionism before the political economy was ready for it.

Gompersism commenced to have hard sledding in the late twenties, and it became temporarily discredited during the depression of the thirties. But the reason for the decline of Gompersism is to be sought, not in Gompers' philosophy, but in the AFL's refusal to organize beltline industries in accordance with the imperatives of mass production. The industrial union no less than the craft union can be organized along pure and simple lines; there is no reason why the locals of the United Automobile Workers, for example, should be torn apart by quarrels over foreign policy. No more than the craft union functionaries do the industrial union leaders have to think for their members on problems of general citizenship.

The rise of the CIO was a response to the failure of Gompersism to adapt pure and simple trade unionism to the conditions of the assembly belt. It may decline, incidentally, with the development of "automated" production lines, which will tend to develop new crafts among the technicians who "program" and watch over the behavior of the lines. But the political thinking of John L. Lewis, of the late Phil Murray and of Walter Reuther, to pick some important CIO names at random, was shaped under the shadow of a business leadership that itself had begun to think in European statist terms. The disease began with big ownership's attitude toward the protective tariff, which is a method of using state power to grab social power from the hands of the ultimate consumer. It reached a high-fever stage when our first great oil-refining company invoked the political means of the rebate. The attempt to control the police and the courts in the coal and steel towns, the insistence by the automobile manufacturers that labor had no rights of association except on company terms, the predilection of big ownership to demand the aid of federal troops in breaking strikes—all of these instances, and many more like them, pushed John L. Lewis and his associates to accepting the methods of continental Europe. The CIO grew up depending on the state. But the end result of state dependence will mean the ultimate collapse of the movement unless a halt is called somewhere.

Fortunately for us all, there are some signs that labor is

becoming increasingly aware that dependence on the state has its dangers. Before he died the late Phil Murray issued a plaintive warning. Yet labor has still to evolve for itself a pattern of belief in economic freedom. Such a pattern might promote belief, not in statism, but in such things as genuine profit sharing; in worker ownership of blocks of voting stock; in consumers' cooperatives to protect living standards; in monetary and tax policies designed to defend purchasing power and leave people in control of their own money; and in the general idea that freedom is what creates jobs. It was freedom, not state compulsion, which created an average of more than $13,000 or more capital investment for every worker that is employed in the U.S. today.

Statist radicals argue, of course, that the political agents of big ownership would prevent any attempt to establish the conditions of freedom, but inasmuch as you have to have power to do anything constructive, why isn't it just as easy to organize behind one programmatic set of beliefs as another? If the majority can't organize to preserve the conditions of freedom, a labor group certainly can't hope to create its own type of socialism, which Americans instinctively reject.

If labor wants to continue part of a free world, labor has got to think in the foregoing terms. It must return to the day when it eschewed trying to gain its economic ends by politics, when it believed in free collective bargaining with management without asking that the state intervene either to set the stage or to affect the result. On Election Day, it must return to Samuel Gompers' prescription: "Reward your friends and punish your enemies." Union members must do this, however, as individuals who may differ with the union leaders over the definition of "friend" and "enemy."

In returning to freedom American labor has a lot of history to "unlearn." In World War I the federal government took over the railroads and put them under a commissar, namely, Secretary of the Treasury William G. McAdoo. This put the state into the business of dealing with both labor and management and exercising the final right of enforcing a "public" decision on both of them. McAdoo encouraged the organization of nonoperating railway workers to the point where labor got the idea that the power of government could work magic if one could only capture and hold it for keeps. After the war, railroad labor put the new theory to the test; and in 1926 it succeeded in getting the Railway Labor Act through both houses of Congress. This was the "entering wedge"; it made Washington a "third party" to labor disputes, and the struggle was on for control of the third-party mechanism.

Donald Richberg, who was instrumental in getting the Railway Labor Act written and passed, has recently expressed his sympathy with the unions' general position in the "dark age" when injunctions were freely granted to put an end to local violence in labor disputes. He still thinks the judiciary sided altogether too flagrantly with the factory and mine owners in the days when the state of Pennsylvania maintained its Coal and Iron Police. He still regards the Clayton Act, the so-called Magna Charta of labor, as a good thing on balance. But now that labor is "top dog" after twenty years, during which the judiciary has sided all too flagrantly with the union bosses, he thinks that such mechanisms as the Railway Labor Act and the Clayton Act are no longer utilized in the proper spirit. Labor has been using its "charter" not as an instrument of freedom, but as a lever for repressive "class" power demands of its own.

The blame for the misuse of the Clayton Act may be

placed squarely on the U.S. Supreme Court. According to the late Chief Justice Charles Evans Hughes, the framers of the Clayton Act merely intended to forbid application of the antitrust laws to unions which were "lawfully carrying out . . . legitimate objects." But the opinion of Chief Justice Hughes was destined to become the minority view of the Supreme Court. Today the Clayton Act is interpreted to mean that unions are exempt from the Sherman Act under any and all circumstances, thus giving labor a total immunity which was never intended in the days of Woodrow Wilson.

As things stand now, a labor union can get away with a whole variety of monopolistic restraints. Electrical workers in New York have made deals with employers to exclude the products of certain manufacturers, and to control prices. There is even one notorious instance in which a union has refused to permit its members to work for one particular employer and simultaneously refused to allow this employer's self-chosen men either to work on a nonunion basis or to join the union after being hired.

This effective denial of the right of an entrepreneur to conduct his business on any terms has been enforced by the state, much to the horror of the late Mr. Justice Robert Jackson. Said Jackson in a strong dissenting opinion: "This court now sustains the claim of a union to the right to deny participation in the economic world to an employer simply because the union dislikes him. This Court permits to employees the same arbitrary dominance over the economic sphere which they control that labor so long, so bitterly, and so rightly, asserted should belong to no man."

It is on the issue of what Mr. Richberg calls "compulsory unionism: the new slavery" that labor has the most to unlearn. The closed shop, or the compulsory union shop, delivers a worker to a union organization without recourse. This means, in practice, that union members must follow their leaders even against the dictates of their own individual consciences. If a man cannot resign from a union if he is displeased with its leadership, its methods, or its philosophy, he has no power to check the tyranny of a majority.

The unions have argued that "majority democratic rule requires the minority to support the majority," and they point to citizenship in a nation as analogous to membership in a union. But the analogy is faulty, for in a free nation one can always organize an opposition with impunity, and one is not required to contribute to the political support of the majority party or its ideas. As Mr. Richberg puts it: "Those who espouse compulsory unionism are essentially adopting the Communist theory that there should be only one party to which everyone should give allegiance and support."

When unions achieve an effective monopoly status, the drive to "industrywide bargaining" becomes virtually irresistible. "Industrywide bargaining" takes no account of local conditions or the means of individual employers. Under industrywide agreements the wage scale of the most prosperous companies tends to be forced on all companies in a given field. Faced with the necessity of paying what is for them an uneconomic wage, the small, weak companies must seek some sort of protection. One way of getting protection is to merge with a bigger unit of the industry. Thus industrywide bargaining helps drive smaller companies out of existence. This may result in narrowing the customer's freedom of choice. Labor suffers for two reasons: first, because it is itself a customer; and second, because the "fringe" employer no longer has much of a chance to become a big fellow (and a big employer) on his own.

Mr. Richberg, who has done the only clear thinking on the subject, offers three propositions to curb union monopoly. He would amend the Clayton Act (or the Supreme Court's own "legislative" extension of the Clayton Act) to make "the creation and exercise of monopoly powers by labor unions . . . unlawful." He would have Congress declare compulsory unionism to be a form of "involuntary servitude" within the definition of the Thirteenth Amendment. And he would make strikes "unlawful" when they are "strikes against the public health, safety and welfare," or "strikes to compel political action," or "strikes without a preceding reasonable effort to avoid a strike," or "strikes conducted with the aid . . . of criminal violence."

It may be quixotic to believe that any type of strike can be stopped by law if free men want to quit work. But Mr. Richberg is quite right in arguing that labor must abandon its hopes of ruling society, through its control of the state. The orginal mistake made by the American people was to permit the government to run the railways during World War I. This was expedient, it was a "national emergency" method of solving a problem. But it was not necessary. One thing led to another, the consequence of it being that not merely railway labor in particular but the labor movement as a whole finally abandoned the Gompers' philosophy of voluntarism.

Is it too late for labor to recover its old belief in the voluntary way? That depends on the course of American economic life in general. For labor has not been alone in running to Washington for a solution of its troubles. Everybody's been doing it since 1933. The bigger question today is: Can anybody stop a trend that is so far gone? Labor can hardly do it unless everyone else pitches in.

Chapter Twelve

Retreat from the American System

In the beginning of modern economics was Say's Law—
the once famous "Law of Markets" or *"Thèorie des
Debouchés"* which holds that production creates its own
purchasing power. First formulated by Jean Baptiste Say—
a Frenchman who remarked, "Lord, let now Thy servant
depart in peace" after sitting for a moment in Adam Smith's
chair at Glasgow—the *Thèorie des Debouchés* seemed quite
obvious to our forefathers. Used to a fairly stable money
system, with gold and silver serving as regulators, nineteenth-century men could look beyond the "lubrication"
function of dollars, pounds and francs to the physical re-
alities of production and exchange. It seemed beyond contest that when a producer handed out cash for raw materials, for wages and salaries, for interest, for dividends and
for the replacement of worn capital equipment and the
purchase of new, that the money so expended would turn
up in the system as available consumption funds. Given no
political distortion of the money supply, the purchasing
power thus released would be sufficient to "clear the market." John Stuart Mill, with his genius for simplicity, re-
phrased the Law of Markets by remarking that "the means

of payment for commodities is simply commodities . . .
Could we suddenly double the productive power of the
country, we should double the supply of commodities in
every market; but we should, by the same stroke, double
the purchasing power . . . every one would have twice as
much to offer in exchange."

This simple explanation disappeared from sight in the
1930s, with the coming of the big depression. Manifestly,
in 1930 and 1933, markets were not being "cleared." The
U.S. in the thirties had a President—Franklin D. Roosevelt
—who publicly disbelieved in the Say formulation (see
Daniel Fusfeld's revealing *The Economic Thought of
Franklin D. Roosevelt and the Origins of the New Deal* for
light on the economic education of our four-time executive).
Far from creating their own purchasing power, goods in the
early thirties seemed interminably stuck in transit. People
with purchasing power refused to buy; employers, therefore,
ceased to employ; and the interest rate hung listlessly in the
air, refusing to perform its office as the regulator of future
investment. A host of lesser prophets—Major Douglas with
his "social credit" idea, the advocates of "stamp scrip," the
Marxian and Fabian believers in a sterilized "surplus
value," the Technocrats—all tried to explain the "leak" in
Say's Law. Their mathematics didn't make sense; nevertheless, the market remained in the doldrums. The time of
"glut," prophesied by Malthus in an aberrant moment when
he suspended his belief that there could never be enough
to go around, was definitely here.

Came the New Deal. There was very little conscious
theory behind any of the New Deals, whether first, second,
or third. Between 1933 and the coming of World War II,
Roosevelt chopped and changed so often that he frequently

appeared to cancel himself. Between his NRA and TNEC phases there was no visible connection; and with such antipodal prophets as General Hugh Johnson (a believer in market limitation) and Thurman Arnold (a trustbuster) clamoring for the President's ear, it often seemed as though the Tower of Babel had been substituted for the Washington Monument. Roosevelt's own metaphorical conception of himself (as the quarterback always willing to change from a passing to a rushing or kicking game) seemed to argue the complete pragmatist. But, where Herbert Hoover thought of him as "that man," Benjamin Cohen and Jerome Frank, though willing to concede the "skipper's" ability to veer and tack, always suspected the President of an abiding hankering for a balanced budget. Rexford Tugwell often wondered audibly at the "internationalism" that kept popping up even when FDR was giving his assent to measures sponsored by doctrinaire nationalists. And Raymond Moley and Cordell Hull went to the London Economic Conference in 1933 with contradictory plans in their pockets, each fully confident that his own plan had unequivocal White House blessings.

The quicksilver quality that was always in Roosevelt was never more apparent than in the legislative program whipped up during the Hundred Days of the First New Deal. The President began by asking for economy. "Too often," he said, "liberal governments have been wrecked on the rocks of loose fiscal policy." But there was no "economy" as such in the Agricultural Adjustment Act, in the Civilian Conservation Corps, in the Works Progress Administration, in the Ickes program of Public Works, or in the Tennessee Valley Authority. All of these involved spending by the state in order to expand the market. The

NRA, on the other hand, presupposed a conscious limitation of markets, of competition, of the number of firms permitted to do business in a given field. A contraption out of the twenties, when the trade association movement was thinking in terms of "stabilized prices" via suspension of the Sherman Antitrust Act, the NRA directly negated the idea that spending must come before, and not after, a price rise.

If there was any rhyme or reason to the various New Deals, it was provided by Rexford Tugwell's theory that the American economy had become "mature" for all time, and that future investment must be consciously controlled, whether by crop limitation and acreage reduction in agriculture (with government payments going to farmers for *not* producing) or by the deliberate allocation of expansion funds to industry. Henceforward, according to Tugwell, the government must "make" the total market in conformity to an overall pattern. Say's Law would be suspended: the state would force consumption, and oversee production.

Tugwell's theory, however, was too direct, too arbitrary, to make a permanent appeal to Roosevelt's nature. "Planning" was all right, but it must be loose planning, the mere stimulation of aggregate purchasing power. The stage was set for the Gross National Product idea, for macroeconomics as opposed to the old microeconomics of the classical thinkers. Roosevelt's sole devotion was to the idea of keeping the volume of purchasing power high. It did not matter how this was to be done, whether by restoring business confidence by first getting prices up, or by getting prices up merely by giving business a volume of orders. Hen or egg, egg or hen—Roosevelt was willing to take it either way. And so there *was* a consistency to the administration which could switch from the NRA to the TNEC to the allocation of war orders without turning a hair. The consistency was in the willingness to do *anything* to increase consumption.

To put the government in control of the effort to stimulate consumption, the First New Deal moved in on the dollar. The President called for the surrender of all privately owned gold, and got a law to enforce it. Then came the devaluation of the dollar, the gold purchase scheme, the issue of paper money, and the repudiation of the gold redemption clause which had been solemnly inscribed on government bonds. With nothing to hobble the government in its role as dictator over the money supply, it was easy to go on from there.

In the old days, the economy had recovered quickly, after sharp pains, through the agency of bankruptcies: marginal producers were bought out at forced sales, and their plants and farms set going again on a basis that did not require the servicing of a vast burden of debt. But from 1933 on the very notion of bankruptcy was repudiated. The RFC (started by the Republicans) would take care of big corporations in trouble; the farmer's solvency would be guaranteed by AAA; home owners would find mortgages easy to finance through the federal government; bank depositors would be insured. As for the unemployed, they were to be supported as a matter of equity: as Isabel Paterson has said, if J. P. Morgan were to be put "on the dole" through the RFC, there could be no good moral reason for denying a dole to any man who happened to be out of work.

In the American past, government had often come to the aid of the citizen in economic trouble. But the general philosophy governing a grant-in-aid was that it should be tem-

porary. The Homestead Act gave a man his farm for a
nominal sum. But, once title was taken, the farmer was
supposed to be on his own. Industry, under the Hamiltonian
dispensation, had frequently received tariff protection. But
the theory, here, was that protection was for "infant industries." The "infant industry" idea had certainly been
honored more in the breach than in the observance, and
some aged industries were taking their benefits from the
Smoot-Hawley tariff when Roosevelt assumed office. But
"liberalism" had never accepted the subsidy idea as a positive boon until Roosevelt decided that "protection" must
be extended to everybody. When Herbert Hoover acquiesced in the idea of government grants-in-aid, he was
insistent that "terminal facilities" be provided for in the
legislation governing the aid. But under Roosevelt the whole
notion of "terminal facilities" was quietly dropped.

When the New Deal first moved out into the area of
underwriting a nation's purchasing power, it did so without
formal theoretical justification. But an economic philosophy
providing the theoretical underpinning for the retreat from
the American system was already in the making in England
when Roosevelt was conducting his first tentative experiments. Roosevelt's own rejection of Say's Law of Markets,
his repudiation of the idea that American production could
be relied upon to expand consumption under its own steam,
was largely a matter of hunch. But in 1936 John Maynard
Keynes published his famous *General Theory of Employment, Interest and Money,* and henceforward the hunch
players could turn to an academic "Bible" when called upon
to cite philosophic justification for what had begun as a shot
in the dark.

Keynes himself had only a sporadic connection with the

New Deal politicians. He met Roosevelt in 1934, and corresponded with him on occasion. If Keynes had any criticism of the New Deal, it was on the score that it mingled "restrictionist" and "expansionist" policies without plan, and that its underwriting of consumption—through doles and government "investment"—seldom went far enough. According to Seymour Harris, one of the early American Keynesians, Keynes approved of the New Deal monetary expansion and reduced rates of interest, its program to raise farm incomes, its encouragement of collective bargaining, its high tax progression, and its relief projects. Writing to Roosevelt in 1938, however, Keynes warned the President that mere pump-priming was not enough, that the government must sustain an increased investment in durable goods such as housing, public utilities, and transport through a long period of time. Keynes warned the President against repeating the "error of optimism" which had caused the New Deal to slacken off on its spending—or "government investment"—in 1937.

Since Keynes' *General Theory* came out in the middle of a decade in which Say's Law of Markets seemed stalled all over the world, it was a most plausible document, at least on first reading. But in the light of the inflation that has accompanied ten years of depression, five years of a major war, and a whole decade more of cold war and minor hot skirmishes, the plausibility of the book seems more and more limited to the short run. Ludwig von Mises has dismissed it with magisterial scorn by calling it "the Santa Claus fable raised . . . to the dignity of an economic doctrine." And there is little doubt that von Mises is right—for the long run.

Keynes seemed justified in the thirties in his call for

"government investment" to turn the tide from undercon-
sumption and unemployment for the very palpable reason
that Say's Law wasn't taking hold. But was it the fault of
the Law? Or was it the fault of the very politicians whom
Keynes himself had damned in his earlier *Economic Consequences of the Peace?* At Versailles the statesmen of the
West—Lloyd George (whom Keynes called the "Welsh
witch"), Clemenceau and the rest—had saddled the Germans with uneconomic reparations. They had insisted on
the delivery of money reparations, but had denied the late
enemy the possibility of selling enough goods in excess of
imports to earn the foreign exchange needed for "transfer."
Say's Law had run foul of what has been termed "carpet-
bag finance." The Germans had to borrow to pay their
reparations debts. In this way money which should have
been fed into consumption by putting men to work through
new investment was simply abstracted from the normal
economic circuit. Keynes himself had predicted that this
would happen. But when it eventually came to pass, he
failed to note its impact on the immediate workings of Say's
Law. Instead, he turned on the law and attacked it savagely.

It has never been the contention of any serious economist
that Say's Law must take effect overnight, or that it must
work out at once in overbuilt and overdeveloped sectors of
the economy, or that it is proof against funny shenanigans
which ostensibly create "purchasing power" without supplying the goods to be purchased. There must always be a
"lag" in the workings of the law when an enterpriser makes
a serious mistake in estimating just what types of goods
will clear the market. The enterpriser who makes aspirin
tablets assuredly puts enough money in motion via wages,
etc., to take the aspirin tablets off the druggists' shelves.
But what if nobody has a headache? Under the classical sys-

tem of thinking, the enterpriser's error serves as a warning signal for investors to deploy their capital elsewhere. The unwanted goods will eventually clear the market at a sacrifice, and the wounded enterpriser, if he is still in business, must make up his mind either to cut his costs or to take up some other line. In the meantime Say's Law, working on what might be called a staggered shift, has resulted in some temporary unemployment.

There are several ways to put the unemployed back to work again. One is to let the debt structure shrink to a point where enterprisers can make money and still service their remaining debts. Another is to cut wages to the point where employers can collectively afford to hire everybody. Still another way is to expand the money supply, either by digging more metal out of the ground, or by creating paper currency of one type or another. But to permit bankruptcies or to cut wages has always been hard politics, whether considered as the politics of the factory, the industry, or of society as a whole. Workers want to be "marginally useful," but no individual worker likes to think of himself as worth only a marginal wage. And to find ways of either cheapening or expanding the production of the monetary metals may not always be feasible. Inflation, so Professor Sumner Schlicter tells us, is preferable to wage cuts, and it is certainly easier than digging more gold out of the ground. The only trouble with inflation is that it feeds on itself: there are natural limits to bankruptcy, natural obstacles to getting gold out of the ground—but only the questionable self-restraint of pressure groups is available when it comes to setting a boundary to inflation. The decision to stop inflation at the "reflation" point inevitably becomes a decision in politics, psychology, sociology and morality, not a decision motivated by pure economics.

The problem, then, is not only to assail the long-run economic relevance of Keynes' system, but to tackle the Master on the score of politics, sociology and morality. The trouble with Keynesian medicine is that the prescriptions can all be refilled without check by the physician. Before dealing with the morality of the Keynesian cures, however, an honest commentator must admit that there are analytical phases of the *General Theory* that are hard to laugh off. Given enough *cumulative* short-term failures of Say's Law, it is obvious that unemployment may reach a point where it must become politically and socially explosive. If employed workers won't accept a wage reduction in order to help put their unemployed brethren back on the payroll, what then?

Keynes insisted that high wages could not in themselves be the *cause* of unemployment, for high wages are part of the consumption power that keeps other people at work. Unemployment, so he argued, must come because money leaks out of the consumption-investment system. Production has put the money there in the first place to be spent on consumption, or to be invested. In the case of investment, it will put new consumer-producers to work or will make old employees more productive on their jobs. Whether the money flows into consumption or investment, there will be no failure of demand. Say's Law can go on working without any "stagger system" or hitch.

How, then, to account for the monetary "leak"? The only way to account for it is to assume the savings—i.e., the money that is not spent directly on consumption—do not *automatically* turn up on the other side of the equation as investment. As Keynes said, the ones who do the saving and the ones who do the investing (i.e., bankers) are frequently different people. Mayhap the "expectancy" of profit will be so low that bankers will quibble about lending and enterprisers may dawdle on expanding their operations. Mayhap the interest rate will be too high to permit ready borrowing. Mayhap businessmen—and even individual hoarders—will be smitten with what Keynes calls "liquidity preference," which will dispose them to hang on to large blocks of cash. For any number of reasons investment may fail—and with it, the possibility of full employment.

The classical economists argued that savings and investment must balance in the nature of things through the mediating office of the interest rate. But to Keynes, with his eye on the short run ("In the long run we're all dead"), it seemed silly to wait for them to balance *"ex post"* when men were starving. He argued that government spending—or "investment"—could have a "multiplier" effect on the economy which might, under ideal circumstances, pay for itself. Money spent by government to put men to work on roads, or public monuments, or cleaning up the forests, or building big dams, would turn up partly as consumption and partly as savings, the exact division being in accordance with the "marginal propensity to consume." (In the case of previously unemployed men, the propensity to consume would be strong.) The new consumption money would go round and round in the economy, "leaking a little into savings with each turn of the spending cycle. The Keynes rationale suggests the verse about the Big Fleas:

> Big fleas have little fleas,
>   Upon their backs to bite 'em;
> And little fleas have lesser fleas,
>   And so *ad infinitum.*

Only in the Keynes version, the fleas are declining increments of consumption as the government money injections
pass from hand to hand, growing smaller all the time as
"savings"—the extinction of debt, the payment of insurance
premiums, etc.—tend, at least momentarily, to sterilize
some of the "purchasing power."

Keynes' mathematical representation of the "multiplier"
must look extremely impressive to the curbstone reader.
But when one realizes that the "representational mathematics" of the professional economist often consists of sym-
bols to which no known figures can properly be attached
(it is like asking how many lollipops Johnny can buy if
both the pennies in his pocket and the price of lollipops
are unknown and unascertainable), the impressiveness of
the formula tends to evaporate. After one has done a
double-take of the *General Theory,* one feels like asking
certain questions. Can one actually predict with any ac-
curacy the effect of government spending on an economy?
The very tax money which goes to swell consumption may
end up not only as savings but as secondary investment.
Conversely, the money saved for investment may end up as
consumption. These considerations have little negative bearing on Keynes' spending "cure" for unemployment, for any
economic activity serves to put people to work. But, since
they imply that everything "multiplies" everything all the
time (unless it disappears under the mattress or into an old
sock or into inert pockets in the banking system), the very
fluidity of the whole process defies mathematical capture.
If money goes abroad to pay for imports, it comes back to
buy exports. If it goes to extinguish old debts, it enables both
lenders and borrowers to undertake new commitments. It
is "consumption" today, "investment" tomorrow, "consump-

tion" again the day after. No doubt meaningful statistics of the Gross National Product can be collected. But to determine in advance just what will happen throughout the economy when the government spends money poses a most difficult problem. Keynes himself made no effort to provide the actual statistical underpinning for his system. He did not really explore the "consumption function" in a way that Madison Avenue, for example, would define as realistic. His "multiplier" might work—but it might also be canceled out if government spending should happen to have adverse effects on investment generally.

The whole Keynes *General Theory* remains in the realm of logical deduction from premises that may or may not be true. Keynes had a fondness for praising ancient Egypt because it could always solve its unemployment problem by building new pyramids. (One can always build two pyramids, but one cannot build two railroads from London to York.) But if government "investment" goes for pyramids —or for any other boondoggle, resplendent or other—it hardly creates the commodities needed to purchase other commodities. Pyramids, by definition, are not for sale, and their lease-value is nil. True, the pyramid builders will have spending power for the moment—but it would have remained potential spending power if it had not been taxed out of free society in the first place. If it had remained in the hands of oversavers it might, admittedly, have "lubricated" nothing, at least for the time being. But the very fact of its being taxed out of society could act to compound the existing "failure of expectation." Why should businessmen even contemplate making extra efforts if their work only leads to seizure by the state of a progressively large portion of their earnings?

Keynes tended to think of "government investment" as merely "something extra," an emergency flywheel which, running concurrently with other wheels, would keep the whole machine spinning merrily. But what does government spending actually do? If it is for pyramids (or stockpiling of copper, say), it makes Say's Law a real dead letter. Nothing is brought to the market to swell the stream of purchasing power in terms of tangibles. The "investment" is in what Isabel Paterson calls a "dead-end appliance." It leads to consumption, yes. But it contributes nothing to the common stock for future consumption.

The "multiplier," then, while it may work out as Keynes says it does, might very well be paralleled in another sector of the economy by a "divisor" effect—if one can presume to work back by "representational mathematics" from "what might have been." Where activity by the state sets consumption going, the same activity might cause enterprisers or private Maecenases to cut back their plans still further in another place. (To put it crudely, if J. P. Morgan is taxed to pay for a third-rate WPA mural, he might forgo the opportunity to buy a new Picasso.) And the workers who would have benefited by the new private spending (say, the employees of the company which would have insured the Picasso in transit) will not turn up at the movies on Saturday night until the government has, in turn, taken care of *them*.

Keynes himself made a good deal of the concept of "expectation" in the *General Theory*. He spoke of the "part played by expectation in economic analysis." The level of employment, he says, depends on past expectations still working themselves out, and present expectations just acted upon. But the *General Theory* is relatively silent on what

"Keynesianism" does to "trade out" diversified future investment for an inefficient and unimaginative deployment of funds in the present. "Macroeconomic" thinking about the "Gross National Product" notes that marginal farms aren't making money and that housing construction is down. Ergo, the answer of the "macroeconomists" is to pump money into agriculture to keep inefficient farmers employed, and to subsidize the sort of flimsy housing that has been referred to aptly as the "slums of tomorrow." Old-fashioned "microeconomic" thinking would, on the other hand, have sought its cure differently, in the "economics of the firm." It would have looked for individual companies with new ideas. Instead of proposing to flood inefficient areas of the economy with funds just to keep marginal producers from going down the drain, it would have directed its attention to new "ladder" industries capable of creating and serving whole new series of wants. If we had had "macroeconomists" in the days of the horse and buggy, they would have proposed flooding carriage companies with subsidy money just to keep the horse-and-buggy sector of the Gross National Product at a peak. And Henry Ford, taxed into adding a couple of hundred dollars to the price of a Tin Lizzy just to provide oats for government-supported horses, would never have gone on to develop mass production of cheap cars.

Keynes' *General Theory of Employment, Interest and Money* adds up to a secular pessimism about the regenerative powers of any advanced capitalistic system. But Keynes himself drew back from contemplation of a steadily increasing socialism. He read Hayek's *The Road to Serfdom* with approval, and he openly put himself on the side of the "educated bourgeoisie." He loved freedom too well to pine for a Tugwellian "planned state"; indeed, at one point in his life he spoke of the state as being relatively "sterile." If he had lived on into the apathetic England of the 1950s, just what would he have said of his own "general theory"? Since his advocacy of inflation was not designed for "full employment" periods, he would surely have had a second go at his book.

In the last analysis it is Keynes the political scientist, and not Keynes the economist, who is the failure. From the standpoint of pure economics his analyses of the failure of demand in a depression era, while not proved by recourse to statistics, do have a general correspondence with the "feel" of the facts. Certainly there is such a thing as "liquidity preference"; E. H. Harriman, the railroad tycoon who made millions in Wall Street, once expressed this preference with a vengeance when he remarked that a depression was a good time in which "to buy money." And when "liquidity preference" is epidemic in an economy, depression will certainly be a concomitant, if not the actual result.

But even though Keynes' analyses of the failure of demand are highly suggestive, the "politics" of Keynesianism must be set down as incredibly naive. Keynes himself tended to think of the "government" as a band of dedicated high priests of the interest rate. The "government," so he thought, could be counted on to turn the stream of spending on and off at will in conformance with a totally disinterested philosophy of the "common good." Though he wrote in a period of deflation, drawing his illustrative examples from a society in the doldrums, his *political* economy provided for a *reversible* system of countercyclical measures to be initiated with calm and magisterial disdain of pressure groups. There would be a jolt of inflation for a depression period, and a corresponding measure of forced saving (via taxation and debt extinction) in a period of overfull employment and general economic euphoria.

Alas for Keynes, he reckoned without the genius politician. To draw a bead on the failures of Keynes as political scientist, sociologist and practical moralist we must go to the "social free market" thinkers of the European continent, to men like Wilhelm Roepke of Geneva. Roepke has gone straight to the heart of Keynes' deficiencies as a social and political scientist. He has tackled Keynesianism where it is weakest: in its failure to understand that *reversible* counter-cyclical action is virtually impossible in a democratic political system, especially in an election year. A dictator can cancel inflation, yes. Nobody in Russia dared complain when the Kremlin wiped out the value of government bonds by suspending the interest thereon. But in a democracy politics tends to go by ratchet action. What has been granted cannot easily be retracted. Inflation, barring heroic forbearance by a majority of the electorate, can only be "corrected" by more inflation. In the best of times the national debt remains stationary. In the worst of times it increases. There is hardly ever a time, however, when it goes down.

Wilhelm Roepke cannily directs our attention to the fact that "government investment," which begins as a policy of robbing rich Peter to pay poor Paul, ends up by robbing Paul to pay Paul. The point is eventually reached where taxation, far from bearing down exclusively on the rich, begins to rob the middle classes of their potential savings and even of some of their "propensity to consume." Finally the masses themselves come under the tax collector's gun. With all classes paying in taxation and/or inflation, "money," as Roepke expresses it, "is juggled from their righthand into their lefthand pockets." This practice, so

Roepke continues, is not only "nonsensical"; it means the death of society as an entity which is counterpoised to the state. "Quite apart from its dampening effect on individual effort and responsibility," so Roepke writes, "it involves the expenditure of large sums on a vast public machine constantly growing in size and power." The ultimate social price is a "dull, grey society, in which public spirit, voluntary service to the community, creative leisure, brotherliness, generosity, and the true sense of belonging to a human family are all smothered by resentment in the higher and envy in the lower income groups. What is left is the pumping system of Leviathan. . . ." This "pumping system is an illusion for all, a purpose in itself."

The operators of the pump, far from being disinterested high priests of the interest rate, soon acquire a vested interest in the gigantic back-and-forth movement. They build their own administrative empires in the capital city. Emissaries from the empires go forth into the hinterlands to keep their pet pressure groups happy, thus assuring themselves of the votes to stay in office. The citizen soon finds himself running the risk of being reduced to the status of what Roepke describes as "an obedient domesticated animal in the state's big stables, crammed together with other similar animals." Changing the metaphor, Roepke argues that the welfare state pumping apparatus eventually degrades human beings to "the status of minors." When a people reaches this stage, it may be lucky for it to lose a total war totally. Then (provided it has not lost the war to a Stalin or a Khrushchev) it can begin all over again, as West Germany has done. And it can begin over again with a Roepke serving as advisor to the Ministry of Economics, not a John Maynard Keynes.

The objection to Keynesianism, finally, is not that it can't put people to work—after all, if it is a mere question of balancing input and output, any system can, theoretically, do the job. The Incas of Peru "balanced" their economy so well that Sir Thomas More fashioned his *Utopia* on what he had heard of New World "planning." In Soviet Russia there is always "full employment"—even though the Soviet state had, at one time in the thirties, to murder three million kulaks in order to get its agricultural "planning" going. The real objection to Keynesianism is not that it can't drum up an "input-output" balance, but that it debases men morally. Since the ratchet action of politics makes a return to the voluntary society more and more unlikely, people become more and more cynical. With every increase in pressure group socialism there is a corresponding increase in the psychology of "what's in it for me." Votes are really for sale. As Roepke points out, Frederic Bastiat's definition of the state becomes all too true: the state is "the grand fiction by which everybody lives at the expense of everybody." And, since nobody has an individual surplus any more to use for cultural expenditures, or for patronage of the arts, or for buying time for creative leisure, all of these things must be taken over by government. Roepke's final damning statement has a most ominous sound: "Charity, honorary functions, liberality, conversation, leisure, everything that Burke included in the expression, 'unbought graces of life,' all these are strangled by the state."

We have not yet reached that point in America. Productivity in this country has, so to speak, managed to outrace inflation. We have become dependent for a sixth of our economic activity on the state "pumping apparatus," but the "dull, grey society," which Roepke discerns in England,

Sweden and other European welfare states, has not yet made its appearance here. It can hardly be held, however, that during the past quarter of a century no inroads have been made upon the idea that the American is one who lives by his own combinations and efforts, in accordance with his own choice, under a limited government that would not dare to curtail any of his "inalienable" rights.

On the European continent the "new" liberals—the men of the "social free market" school who are dog-tired of the Keynesian Pied Pipers—have become an inspiriting group. They are close to the Adenauer government of West Germany, where, according to economist David McCord Wright, they have succeeded in establishing a free policy which has pushed German productivity almost unbelievably high. Germany has recovered faster than post-1945 Britain simply by *abolishing* controls, rationing, state-directed investment, sharply progressive taxation and the "fair shares" mentality which insists that all people must be equal in their misery. In West Germany the top progressive tax rate is around fifty percent; in "rich" America the top rate stands at ninety-one percent. Yet in Germany, with a relatively low rate of tax progression, the government has still been able to restore monuments, to take care of its distress cases, and to behave in a generally humane way.

Could American "liberals," since they have forsworn their own American tradition, find it within their capacity to take a tip from the resurgent true liberalism of continental Europe? For two generations of "Fabianism," "Keynesianism" and neo-Marxism in general, the American liberals have made it a habit of importing their mental clothes from abroad. Every time there has been a crisis they have met it with the same old Fabian or Keynesian plea, "Let Washington do it." But now that they have modern European—as well as old American—proof that the individual can "do it," either by himself or in voluntary association with others, they have an opportunity to bring in an entirely new fashion. One awaits their decision with interest, for it is the "liberals" who have the "swing vote" in America.

As they go, so go the totems of the tribe.

Forward Once More?

Keynesianism in America has tended to blend with the Veblenian tradition. The strangely homogenized product of two highly conscious iconoclasts now presents a new orthodoxy, solid, entrenched and, like all other orthodoxics, utterly intolerant of basic challenge. Keynes and Veblen were alike in stressing the supposed inability of a business society to give scope and function to the "engineer." Where Keynesianism speaks of a chronic "failure of demand," Veblenism speaks of "business sabotage," of a "conscious" or a "conscientious withdrawal of efficiency." But the rude facts of American life belie the impeachments offered in both the Keynesian and the Veblenian texts. The truth is that the new orthodoxy is hollow.

Indeed, the productivity of America has burst all bounds, and the engineer rides triumphant over the supposed ogres of "finance capitalism." What Keynes failed to note about the American economy was its tremendous urge to combine more and more capital with a given unit of labor: he missed the whole point of Eli Whitney, of Frederick Taylor, of Henry Ford, of the Cross brothers and the other high priests of "automation." Here the "marginal efficiency" of

capital has remained high. The productivity figures collected by Professor Seymour Harris of Harvard, himself
a leading Keynesian, contradict everything which Harris
himself has to say about Keynes' "prophetic" ability. "Consider," says Professor Harris, "the twenty years 1932–1952.
Output increased relatively twice as much as prices. Inflation was one of the costs of this advance; and certainly has
to be put against the gains. But would many contend that
the cost was excessive even granting (as I would) the inflation might have been cut by fifty percent? When the
gains outputwise are large relative to the inflation, the case
for an expansionist money policy becomes stronger. . . ."

Professor Harris speaks as if the inflation had created
the technological advances of American industry. But this
is to slander a thousand inventors, enterprisers and production men. Eli Whitney and Henry Ford came long before
the money doctors. We may grant that the forward surge
of American business was interrupted in 1929 and that the
"New Era" of the late 1920s was a period of delusion. We
may also admit that the American banking system needed
overhauling in 1933, and that the SEC regulation of the
Stock Exchange was long overdue. But the 1929–33 need
for technical improvements in the business system did not
constitute a call for "institutionalizing" the depression. The
climb from the pit could have been made without breaking
the dollar in two. The statistics offered by Herbert Hoover
as an *apologia pro vita sua* show the bottom of the depression had been reached in the summer of 1932, and that
recovery would have come under its own steam. Productivity would have taken over in any event.

Instead, the spending school injected a permanent "inflationary bias" into the economy, forcing productivity to

outdo itself in the race to douse the price rise. "Consider," says Professor Harris, "the expansion of money in the United States—about eight times since 1914 and prices little more than doubled; or from 1800 to 1940, a rise of money of about ten to fifteen times that of income, and relatively small net price increases." Professor Harris does not distinguish between inflationary injections and the normal addition to the money supply created by the functioning of the mining industry, the influx of foreign capital and the operations of the credit system when goods create a demand for goods in exchange. He lumps everything together, good money, sound credit and mere multiplication of paper. But what if productivity could have resumed its upward march in 1933 without any political onslaught on the dollar? What if the war could have been financed by much stiffer taxes? The U.S. would still be a low-price economy; men would still be able to retire on $200 a month. And inordinate taxes would not now be needed to keep the dynamic balance of an inflationary economy from collapse.

Instead of inflation financing productivity, it is the productivity which has kept the American inflation from going the way of the German inflation after World War I. This productivity has had to survive staggering blows from the pressure groups and the politicians, in order to keep the entrepreneur's head above red ink. Despite Veblen, the American corporation has not sought to combine with other corporations in cartels designed to share the market and to keep prices high. There has been no "withdrawal of efficiency," whether "conscious" or "conscientious." To balance the mergers, new businesses have proliferated in many directions. As we have already noted, where U.S. Steel once lorded it over the landscape, there are now dozens of steel companies. And when one of the newer companies—say Allegheny Ludlum—pioneers in the making of the newer "grain steels," another company—Crucible Steel—is quick to invade its province. As we have seen, this sort of proliferation has been part of the "true perfection of competition" working to fulfill the commands of the "consumer's plebiscite."

The drive of American life, the enthronement of the consumer, has made Veblen "old hat." Once upon a time it was the rich who had "conspicuous leisure" in which to indulge in "conspicuous waste." But now both leisure and so-called waste are virtually every man's portion. Veblen hated sport, and he lashed out at wealthy yacht owners and polo players. But who are the sportsmen of today? Who throngs the motels of Vermont and the lodges of the mountainous West at the height of the skiing season? Who plays shuffleboard in St. Petersburg, Florida, all winter? Who makes the trout streams look like main traveled arteries on the opening day of the fishing season? Who buys the sports shirts which are worn even on the subway? It is certainly not the rich practicing "conspicuous leisure." No, it is just the Veblenian "underlying population," the common man who has been the main beneficiary of the capitalist order.

The truth is that Veblen has conquered. But it has been the derided industrialist who has provided the basis for the conquest by harnessing the engineer to the demands of productivity. Moreover, it has not been the progressive income tax which has created the purchasing power to take the goods off the market. It has been the machine itself— $13,000 or more of investment per worker, a multiplication of the individual unit's arms, legs and brains which has pushed the wage to a point where everyone can have his own bit of conspicuous leisure and even conspicuous waste.

The answer of the Keynesians and the Veblenians to this emphasis on productivity will come wearisomely and insistently, and it will take the form of the same old litany. "Capitalism," so they will say, "cannot be trusted to provide security without state intervention." But there are voluntary ways of doing all the things which the state is now doing at such a high inflationary cost.

Is it Social Security that the Keynesian is worried about? Well, why not permit any man who can prove that he is already paying his own insurance premiums to be exempted from the Social Security law? (The state might require for a transition period that he keep up a basic amount of private insurance at all times, but it makes no sense for Washington to insure Nelson Rockefeller.) Is it medical care that bothers our Veblenian? Well, the Blue Cross system, not to mention the private medical cooperative, is certainly capable of vast extension. Is it "urban redevelopment" that seemingly requires federal support of slum clearance? Well, what is there to prevent the owners of urban property from pooling their titles and taking over the reconstruction of blighted areas? (William Zeckendorf has shown what can be done to clear slums at a profit all around, and Spencer Heath has pointed out that private real estate interests might do far better for themselves and their tenants by assuming certain municipal functions.) Is it the relief of the unemployed that seems an insurmountable obstacle under "laissez-faire"? Well, why not grant tax rebates to any corporation which is willing to adapt the principle of the guaranteed annual wage to its operations? Is it the alleged inability of a "nationalized economy" to unwind which bothers the "liberal"? Well, the proof of the pudding is in the eating—and it re-

mains a fact that the British government has already managed to sell some of its steel companies back to private
owners. Is it "housing" that troubles the Keynesian's conscience? Well, the private building societies financed a
whopping construction boom in England of the thirties, and
there is no reason why there should not be a recrudescence
of the building-society idea today. Finally, is it the "farm
problem" that seems a perennial Old Man of the Sea? Well,
just the other day the Committee for Economic Development suggested that the federal government take whole
"marginal" farms out of production by compensating their
owners for a limited period while they are learning new
trades.

It is not here alleged that these methods of returning to
voluntary action would result in a recovery of the free society overnight. Some of them would require the temporary
continuation of government aid. Our sole desire at this
point is to suggest that there are ways of dismantling the
welfare state without turning old people out to stony pas-
tures and without heaving inefficient farmers into the midst
of an urban society that is unprepared to absorb them. A
Fabian "gradualism" brought us to the socialism we now
have; a Fabianism-in-reverse could help us to unwind without being brutal to anyone.

Welfarism was private before it was public—and with
productivity once delivered from the incubus of political
inflation, the welfare society could easily outmatch and take
over from the welfare state.

Index

This book was linotype set in the Times Roman series of type. The face was designed to be used in the news columns of the *London Times*. The *Times* was seeking a type face that would be condensed enough to accommodate a substantial number of words per column without sacrificing readability and still have an attractive, contemporary appearance. This design was an immediate success. It is used in many periodicals throughout the world and is one of the most popular text faces presently in use for book work.

Book design by Design Center, Inc., Indianapolis
Typography by Typoservice Corporation, Indianapolis
Printed by North Central Publishing Co., Saint Paul